Jay Shetler, Psy D

SCHOOL CRISIS
MANAGEMENT

"*School Crisis Management* is one of the most clearly written and most useful psychological trauma intervention texts to come off the presses in a very long time. The text is filled with a great deal of traumatic stress information, practical guidelines for critical incident stress reduction, and instructive graphics that will be of great benefit to educators in the field of traumatic stress.

"*School Crisis Management* fills a huge gap in the literature on traumatic events that affect children and adolescents. It leaps forward from the theoretical and plants itself firmly as a benchmark for realistic crisis intervention programs in the school systems of English-speaking countries. It should not be long before the book is translated into other languages.

"Although written for school systems, the usefulness of *School Crisis Management* is not limited to educational institutions alone. Crisis intervention personnel connected with industry, emergency services, and other programs will benefit from the many critical incident stress management suggestions made in the text."

JEFFREY T. MITCHELL, PH.D.
President, International Critical Incident Stress Foundation
Clinical Associate Professor of Emergency Health Services
The University of Maryland, Baltimore County

"Dr. Kendall Johnson has developed an invaluable training guide that offers numerous practical strategies for dealing with trauma. This manual is essential reading for all Crisis Response Teams and is highly recommended for turnkey training of staff."

HOWARD LERNER, M.S., PH.D.
Supervisor of Psychologists
Brooklyn High School Clinical Services Unit
New York City Board of Education

"Kendall Johnson's book fills a gap that has been waiting to be bridged between theory and practice. This important contribution will be welcomed by teachers and educationists around the world—both for its accessible information on posttrauma psychology and the understanding of the practical needs of busy classroom teachers. It will give them the confidence to take on their vital role in reducing stress on their pupils following a traumatic event."

ELIZABETH CAPEWELL, M.A.
Director, Centre for Crisis Management and Education, Newbury, Berkshire, England

Dedication

While watching the courageous manner in which he faced his final adversity, I learned much from my father about sacrifice, integrity, and grace. For this, and for being who he was, this book is dedicated to Roger K. Johnson.

This second edition is dedicated to my father-in-law Kenneth Losh. As a missionary to the postwar Philippines, church leader, father, and grandfather, Ken brought care and compassion to a world of suffering and injustice.

Both of these men are missed.

To contact the author

Kendall Johnson can be reached for consultation or training at (909) 626-2207.

Ordering

Trade bookstores in the U.S. and Canada please contact:

Publishers Group West
1700 Fourth Street, Berkeley CA 94710
Phone: (800) 788-3123   Fax: (510) 528-3444

Hunter House books are available at bulk discounts for textbook course adoptions; to qualifying community, healthcare, and government organizations; and for special promotions and fund-raising. For details please contact:

Special Sales Department
Hunter House Inc.
P.O. Box 2914
Alameda CA 94501-0914
Tel. (510) 865-5282
Fax (510) 865-4295
e-mail: ordering@hunterhouse.com

Individuals can view our books on the Web at www.hunterhouse.com and can order our books from most bookstores or by calling toll-free:

1-800-266-5592

SCHOOL CRISIS MANAGEMENT

A Hands-on Guide to Training Crisis Response Teams

Second Edition

Kendall Johnson, Ph.D.

Foreword by Ronald D. Stephens, Executive Director, National School Safety Center

Hunter House PUBLISHERS

> Hunter House Inc., Publishers
> P.O. Box 2914
> Alameda CA 94501-0914

**Library of Congress
Cataloging-in-Publication Data**

Johnson, Kendal, 1945-
    School crisis management : a hands-on guide to
training crisis response teams / Kendal Johnson ;
foreword by Ronald D. Stephens. — 2nd ed.
        p.cm.
    Includes bibliographical references.
    ISBN 0-89793-305-2 (pb)
    ISBN 0-89793-306-0 (spiral)
        1. School crisis management—United
States—Planning. 2. School psychology—United
States. 3. Crisis intervention (Mental health
services)—United States. I. Title.
    LB2866.5 .J64 2000
    371.7'13—dc21   00-036973

Project credits:
Cover Design: Jinni Fontana
Book Design and Production: Hunter House
Copy Editor: Lydia Bird
Proofreader: John David Marion
Indexer: Kathy Talley-Jones
Production Director: Virginia Fontana
Acquisitions Editor: Jeanne Brondino
Associate Editor: Alexandra Mummery
Publicity Director: Marisa Spatafore
Customer Service Manager: Christina Sverdrup
Order Fulfillment: Joel Irons
Publisher: Kiran S. Rana

Printed and Bound by
Publishers Press, Salt Lake City, Utah

Manufactured in the United States of America
9 8 7 6 5 4 3 2 1
Second Edition   00 01 02 03 04

Table of Contents

Table of Contents (contd)

List of Figures

List of Figures (contd)

Foreword

There are two kinds of school administrators: those who have faced a crisis and those who are about to. Being prepared is essential for today's school administrators. Crisis preparation can make a lifesaving difference in an emergency. It is important not only to have a plan, but also to know who will carry out that plan. Successful crisis management is an inside job. It begins with a well-prepared staff, specifically assigned roles, student participation, and, perhaps most significantly, a well-defined interagency agreement with local community resources, particularly law enforcement officials.

Kendall Johnson's book *School Crisis Management* provides the administrator with some excellent training resources. Dr. Johnson's perspectives into the effects and implication of Cumulative Traumatic Stress are particularly insightful. The changing climate of public education—where fire drills of yesteryear are being replaced by crisis drills, and where the severity of incidents is increasing—makes these valuable tools all the more important.

Developing a workable and meaningful crisis plan is not simply a task for the big-city schools. The need for such a strategy extends to rural and suburban campuses as well. A recent study by researchers at Texas A and M University indicates that suburban and rural schools are having to cope with student fights, weapons on campus, drug abuse, and other forms of violence once thought to be the exclusive problems of large, inner-city schools.

While we may never be able to completely protect a school district from criminal activity, a comprehensive and collaboratively developed school safety plan can go a long way toward reducing potential problems and looming liability. The best crisis strategy is one that focuses on crisis prevention and preparation, crisis management, and crisis response. Kendall Johnson's book will assist you in properly developing these components.

When these comprehensive strategies are in place, school personnel can protect the young people they serve more responsibly and effectively. Safe schools and quality learning are directly related. Creating safe schools and positive campus climate begins with a good physical design, followed closely by caring school administrators and teachers who are trained not only to manage and prepare for inevitable crises, but perhaps, most importantly, to prevent a crisis.

RONALD D. STEPHENS
Executive Director,
National School Safety Center
Westlake Village, California, 1993

Important Notice

The material in this book is intended to provide a review of information regarding school crisis management. The publisher, author, editors, and professionals quoted in this book cannot be held responsible for any error, omission, or dated material, nor can the publishers, author, or editors be held responsible for the judgement and knowledge of trainers using this book. This material cannot be applied without sound professional judgement regarding the particular circumstances of its application.

Introduction

The seven years since the first publication of this book have seen unprecedented technical, social, and political upheaval. School officials across the country are faced with a seemingly unending escalation in the number and intensity of critical incidents in their schools. As these deliciously newsworthy events gain headline status, the public expects timely and effective response.

Providing psychological first aid—school crisis intervention—following such incidents is rapidly becoming accepted as a helpful and appropriate response. Until several years ago such interventions were done primarily by outside mental health resources. Because of their unfamiliarity with school personnel and procedures, however, outside resources are increasingly being replaced by teams made up of district personnel.

About a hundred years ago Emile Durkheim made the observation that the rate of suicide climbs when society is fractured by opposing cultural forces that tear away the individual's psychological underpinnings. He theorized that the internalization of external conflict results in violence, often directed against self; without an external norm, the internal life fragments. One wonders what Durkheim would have made of the latest wave of global change: the homogenization of global culture that undercuts our sense of place. He might have speculated about the connection between anonymity and the random, cataclysmic violence we are seeing in the workplace, the community, and in the schools.

In my consulting capacity I am called in to conduct trainings for the Crisis Response Teams that respond to such violence in our schools. A very typical call involves giving training to a team that was formed a year or two following a problematic situation and prior to an even more problematic critical incident. The team has received some training and has had enough experience to realize the need for more. As I talk to these team leaders, a general pattern of needs emerges.

Crisis Response Team (CRT) leaders repeatedly express the following training needs for their teams:

1. More comprehensive training that moves beyond the introductory concepts of crisis response and intervention

2. More practical training that emphasizes transition from concepts to practical applications

3. Emphasis on training procedures, strategies, and skills specific to school contexts

4. Concepts and language that bridge the gap between schools and the mental health community

5. Models that link school intervention with the larger crisis intervention movement in other disciplines, such as public service agencies and community disaster resources

6. Approaches and adaptations that are applicable beyond the scope of single, small-scale incidents to larger emergencies, such as natural disasters or mass shootings

7. Specific techniques, strategies, and considerations for dealing with special problems, such as staff trauma, suicides or murders, or sudden traumatic loss

8. Materials that can be used not only for Crisis Response Team training but also for raising administrative and community awareness and for classroom-teacher and support-staff training

This book was conceived in response to those needs. The major training areas listed above are addressed in depth here. Full-page copy masters are provided that can be duplicated to produce handouts or overhead transparencies. These can be used as a basis for training the Crisis Response Team, other staff members, or the general public. The copy masters or figures referred to in the text are all located at the end of the book, starting on page 125. Readers are free to select those that are needed to meet their specific training requirements.

Staff and students who have been victimized by a school crisis need appropriate and skillful care. Those who choose to accept the challenge of response need to be prepared to do the very best job possible. They themselves need support in this important work. It is hoped and anticipated that this book will be useful in providing direction and resources for training school Crisis Response Teams.

Copy masters (Figures 1-1 to 1-27) for this chapter can be found on pages 126–152.

CHAPTER 1

Crisis, Trauma, and the Schools

Crises are those events that challenge our position in the world. They threaten us and the things we hold dear. To function optimally in the world we need to be assured that

- we can count on others and the world to meet our needs

- the world will not hurt us unduly

- we can affect the world and create change

- we can stand alone

- we can respect others and ourselves

- we can count on things remaining fairly constant and predictable

We need these assurances to plan how much energy to invest in our lives and how to direct that energy.

Crisis events challenge these beliefs, undermining our security and sense of power. They provide counterexamples to these beliefs and can destroy our spirit.

Crises can contain three problematic elements. First, they may threaten or actually harm people—they may result in pain, suffering, and sometimes loss of life. Second, they usually involve loss. Through crisis events we stand to lose loved ones, material things we need and have become attached to, and sometimes possibilities for our future. Finally, crises may expose us to grotesque and unforgettable sights and sounds. These three elements of threat, loss, and traumatic stimulus have the

capacity to spoil our cherished beliefs in ourselves and the world (see Figure 1-1).

In general, the stronger these elements figure in a particular situation, the greater the impact it has on us. And the greater the impact (both in threat to our basic needs and in intensity of experience), the stronger our reactions and responses at the time—and later (see Figure 1-2).

Basics of Psychotraumatology

Critical incidents trigger profound reactions. These reactions often have two phases. The initial reaction, which can last days or even weeks, consists of an inability to cope with the intense feelings, confusion, and physical reactions that follow a crisis. During the incident the mind seems unusually open to learning. Unfortunately, much of the learning consists of negative messages about the world (its capriciousness, lethality, chaotic nature) or the individual (his or her powerlessness, inadequacies, "cowardice"). A person seems to have a heightened suggestibility in this first phase, which makes it difficult to relearn these negative assessments. Thus, the initial reaction to crisis often results in residual fear and feelings of diminished self-worth (see Figure 1-3). Fortunately, most humans are fairly resilient. Following a period of adjustment, most people in most circumstances resume their lives fully recovered.

Many, however, do not. Their initial reactions are compounded and result in secondary

3

reaction cycles. Secondary reactions can take many forms, as enumerated in Figure 1-3. A person's heightened suggestibility during crisis can result in negative expectations regarding the world and negative judgements of oneself and others. Cognitive sets, or the tendency to interpret experience in predetermined ways, may also be negative or self-defeating. Various difficulties in thought processing are also possible. Emotional over- or underreactivity is common, such as anxiety, depression, specific fears, or detachment. Finally, attempts to cope with unpleasant memories, changed conditions, and uncontrollable feelings may do more harm than good. Maladaptive coping can include substance abuse, withdrawal, flight, dramatic lifestyle changes, and compulsions.

These secondary cognitive, emotional, physical, and behavioral reactions generally make things worse by creating a negative impact on the person's environment. As a result, the situation worsens, which tends only to reinforce the secondary reactions; thus, the cycle becomes increasingly difficult to manage (see Figure 1-4).

Individuals react to crises in their own ways. Some persons are more resilient, some are more vulnerable depending on their personality and constitution. Other factors from their personal histories may also influence their reactions. Having experienced prior crises may render certain individuals more vulnerable to specific types of incidents, while previous experience in successful coping may contribute to resilience in others. No crisis occurs in a vacuum; situational factors such as current stress levels and available resources may make a given situation better or worse.

Figure 1-5 illustrates the potential progression of reactions over time to a serious crisis. Following impact, an individual has an initial reaction. If this reaction is sufficiently disorienting or debilitating to the person, it is called an Acute Stress Response (ASR). This reaction is elaborated in the next section.

A secondary reaction may follow the initial reaction in the ensuing days, weeks, and months. If the reaction is adverse, it is called a Delayed Stress Response (DSR). Signs and symptoms of DSR are elaborated further on.

Complete recovery from either Acute or Delayed Stress Response may occur spontaneously or with intervention. Delayed Stress Response can, however, degenerate into one of various posttraumatic clinical syndromes. The most renowned of these is Posttraumatic Stress Disorder (PTSD) (American Psychiatric Association 1994). PTSD is a clinical condition with an elaborate diagnostic definition; it is discussed at length later in this chapter. It should be remembered, however, that PTSD is only one of several posttraumatic conditions that may follow exposure to overwhelming crisis situations.

Little empirical evidence exists to indicate rates of ASR and DSR impairment following crises. Dr. Jeffrey Mitchell of the University of Maryland Department of Emergency Medical Services estimates that of those normal individuals experiencing serious and potentially traumatic crises, approximately 15 percent will show Acute Stress Response signs, some 15 percent of these will exhibit Delayed Stress Response symptoms, and 15 percent of the individuals with Delayed Stress Response will eventually be diagnosed PTSD (personal communication). This latter figure does not take into account other posttraumatic syndromes. Calvin Fredricks, M.D., Professor of Psychiatry at the University of California at Los Angeles and former Director of the National Institute of Mental Health, has indicated that as many as 25 to 50 percent of persons involved in potentially traumatic situations—such as assaults, shootings, and natural disasters—are likely to show psychological impairment at the time of crisis and later (personal communication). Several sociologists have predicted dramatically lower rates of PTSD following emergencies, although they tend to focus on natural disasters and base their predictions on surveys rather than clinical observation.

Delayed Stress Response may in fact be more prevalent than Acute Stress Response, especially if subclinical conditions are taken into account. These include demoralization, changes in lifestyle, relationship difficulties, premature attrition, maladaptive coping styles, and subclinical depression.

While various background factors can mitigate the response to crisis, it can generally be said that the worse the crisis, the stronger the reaction. The death of a parent, spouse, or child is generally more serious than the death of a friend. Witnessing the violent death of a loved one is worse than hearing about it. Being partly responsible for the death is worse than being a spectator. The more a person's basic needs are threatened, the greater the intensity of the experience; the more extensive the loss, the stronger and deeper the reaction.

Acute Stress Response

The human response to crisis is complex. It manifests in four general areas: cognitive functioning, physical symptoms, emotional reactivity, and specific behaviors. Our initial reactions in a crisis situation are our attempts to survive despite the traumatic sights and sounds or the impact of loss. During an emergency the functioning in each of these domains heightens to meet the demands of the situation. To the extent the emergency takes on crisis proportions—that is, presents personal threat, loss, and traumatic stimuli—our functioning in the four domains is at risk of impairment.

Cognitive operations can be impaired in several ways. The individual in crisis may find that events are confusing and difficult to understand. The individual in crisis may experience difficulties solving otherwise simple problems or may have trouble prioritizing activities and needs. Time may appear to speed up or slow down. Short-term memory may be affected, and names of common objects may be forgotten. Dissociation may render the person seemingly "disconnected" from the event (see Figure 1-6).

A wide variety of **physical reactions** are common during crisis. An individual may experience headaches and heart palpitations, as well as difficulty hearing, nausea, various muscular cramps, or profuse sweating. He or she may become faint or exhibit other signs of shock. Extreme sudden trauma has even been known to induce cardiac arrest (see Figure 1-6).

Emotional reactions may be blunted or even nonexistent. Common reactions include intense fear and anxiety, anger, irritability, and frustration. Displaced anger and aggression may also plague organizations, especially during prolonged crisis (see Figure 1-7).

Behavioral responses are similarly varied. An individual in crisis may respond with "hysteria," that is, screaming and crying, panic, and uncontrolled movement. On the other hand, a person may react with slowness, aimless wandering, little expressiveness, and general dejection (see Figure 1-7).

Although this wide variety of reactions presents a confusing picture, Acute Stress Response in each of these four domains tends to converge into two general patterns. Approximately 25 percent of those experiencing Acute Stress Response tend to show a pattern of overall agitation or overreactive response. The remaining 75 percent tend to exhibit a depressive or underreactive response pattern. It is the latter who are most easily missed by crisis managers and who are the majority at risk for posttrauma impairment. These reactions will be discussed further on.

In 1994, the American Psychiatric Association published the fourth edition of the *Diagnostic and Statistical Manual*. In this edition a new diagnostic entity, Acute Stress Disorder (ASD), was discussed. This disorder generally follows the symptomology of Posttraumatic Stress Disorder. Those symptoms will be presented in the next section. ASD represents a clinically serious psychological reaction to critical incidents that warrants prompt referral to medical care. The major differences have to do with the onset (within four weeks of event for ASD) and duration of symptoms (less than one month for ASD).

Delayed Stress Response

In the period following a crisis, a number of delayed reactions may emerge within the four domains identified during initial reactions. Once the emergency is over, it is no longer critical to focus on survival. It is now time to sort through the experience, determine its meaning, and put it to rest. This can be a troubling process, particularly if the incident

- exposed ongoing threats and vulnerabilities that were not previously acknowledged

- caused loss of persons or things that were of central importance in the individual's life

- exposed the individual to highly traumatic sights and sounds

- undermined the individual's self-confidence and trust in the world

As we grow, we constantly modify and add to our world view, including ideas of causation, meaning, goodness, and purpose. Each of our experiences is incorporated into this construct. Traumatic experiences tear this fabric of personal philosophy. The more bizarre, unusual, and threatening the experience, the larger its reverberations through our system. Recovering from crisis amounts to restructuring or reweaving ourselves.

As the individual struggles to overcome the crisis, accept his or her reactions to the incident, and adjust to the changes brought about by the incident, the individual's specific reactions in each of the four domains can prove troublesome (see Figure 1-8).

The initial cognitive reactions during the primary response stage, combined with subsequent secondary reactions, can make a person feel as if she is losing her mind and going crazy. Because much energy is spent in efforts to understand the incident and incorporate it into a newly emerging world view, a person's frequent reaction to crisis is preoccupation with the event. This can constitute an orientation toward the past; for example, a familiar sight around the Vietnam Memorial in Washington, D.C., is the veteran still wearing his field jacket and various memorabilia.

Another cognitive sign of Delayed Stress Response is denial of the importance of the incident, particularly when such denial is incongruent with obvious behavioral signs. Finally, difficulty focusing or concentrating frequently plagues those who have undergone critical incidents. This often results in performance problems in school and on the job.

Delayed emotional reactions to crisis include depression, grief, and numbing (see Figure 1-9). Depressive reactions may be part of the grieving process or may be part of a more general numbing and blunting of emotional response. This may be partially caused by the enormity or frightful nature of the experience or by a person shutting down emotionally in order to cope with the changes brought about by the crisis. Resentment and rages can be intense and difficult to control. Finally, a person may experience phobic and anxiety reactions to situations or themes that are similar to the original threatening crisis.

A frequent delayed emotional response is guilt. Guilt may surface as a reaction to specific real or imagined obligations, or it may be a more general, free-floating survivor's guilt: "If good people (or things) were lost and I survived, then I must find out why. Either the world is chaotic (I can't live with that), or it must have been more important that I live (and I'm not sure I can live with that responsibility)."

Physical reactions vary widely (see Figure 1-8). Central reactions can include fatigue, psychosomatic symptoms, increased illness, and inordinate physical concerns. Crisis creates new demands brought about by changes in the world or between people. These demands are physically fatiguing. In addition, the work involved in processing psychological changes contributes to fatigue. Some distress manifests itself in psychosomatic conditions. Digestive, respiratory, and circulatory disorders occur with greater frequency following a crisis. As these various stressors drain physical resources, they also depress the immune system, which results in increased physical illness.

While behavioral reactions during or shortly after crisis tend to coalesce into two general patterns, this is not so for delayed reactions (see Figure 1-9). Delayed behavioral reactions can focus on one or several of the following:

Substance abuse. Abuse rates increase following crisis. Self-medication, which initially provides relief from crisis-related stress, can soon become the problem itself.

Withdrawal. Self-destructive behavior (such as high-risk, self-harming, or even suicidal behavior) is not uncommon following crisis, nor are sudden lifestyle changes. Both may be related to guilt reactions and correspond with a more general withdrawal from social contact.

Arousal. Difficulty relaxing is often prevalent. This can include problems sleeping, talking compulsively about the incident, or various kinds of avoidance. The individual might avoid certain types of people, places, or situations. A person might also avoid certain thoughts, feelings, reminders, and memories.

Relationship problems. Due to problems of concentration, irritability, or avoidance, work may become difficult. These symptoms and the resultant stress on the job can, in turn, cause stress for the family. Relationships on the job and at home often suffer, especially if little resistance to stress is available.

Intrusive imagery. Unwanted images of the incident may intrude in the form of daydreams, nightmares, flashbacks, or compulsive memories.

These cognitive, emotional, physical, and behavioral signs and symptoms of trauma each represent an attempt, or a reaction to an attempt, to integrate the experience. The incident must be put into perspective, lessons must be learned, and the individual must go on with life. Most symptoms are normal and temporary. When they become entrenched, however, they bring about one of several posttraumatic syndromes, such as the well-known Posttraumatic Stress Disorder.

Prior to discussing PTSD, more must be said about the factors influencing an individual's vulnerability to crisis.

Vulnerability

A crisis affects different people differently. The factors influencing vulnerability were mentioned earlier; however, some elaboration will be helpful (see Figure 1-10).

Even though some measure of resilience is gained from the experience of overcoming previous crises, rarely does a person completely master prior traumas. Usually a residue of partially resolved issues and a disproportionate sensitivity to current crises of similar nature remain. Previous losses can make a present loss less bearable; prior victimization often leaves a person vulnerable to the trauma of present victimization.

The amount of background stress also lowers an individual's resistance to crisis. For example, if a person is going through a divorce, is on the verge of losing his job, or is facing an income tax audit, a minor traffic accident can be overwhelming.

Family stability is critical to a sense of well-being. Changes in family functioning, discord, and separation undermine personal confidence and reduce social support, which are key aspects of resilience to crisis.

Feelings of inadequacy stemming from personal traits, family training, or life experience can prove critical to one's ability to cope with crisis. While popular literature is full of stories of inadequate people rising to meet the demands of a crisis and thereby saving themselves, the opposite is more often the case.

Similar outcomes can be seen in relation to psychological needfulness, physical fatigue, or personal needs due to recent changes or loss; each creates special vulnerabilities to crisis. In addition, certain beliefs (such as invulnerability, "specialness," or rigid religious beliefs) or overly positive or negative attitudes can lend to disillusionment and despair following a crisis.

In assessing the likelihood of impairment pursuant to a crisis or disaster, it is important to look not only at the nature of the incident but also at the individual's reactions.

Recent Advances in PTSD Research

While references to psychological responses to crises have appeared throughout world literature, it was not until the nineteenth century that discussion began in earnest. During that time industrial accidents became more frequent, and the issue of compensation for nonphysical impairment due to such accidents was argued in court in England. Later, Sigmund Freud (1920, 1926) and then Trimble (1985) made seminal observations regarding trauma and the development of neuroses; this discussion intensified during World Wars I and II. Since then there has been much confusion, with various models being utilized.

Horowitz outlined the essential elements of the posttraumatic response at the San Francisco Veteran's Administration Hospital (Horowitz 1975). They described an alternating process of intrusive traumatic imagery (memories, dreams, flashbacks) and corresponding efforts at denial (depression, amnesia, alienation). The result was a chronic debilitating condition with a wide variety of specific symptoms.

In 1980, the American Psychiatric Association (APA) introduced the term Posttraumatic Stress Disorder in the third edition of the *Diagnostic and Statistical Manual*. The term referred to a set of symptoms following the experience of an event that is "outside the range of usual human experience and that would be markedly distressing to almost anyone" (American Psychiatric Association 1980, 250). Much of the conceptualization of PTSD comes out of the study of Vietnam War veterans.

In recent years PTSD has gained media attention as the public's awareness of terrorist crimes against children and of school violence has increased. It is important for school crisis planners and responders to be familiar with both the nature and the limitations of the PTSD diagnosis.

In 1987, and then again 1994, the APA revised its criteria for diagnosis of PTSD. These conditions include the nature of the traumatic incident, the convergence of three sets of symptoms, the time of onset and duration of the symptoms, and effect of the disturbance on functioning (see Figure 1-11).

Criterion B refers to the set of intrusive imagery and concomitant reactions referred to by Horowitz (see Figure 1-12). Memories and recollections may occur spontaneously and may be troubling; they may be obsessive or they may be involuntary, as in the case of flashbacks. Dreams and nightmares of the incident, or of

content having parallel themes, may be recurrent. Traumatized individuals may suddenly sense that the incident is recurring or may feel great distress in a similar situation. Children often engage in play activities that repeat traumatic themes without successful resolution.

Criterion C refers to both avoidance and numbing phenomena (see Figure 1-13), which can include avoidance of thoughts and feelings associated with the incident or avoidance of similar situations. One firefighter was unable to bring himself to drive over the bridge he had worked on during the aftermath of an airline disaster. The bridge lay between his home and workplace, and avoiding it cost him an additional hour of commuting in heavy traffic every day for two years.

Numbing symptoms include amnesia, diminished interest in significant activities, detachment, constricted affect (limited emotionality), and a sense of foreshortened future (not having long to live). Some children may display regressive behavior.

Of the avoidance and numbing symptoms, three must be present to warrant a PTSD diagnosis. In other words, even if all other criteria are met, but only two avoidance or numbing symptoms are present, a PTSD diagnosis could not be made. The individual would be considered to be suffering from some other posttraumatic syndrome.

Criterion D refers to problems of inappropriate arousal (see Figure 1-14). Crisis victims are plagued with difficulties falling and staying asleep; irritability with family, friends, and coworkers; and problems concentrating on tasks at hand. They are often unable to relax because they feel a need to scan for further threat (hypervigilance); they suffer from a delicate startle response and general overreactivity. Minor stimuli will trigger a disproportionately large response from them.

To give an example: I was called upon to consult with an insurance company following the 1989 Loma Prieta earthquake in the San Francisco Bay Area. Claims department telephone operators who did the initial screenings for property damage claims worked at an all-time low rate of efficiency one week following

Diagnostic Criteria for 309.81: Posttraumatic Stress Disorder

A. The person has been exposed to a traumatic event in which both of the following were present:

1. the person experienced, witnessed, or was confronted with an event or events that involved actual or threatened death or serious injury, or a threat to the physical integrity of self or others

2. the person's response involved intense fear, helplessness, or horror. **Note:** In children, this may be expressed instead by disorganized or agitated behavior

B. The traumatic event is persistently reexperienced in one (or more) of the following ways:

1. recurrent and intrusive distressing recollections of the event, including images, thoughts, or perceptions. **Note:** In young children, repetitive play may occur in which themes or aspects of the trauma are expressed

2. recurrent distressing dreams of the event. **Note:** In children, there may be frightening dreams without recognizable content

3. acting or feeling as if the traumatic event were recurring (includes a sense of reliving the experience, illusions, hallucinations, and dissociative flashback episodes, including those that occur on awakening or when intoxicated). **Note:** In young children, trauma-specific reenactment may occur

4. intense psychological distress at exposure to internal or external cues that symbolize or resemble an aspect of the traumatic event

5. physiological reactivity on exposure to internal or external cues that symbolize or resemble an aspect of the traumatic event

C. Persistent avoidance of stimuli associated with the trauma and numbing of general responsiveness (not present before the trauma), as indicated by three (or more) of the following:

1. efforts to avoid thoughts, feelings, or conversations associated with the trauma

2. efforts to avoid activities, places, or people that arouse recollections of the trauma

3. inability to recall an important aspect of the trauma

4. markedly diminished interest or participation in significant activities

5. feeling of detachment or estrangement from others

6. restricted range of affect (e.g., unable to have loving feelings)

7. sense of a foreshortened future (e.g., does not expect to have a career, marriage, children, or a normal life span)

D. Persistent symptoms of increased arousal (not present before the trauma), as indicated by two (or more) of the following:

1. difficulty falling or staying asleep

2. irritability or outbursts of anger

3. difficulty concentrating

4. hypervigilance

5. exaggerated startle response

E. Duration of the disturbance (symptoms in Criteria B, C, and D) is more than one month.

F. The disturbance causes clinically significant distress or impairment on social, occupational, or other important areas of functioning.

Specify if:

Acute: if duration of symptoms is less than three months

Chronic: if duration of symptoms is three months or more

Specify if:

With Delayed Onset: if onset of symptoms is at least six months after the stressor

(American Psychiatric Association 1994, 424–429)

the quake. By their own estimates, their productivity had dropped to 10 percent of normal prior to the quake. Three factors contributed to this. First, each lived and worked in the quake impact zone and thus experienced the extreme shaking and immediate aftermath. Second, the four-story building where they worked was repeatedly shaken by small and large aftershocks. Third, whether or not it was relevant to the claim, each caller, because of the need to talk, was telling the operator everything he or she had experienced during the quake. Each call reminded the operators of their own experiences, keeping them in a state of chronic arousal. Thus, their distractibility, hypervigilance, startle responses, and overreactivity reduced their efficiency.

Taken together, disparate PTSD symptoms can create troubling life conditions. One 25-year-old former firefighter and Vietnam veteran would wake suddenly out of a sound sleep convinced that the fire bell had rung or that battle stations had been sounded. He would spring upright, leap out of bed, and dash headlong into the adjacent closet. His terrified wife would try to wake him while he was fighting with clothing or searching wildly for his shoes.

One attempt at making the spectrum of PTSD symptoms more cohesive is the recent work of George Everly (Everly and Lating 1995) of Johns Hopkins University (see Figure 1-15). Dr. Everly's neurophysiological model points to a lowered activation threshold of the brain's arousal system. According to Everly, both the structure and function of neurons in the limbic system are altered following trauma. This results in a greater propensity for arousal. The various recollective processes necessary for integration of traumatic experience trigger arousal of the limbic system. Thus, he considers PTSD to be a disorder of arousal.

Children's Posttrauma Behavior

Children's posttrauma behavior closely follows that of adults, with allowances for developmental differences. Awareness of these differences,

however, is critical to the identification of children in crisis and the planning of appropriate interventions.

This section reviews the basics of child development as they affect crisis response, outlines general crisis reactions, and discusses posttrauma responses at different age levels.

Crisis and Development

Perhaps the most widely accepted schema for understanding child development is that of Erik Erikson (1968). Erikson's concept of developmental stages and crises provides a useful starting point for predicting the effects of traumatic stress at various developmental levels.

Erikson held that each level of development presents a normal crisis that must be resolved before the next level can be fully attained. Incomplete resolution not only results in ongoing vulnerabilities and difficulties, but also it makes resolution of the next level's crisis more difficult. For example, for infants up to two years of age, the major issue is whether or not the world, other people, and even oneself can be trusted. Without such trust, individuals develop attributes of anxiety, dependency, and withdrawal. When older people exhibit these character traits because of incomplete development during infancy, they now have attributes that are considered to be regressive. Erikson believed that traumas experienced during infancy would likely result in such regressive attributes later.

Erikson's work has received much support. In a notable empirical investigation John Wilson (1978) discovered that Vietnam veterans traumatized in combat had difficulty completing developmental tasks. These veterans, traumatized during one stage in their lives, showed a changing and predictable configuration of difficulties during later stages.

Trauma during play age (three to five years), when autonomy is at issue, is likely to lead to shame and doubt, overcontrol, impulsiveness, and helplessness in response to crises. These regressive attributes may linger into subsequent stages. Further, the child is at risk for unsatisfactory resolution of tasks in subsequent stages and may manifest the regressive attributes of those later stages as well. Issues and regressive attributes of the younger and older school-age and adolescent stages are illustrated in Figure 1-16.

Children's Immediate Signs of Distress

Spencer Eth and Robert Pynoos (1985) studied children who witnessed the murder of their parents. These children had experienced serious sudden loss, personal threat, and traumatic sights and sounds. Eth and Pynoos conceptualize four general responses common to children (see Figure 1-17). They report:

Disorganization. The extreme stress of crisis threatens children's newly won and tentatively held conceptual organization; thus, children tend to become disorganized under such stress. Signs of disorganization are loss of attention span, confusion, immobility, and lack of perspective.

Primitivization. Children become less sophisticated, regressing to earlier, more primitive forms of functioning. Among these are loss of toileting or other independent living skills, dependency, generalized fears, and a return to earlier forms of coping.

Deverbalization. Children tend to show their distress rather than tell of it. They rely on less verbal means of communication, such as thematic play, anxious clinging, acting out, and avoidances.

Somatization. Much of children's distress manifests itself physically. Appetite and respiratory and digestive functions can all be affected. Aches and pains are common.

Eth and Pynoos (1985) found that Acute Stress Response in children fell into either an "agitated" or a "depressed" category (see Figure 1-18). Children's agitated reactions include a flushed, sweating and frenzied appearance; panicked, enraged, or "hysterical" emotional reaction; and frenzied, ineffectual, and uncontrolled behavior. These are overreactions to the situation.

A depressive reaction, or underreaction,

can include a pale, submissive, and shocklike appearance; blunted or numb emotional state; and slowed, automatic, paralyzed, or immobilized behavior. It is critical that staff be aware of the signs of depressed Acute Stress Response because the majority of ASR responses are of this type. If crisis managers focus only on agitated responders, the majority of at-risk students will not be identified. In that event, many of those children who need it will not receive further assessment and services following a crisis.

Children's Delayed Signs of Distress

Children have long-lasting reactions to crises, consisting of a wide variety of specific signs that overlap to configure an individual pattern. These reactions can be more easily identified in clusters of regressive physical and emotional signs of distress. Further, each cluster differs according to developmental level.

Preschool and Kindergarten. Regressive signs among three-to-five-year-olds include resumption of bedwetting and loss of toileting skills, thumb sucking and other childish attempts at coping, and generalized fears (see Figures 1-19 and 1-20). Physical symptoms include loss of appetite or overeating, various bowel and bladder problems, and difficulties with sleeping and nightmares. Young children's behavioral signs are rooted in their overall life concerns which are focused on autonomous functions. Anxiety, dependency, control, and helplessness are at issue. Signs of distress include nervousness, anxiety, and irritability. Young children will engage in repetitive play, reenacting the trauma. Their attention spans become shorter, and they cling more to adults. They may also become more aggressive and tend to disobey adults who are attempting to manage the children's acting out. They are frequently fearful of reminders of the crisis and appear confused about the incident, its location, sequencing, and meaning. Young children find loss particularly troubling because they do not understand it.

Elementary. Elementary students' developmental focus has evolved from trust and autonomy to initiative and industry. A loss of purpose, a need for protectors, and feelings of inferiority and incompetence are critical issues. Regressive signs include clinging to parents and competition with siblings (see Figures 1-21 and 1-22). Sometimes children wish to be fed and dressed; they resort to outworn habits they had previously discarded. Their physical complaints are frequent and may include vision problems and stomach pains. Often they experience headaches or nausea. Difficulties with sleeping and nightmares continue. The elementary child's increased concern with peer and school involvement and his or her immature conceptual development are reflected in emotional and behavioral signs.

Middle School and Senior High School.
The central task of adolescence is to develop personal identity. This comes about through a swing of allegiance and identification from parents to peers and from peers to self. At issue is identity diffusion, lack of commitment, self-consciousness, and prolonged psychosocial moratorium on maturing to adulthood. Regressive signs of distress include the failure to meet responsibilities and the resumption of earlier forms of coping (see Figures 1-23 and 1-24). The process of emancipation from family can make setbacks uncomfortable for both the adolescent and his or her family. Social interests—normally piqued during this period—may decline. Physical signs of distress include headaches and other vague pains. Overconcern with health and vague health complaints are common. Skin rashes and appetite disorders are frequent. More notable are the full range of maladaptive adolescent behaviors, spanning from survivor's guilt to antisocial behavior. Increased substance abuse, addictive behavior, and sexual acting out are common, as is a drop in school performance. Depression, not uncommon during later adolescence, often occurs following a crisis. There can be sudden and dramatic changes in attitude, lifestyles, or relationships. Adolescents can appear "too old too soon," adopting new lifestyles or habits and precipitously making binding life choices, such as pregnancy, dropping out of school, and early marriage.

Trauma, Brain Chemistry, and Learning

Much recent work on understanding how trauma occurs has focused upon neurobiological dimensions of brain changes following overwhelming incidents and upon memory research. In reviewing recent work on the psychobiology of Posttraumatic Stress Disorder, Bessel Van der Kolk (1996) points out two different types of abnormalities following trauma. The first consists of heightened responsiveness to trauma-specific stimulus. Reminders of the event(s) can result in increased levels of the chemicals that trigger autonomic nervous system arousal. A second abnormality consists of overarousal to intense stimuli that are not even trauma-related. Victims of trauma tend to have a pronounced startle reaction as well as other arousal symptoms to loud noises or other abrupt but trauma-neutral experiences. This overactivation of the autonomic nervous system, Van der Kolk feels, results from a lack of integration of highly emotionally charged memories with the cognitive structuring of experience.

Van der Kolk points out that specific psychophysiological effects include release of those neurohormones that accompany stress reactions. These include:

- increased levels of catecholamines (epinephrine and norepinephrine), resulting in increased sympathetic nervous system activity

- decreased corticosteriods and serotonin, resulting in inability to moderate the catecholamine-triggered fight-or-flight response

- increased levels of endogenous opioids, resulting in pain analgesia, emotional blunting, and memory impairment

Van der Kolk cites a recently growing body of research that is beginning to outline the psychophysiology of trauma among children. The developmental effects of these neurohormonal responses appear to include disruption of the functional areas of numerous cortical and subcortical areas, including loss of synchronization and integration. Left hemisphere activities seem to be more affected, impacting language and recall abilities in particular. While the evidence is limited so far, it seems to provide support for observations leading to the new complex Posttraumatic Stress Disorder discussed later in this chapter, which has particular relevance for children traumatized early and for prolonged periods. The potential for connections with a wide range of thus far poorly understood learning and adjustment problems among young people seems to be great.

Finally, as indicated above, researchers have narrowed the search for the brain centers responsible for these posttraumatic biological changes (Van der Kolk 1996). Two structures in the limbic system (that part of the subcortical brain which is responsible for self-preservation and survival), the amygdala and the hippocampus, are impacted negatively. The amygdala evaluates the emotional meaning of incoming stimuli and integrates the representation of external events with emotional experiences associated with their memory. The hippocampus categorizes, relates, and stores incoming stimuli in memory, a vital part of the process of creating declarative memory.

Van der Kolk cites reports linking posttrauma chemical activity as described above with shrinking of the hippocampus (due to increased levels of cortisol—a hormone toxic to the hippocampus) and increased activity in the right hemisphere, the site of parts of the limbic system connected with the amygdala. This would correlate with findings that activity in these various areas correspond with posttrauma symptoms. As research develops in the psychobiology of stress disorders, new avenues of prevention and treatment will emerge.

The effects of trauma are of far more than clinical interest for educators. Indeed, the very mission of the school—student learning—is compromised on the individual, classroom, and entire school levels by posttrauma reactions. This occurs in a variety of ways (see Figure 1-25):

1. **ADHD students have disproportionate rates of prior trauma; posttrauma behavior mimics ADHD.** Studies of background factors among Attention Deficit Hyperactivity Disorder (ADHD) students show relatively high rates of background trauma in comparison to students not identified as ADHD. This may be a result of ADHD behavior precipitating conditions conducive to critical incidents, or, more likely, it may be that the traumatic incidents create changes in the traumatized child. During the process of recovery from trauma, children must reexperience the event in order to integrate it into their construction of the world and their sense of self. This reexperiencing creates several reactions that affect learning.

2. **Heightened physiological arousal disturbs concentration.** Of the three major chemical groups involved in the reaction to intrusive imagery, catecholamines and corticosteroids directly affect the ability to concentrate. Increased levels of catecholamines heighten physiological arousal, and decreased levels of corticosteroids allow the level of activity to escalate. Impulses—such as aggression or emotionality—cannot be modulated and overcome cognitive controls.

3. **Heightened startle reflex disrupts attention.** One typical result of overarousal is an inability to modulate the startle reflex. Any distraction spirals into a prolonged fight-or-flight response. Students are then victimized by the myriad of distractions that characterize a normal classroom.

4. **Regression and reenactments interfere with socialization.** When faced with overwhelming stress, children tend to react to trauma by regressing to an earlier level of coping and its associated interests and behaviors. In addition, one very natural way they integrate new experiences is to incorpo-

rate them in their play. This amounts to reenactments of the trauma. Both regression and reenactments, however, put off other children and lead to social rejection. This process interferes with socialization.

5. **Memory difficulties frustrate retention and retrieval.** Increased levels of endogenous opioids, triggered by the flooding of catecholamines, have several effects upon learning. The first is difficulty in memory retention and retrieval. Students who cannot classify, store, and retrieve information are at an obvious disadvantage in many classroom situations.

6. **Dissociative reactions affect attention.** Dissociative reactions are another effect of endogenous opioid flooding. Dissociation is considered a key sign of trauma, both at the time of the incident and during the recovery period. Not only do dissociative reactions impact retention, they affect motivation and socialization. Attention suffers when the child is shut down to the world.

7. **Behavior caused by dissociative, attention, and concentration difficulties is interpreted as a conduct and discipline issue.** As teachers and parents observe students who are having difficulty paying attention and staying on task, they see children who are "avoiding work," "refusing to cooperate," and "daydreaming." This creates a secondary source of stress for the child: adults who can neither understand nor tolerate the behavior. Many traumatized children are inadvertently punished by well-meaning adults who are just trying to help.

8. **Preoccupation with traumatic experience disengages child from schooling process.** When experiences do not fit existing models, the models must be revised and experiences reinterpreted until a "fit" is made. Horowitz calls the predisposition to actively store and continually rework memories of incompletely processed experience a "completion tendency." To the extent the child is engaged in the attempt to process the memories and newly experienced reali-

ties presented by the traumatic experience, he or she is too preoccupied to fully benefit from the school experience. His or her behavior is likely to pose a significant distraction to others, earning the child the label of a troublemaker.

Group-Level Effects

Schooling takes up a large part of the child's day for the better part of each year. Whatever affects the mood, climate, and effectiveness of the school directly affects the child. To the extent that a crisis impacts the classroom, it impacts the child. To the extent that staff are affected, so is the child. If a localized incident impacts a particular class, it also affects the rest of the staff, along with the siblings and friends of the students in that class. Crisis managers must understand this ripple effect in order to plan a comprehensive intervention.

Groups have their own responses to crises that affect their members. This principle extends from peer group to classroom, from site staff to district office, and from district office to community. The real cost of crisis must be measured not only in terms of the impairment of directly involved individuals but also in consideration of the diminished functioning of the entire group. The total cost encompasses cumulative lost time, diminished performance, morale and climate problems, and other subtle effects of the crisis; all of these are pervasive. Group costs usually far outweigh the cost to the obviously impacted individuals.

Each group evolves its own character, including its level of social cohesiveness. Although this solidarity level varies from hour to hour, day to day, over time it is generally consistent. There is no "best" formula. The greater the level of cohesiveness, the less room for individuality and self-expression. The lower the level of cohesiveness, the less group identity and support are available. Each group will work out its own level, which is necessarily a compromise.

Bonding forces, which develop over time, determine a particular group's solidarity level.

These forces are balanced by the forces of fragmentation and differentiation, territorial disputes, old animosities, and divergent interests that are common in any organization. The overall balance between bonding and fragmentation factors determines the level of cohesiveness.

Crisis impacts group solidarity in three stages: recoil, reorganization, and restabilization (see Figure 1-26). Immediately following impact, the organization typically recoils in initial disorganization, which is followed by a focused effort at meeting the crisis. Old animosities, disputes, and divergences are temporarily put aside. This "circle the wagons" reaction results in an unusually high surge of cohesiveness. The recoil stage can last from hours to days or weeks.

Following the recoil stage is a relatively long period during which the group tries to reorganize itself. Various factors work together toward reestablishing a new level of general cohesiveness. Crises normally force changes. They create new conditions and realities that interfere with the previous ways of doing things. These new conditions are the first factor. The group's realization of its capacity for greater solidarity and strength, revealed during the recoil stage, is the second. But old fights and old animosities return, fueled by the increased stress of changed conditions. These reemerging forces of fragmentation are the third factor. The relative influence of each of these three factors alternates, and the overall solidarity level varies more widely than it did before the crisis. The reorganization stage can last weeks, months, or even years.

Critical areas of impact on organizational dynamics include both the group's content and its process (see Figure 1-27). Affected process dynamics can include patterns of communication and decision making, operational expectations, distance regulation, and adjustment to change. Key indicators include informal and formal contractual disputes, role rigidity, homeostatic resistance to change, and emerging polarity in the felt distance between group members.

The crisis can precipitate difficulties in the content dynamics of organizational identity and purpose. Key indicators can include changes in patterns of attachment and affiliation among group members and alteration in key shared values, goals, and beliefs.

The reorganization stage of response to crisis includes renegotiation and adjustment in these areas of organizational dynamics, and the stage is sometimes punctuated by much painful fluctuation.

When these factors finally settle into a new stability, the organizational adjustment process is complete. A new solidarity level becomes the norm, and the swings in cohesiveness become less variable and more routine. New territorial boundaries are established, new alliances form, new ledgers of obligation and entitlement are drawn, and new conflicts are defined. Usually group solidarity will restabilize at a higher or lower level than before. If the crisis has any impact at all, the group rarely emerges unchanged.

A single death by accident does not call the bonds, structure, and procedures of a school into question. However, the unexpected suicide of a long-respected teacher coupled with a scandal might. A drive-by shooting is serious, but a shooting between rival groups within a school, where attempts to control such groups in the past have failed, is much more serious. To the extent that a crisis challenges the effectiveness of the organization itself, reorganization can be expected in the wake of the event.

Because students are deeply affected by the climate and effectiveness of the school, Crisis Response Teams must take into consideration the group dimensions of any crisis. The tendency of many officials is to minimize a crisis by minimizing the extent of the intervention, but this may result in a widespread decline of cohesiveness within the school and a widespread cost to both students and staff in the areas of school climate, staff morale, delayed stress reactions, and diminished performance at all levels.

This chapter focused on the traumatic stress response seen in individual reactions to crisis, the significance of developmental differences, and the impact on the larger system. Given the significant threat to the schooling process posed by crisis, strategies to manage such incidents and mitigate their effects are crucial tools for school leaders. Chapter 2 discusses the goals and objectives of school crisis management and sets the stage for further exploration of specific strategies and their coordination.

mands of staff. Provide charts and handouts for reference. Make yourself available for follow-up clarification and support. Understand that teaching is a relational profession, and school crisis affects teachers personally.

Suggestions for Community Mental Health and Crisis Response Teams

This section, and the similar sections at the end of each of the subsequent chapters, provides additional perspective, context, and direction for mental health or crisis response professionals who assist schools following crisis. Schools are unique environments; they tend to be surprisingly political and territorial and at the same time intent upon serving the well-being of their students. Because of the differing organization, scope of practice, language, and culture of schools compared to other organizations, each chapter in this book will provide nonschool professionals with information that aims at bridging the school-community gap.

Outside professionals can assist school personnel in recognizing and addressing the effects of acute and posttraumatic stress reactions. Traditionally following a crisis, students are referred to outsiders for evaluation and support if staff feels it is needed. While school people often lack specialized knowledge necessary to make such clinical distinctions, this arrangement does acknowledge that school personnel are those with the most exposure to the child and best know the child's background and normal reaction patterns. Training teachers and other staff to observe signs of over- or underreactivity, exacerbated startle reflex, and signs of dissociation can do much to sharpen perceptivity and utilize staff as the screening eyes and ears of the assessment process.

When training school personnel, use clear, nonclinical language and provide clear descriptions of dysfunctional behavior. Respect the background, experience, and workplace de-

Columbine High School at Year's End: Challenges to Reestablish the Educational Process

Betty Fitzpatrick

The number of traumatized victims of the Columbine shooting is estimated at several hundred. At year's end, all these individuals—those who were physically wounded and are returning to school in wheelchairs, those who had family members or close friends die, those who directly witnessed horror, those who were trapped in the building for several hours, those who were waiting outside with the unknown—are still affected to differing degrees and are in differing phases of their emotional recovery. Eight months after the event we continue to add to the number of victims, because of new events and the continuous retelling of the event through media and the ongoing investigation.

The challenge of "taking back our school" has now receded. The reality of "back to school as usual" becomes an ongoing challenge. How does a student stay focused, prevent intrusive thoughts, or hold important trigonometry, AP world history, and chemistry concepts in his or her head after such a horrific event? The year began with 11 students on Homebound Support service, and as we end the first semester, the number has increased to 30. While still a small number given the total enrollment of over 2,000, this creates a demand for accommodation that was not anticipated.

Some of our students may never be able to return to their school. Alternatives for these students must be explored, which will be a challenge to the school system itself. A public school is not designed to be flexible. It is designed for continual attendance, consistency of effort, and no lapses in comprehension and requires one class to build on another. If you falter at Math 1, second semester does not necessarily provide the opportunity to try again. Your entire sequencing of credits may be affected. The education system, as we know it today across the entire U.S., does not make room for the cognitive deficits that will occur with posttraumatic stress symptoms or those of anxiety and depression. All are symptoms that we can expect after any type of major disaster: man-made or natural.

Many members of the community continue to be traumatized, either directly or vicariously. Our culture expects us to return to normalcy—to put it all behind us. But new events—a new arrest, a suicide in a family, release of videotapes to a national magazine, a criminal investigation not yet concluded—prevent that from occurring. In Littleton, "When will it end?" is a collective refrain.

Partnering with outside agencies for much needed help is a challenge for the school district. School districts are not equipped to respond to the multiple emotional needs that are now present. We rely heavily on our local community mental health agency (Jefferson Center for Mental Health) for services. This is in a community and school that has never needed this type of support before. We continue to partner with private therapists and our university to provide risk assessment as well as treatment and psychoeducation to staff, students, parents, and community.

While many of the victims of this event are in therapy and others seek counseling services through their local church groups, we continue to do outreach. The mental health counselors assigned to the school as a result of the shootings and its aftermath have logged in over 600 visits in the first semester. We do not anticipate this demand to decrease. In addition, the full-time nurse placed in the school to serve the increased number of students with physical needs—and on medications—has recorded over 1,100 visits this first semester. Clearly the need is there. We must have the support that an event like this requires!

As we begin a school year after such a traumatic event, our school system and community face a multitude of new challenges—challenges that were never anticipated and had never crossed our minds prior to April 20, 1999.

Betty Fitzpatrick, R.N., M.S., is Director of Health Services, Jefferson County Public Schools.

Copy masters (Figures 2-1 to 2-13) for this chapter can be found on pages 153–165.

CHAPTER 2

School Crisis Management: Goals and Objectives

"Graduate school never prepared me for this. Heavens, all my teaching never prepared me for this!"

— *Twenty-year veteran teacher following a campus shooting*

Crisis brings chaos, and chaos undermines the safety and stability of the entire school. Some crises are generated in the community and follow students to school (such as domestic or community violence or disaster). Some are generated within the school itself (such as campus violence, sudden loss, or suicide of a student). In either case, when crisis becomes the unwelcome visitor to school, the proper role of the school is to respond in such a way as to mitigate the effects of the crisis upon its students.

Next to the family, the school is the single most important social structure in the life of the child. The family is called upon to provide sanctuary from the storms of the world; disorganization and turmoil within the family undermine the growing sense of identity and security of the child. The school is also called upon to provide respite from chaos, and turmoil in the school can be as disruptive as turmoil in the family.

Goals for School Crisis Management

The role of the school within the community, and the role it plays in the life of the growing child, dictate that it meet crucial needs of students and staff following crisis (see Figure 2-1).This in turn generates the following sets of goals for school crisis management, each of which will be discussed in detail in this chapter:

- Safety
- Stability
- Consistency
- Leadership
- Prevention of further injury
- Individual contact and support
- Skills in coping
- Family-school solidarity
- Group support
- Sense of community
- Empowerment
- Support during recovery period

Safety

Of all the concerns that should occupy the attention of administrators and crisis managers following emergencies, first and foremost is the safety of students (see Figure 2-2). Mitigating physical danger and protecting young people from further harm take priority over all else. To do this, good intelligence is critical. One source is the information available from police, fire, and other emergency services.

Shooting at a Middle School Dance

Barb Ertl

They said it sounded like balloons popping. One, two, five in all. When the last pop was heard, one teacher lay dead, two students and a teacher were wounded, and approximately 270 people experienced a sense of fear like none they'd ever known.

On Friday, April 24, 1999, the eighth-grade students of James W. Parker Middle School were attending their annual spring dance when 14-year-old Andrew Wurst pulled his father's revolver from his pocket and opened fire. He killed teacher John Gillette, who had organized the dance and who by all accounts was well loved by students and faculty alike.

Within an hour of the incident, the General McLane School District's Crisis Team was notified, and efforts were coordinated to respond to the school the following day. The team—consisting of 29 mental health professionals and clergy members from within the school district and the surrounding community—had previously agreed to respond to just such an incident.

The morning of April 25 began with an administrative council meeting during which the school superintendent and her fellow administrators developed what would be an overall game plan for providing support and intervention to the students, faculty, staff, and parents of the District. Following this meeting, the Crisis Team was briefed as to the details of the previous night's incident and given a general overview of when and how specific interventions would occur.

Later that same day, a large-group informational briefing was provided to all interested parties. The Pennsylvania State Police and the school principal, who had been present at the dance, provided an overview of the incident. Parents and other interested parties were encouraged to ask questions and get the facts so as to prevent the perpetuation of rumors. All were given a preliminary outline of interventions to be utilized during the coming weeks and a list of available community resources.

Throughout the weekend, and for the remainder of the school year, all of the community churches opened their doors to act as gathering places for people who were hurting. Formal supports—such as counselors and clergy—were available to all who were interested. Informal support people, such as members of church youth groups and neighbors, were encouraged to reach out to those impacted by the shooting.

Sunday, April 26 was utilized by the Crisis Team to prepare for the opening of school on Monday. The team developed plans to help faculty and staff provide a supportive environment to what was anticipated to be a very fearful group of students and parents. On Monday, Crisis Team members were disbursed throughout all four of the District school buildings, providing both group and individual interventions as required and distributing handouts to be sent home to parents regarding "normal reactions to abnormal events."

Throughout that first week back to school, team members focused most of their attention on the students and their family members. By the beginning of the second week, however, it became abundantly clear that the faculty, staff, and administration were weary and needed to begin their own process of grieving. During this second week, the Crisis Team focused on taking care of the previous week's caregivers. A support group was begun for the 13 chaperones of the dance (this group continued to meet on a regular basis for the 18 months that it took to bring the legal proceedings to a close). Meetings with the spouses, children, and other family members of the faculty were scheduled to give them some sense of what to expect and how to deal with it. Interested faculty members, staff, and administrators were given the opportunity to meet individually with counselors—either on campus or off campus.

In the weeks and months that followed this one incident, thousands of man-hours were spent in providing students, faculty, staff, administrators, and their families the support and information necessary to adapt to a new sense of "normal." Nothing can prepare a person to cope with this kind of tragedy, but much can be done in its aftermath to help those who experience it deal with their feelings of fear, anger, and vulnerability.

At the time of this incident, Barbara Ertl, M.S., served as School Social Worker for the Northwest Tri-county Intermediate Unit (IU) and was team leader for the Erie County Critical Incident Stress Management Team.

Crises are often potentially politically sensitive. Thus the site administrator's supervisors should approve all actions that deviate from preplanned emergency procedures. Sometimes time constraints do not allow for approval; in this case act conservatively, document the decision, and clear it with supervisors as soon as possible.

Inform staff members of all extraordinary procedures so that they can best coordinate and support their own decisions to meet the changed circumstances. Information should be regularly updated through verbal or written messages. The most efficient way is through an emergency staff meeting, in the form of an Informational Briefing (discussed elsewhere). More in-depth brief inservice training can be provided on various aspects of the crisis and response surrounding security issues. Further, as the students' perception of security is shaped by staff response, monitor staff reactions to the crisis and determine the type of leadership needed.

Unnecessary exposure to crisis-related sights and sounds reinforces feelings of insecurity. To the extent possible, provide some sort of buffer to block such exposure. This facilitates the return to routine. Finally, keep students, parents, and community informed of the proactive measures taken by the school to guarantee that students are safe.

Stability

Children thrive in a stable environment. Thus they are especially vulnerable to sudden changes in their daily routine. This vulnerability is compounded when adults around them are upset, dysfunctional, and unable to provide the protective barrier children need against rapid change.

To maximize stability, routines must be reestablished as soon as possible with as little disruption as possible (see Figure 2-3). Once safety is assured and necessary crisis-related logistical adjustments made, the normal class schedule should be resumed.

Apprise teaching and office staff members of the situation and resulting changes as thor-

oughly as possible, and provide them with the "official" description of the incident. They need to know what to expect next, or at least when the next update of information will be given. Staff should be given directions as to how to conduct informational briefings and classroom discussions with students. If any information is sensitive and confidential, care must be taken to communicate that fact to staff.

Specific crisis response activities should be orchestrated with minimal disruption to normal routine. Particular areas on campus, or groups of particularly affected students, should be isolated. Establish catchment areas, crisis response personnel, and referral mechanisms for those students showing signs of psychological distress or behavior that would interfere with classroom functioning.

Consistency

Chaos thrives on rumor. Information flow can be the best asset or the worst liability to crisis managers. News travels quickly in schools, whether it is accurate and constructive or distorted, inflammatory, and destructive. The flow of information must be controlled (see Figure 2-4).

The first step in controlling the flow of information is to develop an official narrative of the event that covers three basic elements: what led up to the crisis, how things stand at the present, and what the school will do next to contain the crisis. Accuracy and sufficient detail support the credibility of the school, although legal and practical ramifications must be considered.

The official narrative is a living story in the sense that it grows, matures, and takes different forms according to the evolving situation. For that reason the information to be included in the story must be current and credible. Incoming information must be managed—it must be sorted, confirmed for accuracy and reliability, organized, and retained. Sources of information must be assessed and cultivated.

Because much valid information comes from other agencies and must be coordinated with central administration, a designated liaison is necessary. Similarly, outgoing information, particularly to news media, should flow through the site administrator to one designated spokesperson.

News reporters can be intrusive and disruptive and can disseminate exaggerated and distorted information. This can exacerbate the crisis and create new emergencies. To do their jobs, news reporters must get interesting stories to their editors and are likely to do so whether or not the school is fairly represented. The central task of information flow focuses upon rumor management, responding to needs and inquiries, and the dispersal of useful information. It is helpful to recognize the needs of reporters and to work with them, rather than trying to work against them.

Leadership

Outsiders often perceive the site administrator, or even the district superintendent, as the source of leadership on campus. Students know better, however, and look to their teachers for direction. Classroom teachers and support staff are the front line troops who implement change and feel the greatest effects of changes in their students' lives. Teaching involves personal relationships with large numbers of students; when those students are reflecting the stress of a crisis in their behavior, the teachers are directly impacted. Support given those teachers pays off in terms of safety, stability, consistency, and leadership in times of crisis (see Figure 2-5).

Teacher training and crisis planning should occur prior to the chaos crisis brings. During and following a critical incident, monitor staff to identify those teachers whose ability to handle their classes is compromised by acute or delayed traumatic reactions of their own. Staff members need timely information and close supervisory contact in order to carry out their responsibilities.

Relief for distressed teachers—as well as support services such as consultation, debriefings, or counseling—may be necessary. Reduce the normal pressures for optimum performance and for nonessential paperwork, and provide basic structure and assistance for bottom-line expectations. Protection from parents

who are especially needful or who are displacing anger and hostility on the institution through the teacher is helpful. Provide informal crisis-related trainings as needed, as well as assistance in networking resources. Teachers tend to be perfectionists and frequently need help in recognizing when they have done all they can for students and need to take care of themselves.

Prevention of Further Injury

Crises can hurt kids, not only during the crisis itself, but long afterwards. Secondary reactions can develop in the weeks and months following crisis and can lead to debilitating physical, emotional, and behavioral reactions. Learning performance is often negatively impacted. A great many students who are at risk of such secondary reactions can be identified and can benefit from intervention (see Figure 2-6).

Strategies for preventing secondary stress and mitigating primary stress reactions to critical incidents can include information sent home to assist parents in observing their children and helping them cope. Observations by both parents and teachers can help identify students at risk for developing postcrisis complications. Once identified, whatever intervention or referral is deemed appropriate and initiated, at-risk students should be periodically monitored. Notify parents of staff concerns, stay in close communication with them, and elicit their help in monitoring the students.

Good observation implies knowing what to observe. Staff should be trained in recognizing distress signs among students and referral procedures. A referral system must be articulated, including a designated "case manager." Some schools and districts have developed resource files categorizing district and community referral resources according to specialties, expertise, and fee arrangements. All referrals should be documented and centrally filed to facilitate monitoring and follow-through.

Individual Contact and Support

Counseling following crisis or loss has been shown to facilitate adjustment and mitigate postincident delayed reactions (see Figure 2-7). Counseling an individual student could minimize the upset to the entire class brought about by postincident maladaptive behavior. Much effective counseling is done informally, and so staff must be prepared through background knowledge of the the involved student's situations and an understanding of the process of postcrisis adjustment. Disaster Response Plans can include provisions for formal planning and intervention.

These plans can utilize trained Crisis Response Team members—especially trained district personnel—or other community resources as available. Carefully screen and approve any person providing counseling to children for reliability, background, and understanding of the purpose and role of crisis intervention in schools. Counseling can be provided individually or in groups and should follow standardized guidelines such as those in this book.

If impacted students have difficulty returning to school following a highly charged incident, counselors can work with them directly, helping them to deal with fears and avoidance reactions. Follow-up activities can include grief support groups, memorials, and anniversary commemorations.

Countries, states and provinces, counties, and municipalities differ as to the legal propriety of providing counseling in schools. It is critical to be knowledgeable of and to observe all applicable laws regarding the scope of practice in schools.

Skills in Coping

Crisis brings change, and change creates stress. Even those students who are unaffected by the crisis must coexist with those who are. Peers who are having postcrisis reactions act differently than they usually do, as do staff members and parents. Overreactions, irritability, difficulty concentrating, and inappropriate behavior create a stressful learning and working environment. Stress management skills can benefit everyone (see Figure 2-8).

Teachers are in a high-stress occupation in the best of times, and that stress level is com-

pounded by the postcrisis reactions of their students. They are in the ideal position both to learn stress skills and then to teach those skills to their students.

Some specific class management strategies can be used to reduce stress levels in the classroom. Televisions should not be allowed to replay the crisis continually, as it adds to the stimulus overload and serves as a constant reminder of the incident. Similarly, although some teachers are tempted to utilize current events themes to carry curricular interest, using crisis themes in this manner can perpetuate the sense of emergency and is not a good idea.

Simple dietary modification (such as cutting caffeine and sugar) can help reduce stress levels, as can the addition of rest periods. Student perceptions of the incident are important and deserve to be heard. The manner and timing of expressive activities, however, should be managed.

Family-School Solidarity

The family is the most influential institution in the life of the child; the school runs a close second. Whatever the school can do to help stabilize the child's family following crisis stabilizes the student. This can be accomplished through a number of orchestrated outreach strategies (see Figure 2-9).

Send home material explaining the nature of the crisis, the manner in which children may be affected, and the steps parents can take to assist their child. Encourage parent-and-teacher-led meetings to assist parents in planning and networking. Emergency baby-sitting pools can be arranged by parent leaders to allow parents the flexibility to meet recovery needs. School staff can visit key homes to assess functioning and provide assistance or can organize visits by others. Suggest that parents put together a newsletter containing crisis-related information, which can be circulated by the school.

Provide staff-child-family conferencing regarding home support for at-risk students, followed by positive and encouraging notes to home. Encourage parents to increase their contact with the school family—through volunteering or participating in crisis-related task force projects—and to regularly update the school on their child's progress.

Classroom and Group Support

All students will benefit from a more supportive classroom climate, and climate is amenable to intervention (see Figure 2-10). Provide support groups for students who have been identified as at risk; the groups should be relatively homogenous in terms of exposure to the crisis, degree of impact, and other relevant factors.

In-class discussions about the crisis or recovery process can be helpful so long as they are, in fact, supportive. Guidelines for such discussion can be found in Chapter 7. Dialogue regarding the crisis must be managed in such a way as to ensure its supportive nature. Critiques of performance, "war stories," and expressions of hostility have no place in postcrisis dialogue.

Opportunities for undirected expression, such as feeling walls (where notes, poems, pictures, etc., can be posted), shrines, letters to editors, and free-form journal entries can also be provided, although these should be monitored for inflammatory content or signs of distress or danger to self or others. Art, writing, or enactment activities can provide opportunity for self-expression and group cohesiveness (see Chapter 7). In each of these, make sure that participation in the activity is optional.

Sense of Community

A solid sense of community at school—particularly those schools whose communities or families are disrupted—provides a psychological grounding for students (see Figure 2-11). Various group-building activities for classes or whole schools are available commercially or can be designed by staff or consultants.

Group or individual communication facilitator skills normally taught in peer-counseling or conflict-mediation classes can be very helpful in increasing the overall sense of school community. Peer counselors can be given extra training in recognizing, assisting, and referring students who are experiencing postcrisis distress.

To further bolster a sense of school community, introduce special crisis-adjustment-related articles or sections in the student newspaper, organize whole-school projects to raise funds or provide crisis-related assistance, or bring in outside speakers to address crisis issues and lend a sense of shared experience.

Empowerment

Crises make people feel powerless and defeated by circumstances. This can have lasting effects in terms of diminished self-esteem and an inability to take risks necessary for learning and results in a decline in the group investments that make schooling an exciting and involving experience. To the extent students can be empowered following crisis, they can resume their normal school activities (see Figure 2-12). Activities that rebuild the sense of personal and collective efficacy help students regain a positive attitude and approach to education. Encourage personal and group expression to further this process.

Community service projects, fund-raising, letter writing, or other projects let students have a tangible effect on a world that has proven itself chaotic. While none of us can control the world or match the power the world can muster, we can nonetheless act in our own behalf. Individual and group action projects teach students that they can still control some parts of their world and can reinvest in their lives.

Following the cessation of a critical incident, people deal with their emotional aftershocks and readjust to the changed realities brought by the emergency. Depending upon the nature of the incident and the damage done, complete recovery can take months or even years. During the recovery period the profound impact of the crisis sets in and delayed crisis reactions can surface. The school can do much for staff and students during this time (see Figure 2-13) and in doing so can change itself for the better.

Psychological first aid will be necessary as delayed reactions arise and affect students and families. Individual conferencing will remain occasionally necessary. This period is a good time to develop strong school counseling, peer coaching and counseling, and community volunteer programs.

Invite students who need extra support into special projects. Increased physical activity helps relieve the physical manifestations of stress, and after-school activities can provide needed social involvement. When possible, monitor students' homes for special needs, and address those needs through proper community agencies.

Suggestions for Community Mental Health and Crisis Response Teams

Community mental health and crisis responders generally tend to be oriented toward individuals in their thinking, their professional models of trauma, and their practice. One of the hardest things for them to accept about working in schools is the subordination of individuals to the school's overall functioning. Outsiders often balk at the decisions that must be made at the school level, and sometimes intervene on behalf of individuals. This is often good, and indeed one of the greatest helps that outside resources provide the school is the chance to allow one-on-one attention for those who need it and would not otherwise get it. It can be bad, however, if outside personnel take their role to be that of intruder and rescuer, which can subvert schoolwide organization and service delivery.

Remember that the school—as an organizational whole—is a stabilizing factor in the lives of children, second only to the family. The family's reactions to an incident mediate and define the meaning of the incident to the child; the school's response gives meaning to the experience in the mind of the child as well. In most cases, the school's response can be more important than the response of any of the individual professionals in the school or in the community.

Thus, the broad schoolwide goals and objectives of school crisis management are likely to take precedence over the strategies of the Crisis Response Team. It is the proper role of outside mental health and Crisis Response Teams and team members to work in conjunction with the school. That is not to say that schools or incidents are never badly managed—many certainly are. It is simply to acknowledge that no matter how good we are individually, working at cross-purposes to the school is only likely to compound matters.

Conclusion

This discussion has focused upon schoolwide administrative strategies to manage the deleterious effects of crisis upon the life of the school and its students. From the initial phases of the crisis through the recovery period, the goals and objectives of school crisis management follow from the needs of the students and aim at stabilizing the school and returning it to proper functioning. The school is central in the lives of children, and its stability is critical during times of chaos.

Copy masters (Figures 3-1 to 3-11) for this chapter can be found on pages 166–176.

CHAPTER 3

School Crisis Response

Schools are not generally in the business of providing psychological care. Crises, however, do not respect school boundaries. When crises occur, they may hurt children, disrupt school functioning, and leave lasting marks that can directly and negatively affect student performance. School interventions, done properly, can assist school staff in containing the crisis and mitigating the long-term effects on the school, its staff, and the students.

Many types of interventions are possible. They include consulting administration and staff, debriefing individuals and classrooms, holding parent conferences, and disseminating appropriate information.

In the middle of a late afternoon practice of a school swim team in Tennessee, high school junior Christie Bates was sitting alone in the bleachers. She quickly but deliberately pulled a small-caliber pistol out of her book bag, put the barrel in her mouth, and shot herself. The ensuing moment of frozen disbelief finally gave way to action as coach Bill Sommers ran over. With the help of Christie's teammates, he carried the wounded girl to the pool deck. They called 911, but to no avail. Christie was pronounced dead on arrival at the hospital. After the police completed questioning of all those present, the students drifted home.

The coach had called Principal Hugh Steinwold immediately and told him what had happened. Hugh Steinwold called a meeting that evening with Bill Sommers and Sandra Evans, who is the head of Student Services for the district and the administrator of the district's Crisis Response Team (CRT). She in turn invited Bill Koernig, district school psychologist and CRT member. They also asked Gloria Paige, a psychologist at the Community Mental Health Center and the team clinician, to attend. The five met at Principal Steinwold's home to discuss the implications of the incident and to determine whether the Crisis Response Team should be utilized.

They decided that since Christie was popular with both students and staff, the reactions to the incident could present problems and affect normal school operations and that students close to Christie might need support.

They developed the following strategy. A team would be organized under the supervision of Principal Steinwold. Psychologist Koernig would be the team leader on site and would maintain contact with Sandra Evans at the district office. She would be able to provide him with backup resources or direction as needed. Bill would also have nine CRT members at his disposal, all of whom had received CRT training: Gloria Paige, who would also act as liaison with Community Mental Health should those services prove necessary; three site counselors; three site teachers; and two district school psychologists.

The CRT was contacted and scheduled to meet at 6:00 AM the following day. They would meet with the remaining site counselors, the health specialist, and several key teachers at 6:45. At 7:30 AM meetings would be held by a CRT member with the teachers of each department to inform them of the details of the incident, the CRTs planned intervention activities, possible reactions of their students, warning signs to look for, and referral procedures. A prepared notice would be provided, along with suggestions on how to handle the ensuing class discussions. During the meeting, staff reactions would be assessed in terms of their level of functioning and need for support. Several substitute teachers would be put on alert in case last-minute relief was needed.

It was also decided that special debriefings would be held with the swim team and with a select group of students who had been especially close to Christie. Further, additional CRT members would be available for individual or small group meetings upon referral from classroom teachers. A security system was devised that would control the numbers and distribution of students referred to CRT members. One student, Christie's boyfriend, had been notified already and had agreed to meet with Gloria Paige at 7:45.

In addition, Sandra Evans would work closely with Principal Steinwold to plan ways to deal with the media, if necessary, and to deal with concerned parents. The principal would produce an informational letter to be sent home with all students, stating that a meeting for all concerned parents would be held two evenings hence.

Besides the informal staff debriefings, the CRT would conduct a special debriefing for any staff member who felt especially affected by Christie's death. A debriefing for all involved CRT members was scheduled for 4:30 PM. They determined that a smaller team of three members would be on hand the following day.

Plans for a student-staff memorial committee were tentatively outlined. Finally, a CRT incident evaluation meeting was scheduled for the following week and plans were made to determine its composition. The meeting would evaluate the CRT performance and assess the need for further services.

Crisis Response Teams like the one at this Tennessee high school are being trained nationwide to respond to crises at schools. Varying in organization, function, and composition, these teams exist to administer care at the site level following a crisis. CRTs can include some or all of the following types of personnel:

- district-level administrators and resource persons
- student service personnel
- school psychologists
- school counselors
- resource teachers
- classroom teachers
- community mental health professionals or social workers
- clergy

Each member of a Crisis Response Team must participate in standardized training in order to function within shared objectives and coordinated operations. It is crucial that all CRT members recognize their own particular limits as well as the limits of the team. School intervention does not aim to provide psychotherapy, healing, preaching, or school reorganization. The objectives of school intervention are to

1. Assist site management as directed

2. Provide assessment of the crisis and of student and staff needs

3. Provide support to staff, students, and parents as appropriate

4. Provide referral and follow-up to staff and students within the guidelines set by district administration

5. Aid the physical, organizational, and psychological well-being of Crisis Response Team members

Crisis Teams

While crisis work is by no means new in schools, Crisis Response Teams are a fairly recent phenomenon. Until the late 1980s, school crisis intervention was conducted informally by school staff or was entrusted to outside professionals. This is beginning to change now, as districts across the country develop their own formal teams.

This change was not motivated by money, since most crisis work was donated by community mental health professionals. The main problem with this type of crisis treatment, however, is that outside professionals typically do not understand school systems, have difficulty relating to classes of students, and are not always able to relate to and establish rapport with school staff.

The composition of a Crisis Response Team must reflect the system the team serves. A team needs to have the highest organizational blessing, which means operationally that a district-level administrator must play a leadership role on the team. It must also have considerable student services firepower, so school psychologists and health specialists must form a strong element. It must have the trust of and a preexisting relationship with those it serves, so site-level administrators, counselors, and teachers are critical. Finally, because schools lack clinical expertise and need the follow-through of community resources, outside private and/or public agency mental health professionals are valuable to have on the team.

A basic training course that provides them with essential background information and skills is necessary for all CRT members. This also builds relationships and group identity and provides a common working lexicon, with shared expectations about CRT operations. A program of ongoing training can reinforce these objectives as well as integrate new members. Any training curriculum should include all areas covered in crisis management.

Organization is crucial to effective team management and intervention. First, everyone should understand that the CRT can only function on site under the direct supervision of the site administrator or his or her designate. The CRT carries only derivative authority at best.

Second, once on site the CRT must have as a team leader someone who is not immediately involved in actual care giving (other than staff consultation). This individual is responsible for maintaining a liaison with site administration, monitoring team operations and personnel functioning, and providing redirection as needed. Consulting the school management team on an ongoing basis is essential.

Third, the site team leader must have ongoing support from and contact with the district-level administrator involved with the CRT program. Policy decisions, district needs, legal issues, and resource mobilization are functions best handled by someone who is not pressured by the management responsibilities of site operations.

Centralized Model

Given these specific operational considerations, there are two main organizational models for CRT teams. The first is the centralized model (see Figure 3-1): one team, composed of the members previously discussed, serves all sites in the district. If an incident occurs on a given site, the administrator calls the district-level contact person, and, if appropriate, the team mobilizes and arrives on site. Operations are under the close control of the district office. This model is highly efficient in small incidents and maximizes quality control over services.

One of the clearest examples of this model was the Secondary Division of the Los Angeles City Schools in the early 1990s. Upon receiving a request for crisis services, the head of Psychological Services would gather up to 17 specially trained school psychologists and descend upon the site. After assessing the school's needs, he sent unnecessary personnel back to the office. The rest stayed on site, planning and implementing the intervention.

The disadvantages of this model are that outside community resources tend to be underutilized; consequently, follow-up services from the community resources are less available. Furthermore, this model promotes the school's dependency on district services. After the team packs up and leaves, school personnel have been diminished in the eyes of the students and in their own eyes in terms of their capacity for meeting the challenges that periodically arise. A final disadvantage is that in the event of communitywide crisis or disaster, a centralized CRT will be easily overwhelmed, no matter how large the team is.

This is illustrated by the plight of the East Whittier School District in Southern California following the Whittier Narrows earthquake.

Because the event occurred during the period prior to the development of school intervention, the school did not have a formal CRT. The four and one-half school psychologists—already overwhelmed with fall Individualized Educational Plan (IEP) meetings and reports—were deluged with requests for assistance at all sites and received over one thousand requests for individual counseling from distraught parents. Requests for assistance from community resources yielded only one counselor for a total of three days.

Decentralized Model

The decentralized model of intervention seeks to meet the deficiencies of the centralized model (see Figure 3-2). Rather than having one team serve all sites, a district coordinating committee trains and supervises small teams at each school. Optimally, mental health resources in the community, through preplanning and prior arrangement, play a role in assisting selected school personnel who have been specially trained. The site teams provide site services, augmented by other district personnel who might be available through the district coordinating committee. This committee assists schools in developing crisis intervention teams according to the district and school disaster plan. It also trains and supervises CRT members, including outside resources.

The decentralized model increases the availability of resources, particularly during districtwide crises such as civil disturbance or disaster. It also empowers school staffs to meet their own needs and become more self-sufficient, which has implications for more general organizational development. Finally, it allows for greater utilization of outside talent and resources during both crisis and noncrisis times.

This model is not without certain disadvantages, however. Some site staff will require training, which tends to increase the overall cost of training. Some of this cost can be offset by training outside resources as staff trainers, which in turn builds increased familiarity and trust between school staff and the outside resources. It is more difficult to control service

quality with this model, and a certain amount of administrative control is compromised. Some would argue that there is lowered efficiency in smaller incidents. This probably results from fewer calls for service.

Whichever model is used to set up a CRT, school intervention basically requires the same skills. The team must be able to make rapid assessments of student and staff needs, plan and carry out appropriate interventions, use individual and group strategies, and meet special problems as they arise. The rest of this book covers these aspects of the process.

Response Team Strategies

School Crisis Response Teams serve the administrative effort to restore normal functioning to the school and manage the effects of crisis. While the size, ability, composition, and function of the team may vary, the team's purpose is to augment the existing resources of the school to handle the unusual situation. While teams may vary in function, several key strategies are especially amenable to team operation. These strategies are not mandatory or necessary, but simply represent frequently employed operational tactics among many formal and informal teams. They include those strategies represented in Figure 3-3:

1. Administrative consultation

2. Staff consultation

3. Informational briefing and fact sheets for home

4. Parent meetings

5. Identification of community, school resources

6. Liaison

7. Individual consultation and assessment

8. Parent consultation

9. Classroom discussion, defusing, debriefing

10. Classroom follow-up activities

Several of these strategies will be discussed in this chapter, and the others will be elaborated in chapters to come. Again, different teams bring different resources and skills, and particular schools, communities, and crises all present differing demands. These response options constitute a set of varied strategies that can be selected as the situation and team strengths allow.

CRT Strategy 1: Administrative Consultation

Administrative consultation usually focuses upon the administrator in charge. It is critical to understand the organizational vulnerability and consequent stress levels of administrators in the crisis situation. They may be held politically responsible for the incident itself, as well as for results of efforts to mitigate the effects of the emergency. Crises have a destabilizing effect and can bring about political disaster. It is important to do nothing to undermine the administrator's authority or efforts. Consultation with administrators should be primarily on an individual basis, and only if necessary and appropriate to the situation in a small group (see Figure 3-4).

Help the administrator size up the crisis, particularly the effects upon student and staff functioning. Keep in mind that administrators may themselves be affected negatively by the emergency and that their stress reactions may affect their ability to provide decisive leadership. Assist with situational assessment and planning and with the carrying out of his or her role as leader. Because of the administrator's professional and career vulnerability, judgements about an administrator's fitness for duty are not a function of the Crisis Response Team. Concerns about mental status, however well intentioned, should never be expressed to anyone other than the administrator, unless the physical safety of students or staff is being compromised. Only in the case of dangerousness should such concerns be expressed and then only to the administrator's superior and with utmost professional discretion.

CRT Strategy 2: Staff Consultation

Teachers, adjunct support staff, and classified and clerical staff may all benefit from consultation (see Figure 3-5). This can occur in individual meetings, small informal groups, informational briefings, didactic sessions, or formal debriefings. The purpose of such support is to provide information to staff regarding the nature of the incident and response efforts, what to expect from students, and how to identify students needing additional assistance. Suggestions can be provided for modifying classroom approaches, and the availability of further resources can be discussed. In some cases tangible assistance in dealing with a variety of unforeseen needs can be provided. Staff consultation includes assessing the impact of the crisis on staff functioning and providing feedback to the administration for staffing and planning purposes. Referral to the administrator or to outside resources may be appropriate.

The staff provides the primary interface with students and families, and thus must be empowered and supported to stabilize the campus. Observe for signs of Acute Stress Response and dysfunction relative to duties, particularly with students. Determine the staff member's ability to provide necessary support to the students and his or her need for supplemental support. Determine if the staff member is open to additional assistance for students or himself or herself. See section in Chapter 5 for further comments on staff intervention.

CRT Strategy 3: Informational Briefing and Fact Sheets

Rumor thrives in an informational blackout and creates confusion, panic, and discontent. Prompt dispersal of basic information regarding the situation, a reasonable explanation, and school response to the situation helps combat rumor and provides understanding (see Figure 3-6). Informational briefings can occur in a wide variety of contexts, from small groups to large-scale media releases. Helpful components of such briefings include situation assessments, explanations, and updates on actions taken by the school. In addition, briefings can include a discussion of of likely reactions to the crisis, steps teachers and families can take to mitigate those reactions, recommended measures for providing family support and stability, and how to access additional resources.

Keep information simple, direct, and current. Learn about rumors circulating in the school and community and address their content directly. Anticipate the needs and questions of the group being addressed. If the information is being communicated directly, leave time for questions and clarification. Time spent in discussion—despite the difficulty of dealing with displaced anger and anxiety—will be well spent. If providing the information on fact sheets for students, staff, media, or home, anticipate the probable effect of the information.

CRT Strategy 4: Parent Meetings

Parents are rightfully concerned about the well-being of their children and hence about the nature of the crisis and the steps the school is taking to manage it. Parent meetings provide them the opportunity to express that concern and receive personal assurance that all reasonable steps are being taken in behalf of their children. Much can be done in parent meetings to reduce the outward impression of cold bureaucratic indifference (see Figure 3-7).

The purpose of such meetings should be to provide information to families regarding the nature and extent of the situation and actions taken by the school. In addition, parents can learn about possible stress reactions their children may exhibit, steps they can take to support their children, and various resources available to them.

On the other hand, such meetings can become the arena for displaced anxiety and anger and a forum for political posturing. Much of this is inevitable, and steps can be taken to minimize the negative sense of discord and chaos.

The best way to handle potential discord is to prepare for a wide range of parental responses and reactions and to be as honest and detailed as possible. Appoint one spokesperson, either the site administrator or someone in a higher position of authority. Make sure representatives of the various community or district resources are available, but do not turn the meeting over to them without first limiting their time and subject matter. Finally, make plans to speak with members of the media beforehand to inform them of the purpose of the meeting and enlist their support in allowing the event to proceed without inflammatory interference.

CRT Strategy 5: Identification of Community, School Resources

Resources for meeting the needs of students, teachers, and families exist in most districts and communities. These resources range from financial to mental health to medical to practical. The greatest obstacle standing between such resources and those who need them is usually lack of awareness.

The crisis team can assist the school in inventorying what resources are available and learning how those resources can be accessed by impacted staff, students, and families. Those providing services can distribute information regarding what is available and how to get it through informational presentations, handouts, and individual contact.

Consider first the wide range of needs for goods and services among those impacted, as well as their cost, availability, and access. Learn names of contact persons, locations, and phone numbers. Obtain necessary forms. Centralize and organize information, and determine means to disperse information to all that might benefit (see Figure 3-8).

CRT Strategy 6: Liaison

District administrators, other district personnel, and outside resources can greatly assist site administrators during crisis. On the other hand, they can get in the way. The CRT can provide a valuable service by assisting with liaison between these various groups. In this process it is important to not interfere with normal chains of command, nor to undercut site level authority. Decision makers can be insulated from unnecessary diversion in order to assist communication. At all times, CRT personnel must be aware of and respect issues of professional "face" at all levels.

Site consultation and intervention must also include liaison with other outside professionals. This means identifying additional resources and providing orientation for incoming assistance, which may include a chronology and details of the event, plus outlines of the current situational status, the leadership structure, the operations, and relevant organizational issues. Where necessary, supervision may be required as well as assistance in the transition between rotating personnel (see Figure 3-9).

Orchestrating Services

Some incidents require a large number of CRT members, while others do not. Sometimes a student needs one-on-one consultation. Even when a full CRT intervention is orchestrated, consulting with site and district administrators is essential and critical.

Site administrators are often severely impacted by an incident and may need help planning how to meet the emergency. While they may have serious emotional reactions themselves, they must maintain order and leadership for everyone's well-being. They are expected by their superiors not to have trouble on their campus and to contain it quickly if it should arise. As the witch in the Broadway production of *The Wiz* proclaimed, "Don't bring me no bad news!" A complicating factor is that, when all is said and done, site administrators are affected occupationally: with every crisis, the site administrator's career is on the line. This makes the site administrator the most vulnerable during crisis.

Take these factors into account when consulting with administrators. They need help managing the crisis, yet they may be reluctant to let others meddle with a situation that could end up costing them their jobs. CRT members should avoid focusing overzealously on their own concerns while portraying administrators as obstacles to good service.

A good rule of thumb is to assume that everyone in the situation may be having an adverse reaction and may be in need of support. The first person to assess informally is the person who first requested crisis management services. The second is the site administrator, with whom it is critical to establish rapport. Reassure the site administrator that he or she is in control of the team.

It is important to assess the administrator immediately because support for and crisis intervention with that individual may be necessary before matters can progress. Help the administrator assess all needs for services and determine which individuals and what means can provide that assessment. To assist in this process, Chapter 4 discusses emergency situational assessment, Chapter 6 discusses rapid assessment, and Appendix II provides a consultant's checklist. Assisting assessment, raising issues, providing a sounding board, making suggestions, and coordinating resources are the main functions of a site consultant. Specific issues for a site consultant to consider are student and staff needs, school routine, resource availability, decision making, planning, information control, and media management.

Assist teachers and other staff members with briefings and orientations detailing the situation, possible student reactions, and suggestions for handling students. Staff can benefit from individual consultation and debriefings as well as group debriefings. Staff members appreciate coaching if they have requested it; they also welcome any available materials and resources.

Students can be served through class debriefings, individual and group consultations, and informational sessions. Drop-in rap sessions may be useful, by permission of the teacher. Such sessions may indicate a need for assessment and referral to further assistance.

Parents should be included in their children's recovery plan as much and as quickly as possible. It is very helpful to notify parents about the nature of the incident, reactions to watch for, and the principles of psychological first aid. Holding meetings and conferences is also very appropriate, as are assessments and referrals for further assistance.

Educators within school systems and therapists in the surrounding community often deal with the same children. Educators teach children who are in therapy; they also refer children to therapy. Therapists treat children who spend most of their waking hours in school. A child in crisis can benefit greatly by cross-disciplinary interaction between school and clinic. Yet educators and therapists often view each other's professional domain as a black box. While each has much to offer the other, often neither professional has much idea what that might be.

In a dialogue with community professionals in the Fort Worth area in August 1990, some one hundred educators and therapists articulated a substantial list of specific information, insights, or services each discipline could provide the other. This set of mutual aids is discussed in Appendix I and should be reviewed by those professionals and administrators who set policies and procedures.

Working with Traumatized Staff

Recent large-scale shootings on campuses such as Jonesboro and Columbine attest to the changing nature of teaching. Particularly difficult teaching situations, such as inner city assignments, defy normal description. Teachers whose duty it is to carry out reading and math programs find themselves in lethal situations where survival becomes a professional goal. Every time a campus is rocked by catastrophe, an entire teaching staff is shaken. What happens when teachers are traumatized? How can administrators be best counseled by school CRT members to manage a traumatized staff?

Acute Stress Response in Staff

When staff members develop an Acute Stress Response to a critical incident, those showing more agitated functioning are fairly easy to identify (see Figure 3-10). However, it is important to also observe unusually quiet staff members for signs of depressed reaction. Rest, refreshments, or even rotation to less critical assignments may be all that affected staff members need. However, those who have a more serious reaction may need to be placed on light-duty assignments or be escorted home. All staff members showing signs of ASR should be referred to counseling with trained personnel.

Whenever possible, assist the site administrator in handling the situation and the staff in such a way as to maintain school safety. When children are present, the work of the staff and the pressure of the situation take priority. If an employee is functional, allow him or her to continue. If not, pull the employee away from the situation, make sure someone can supervise the person, and return as soon as you are able.

When talking to a traumatized staff member, remember that he or she may be in shock or particularly vulnerable. In a crisis, employees need a benevolent authority figure to convince them that the world is under control. Let them cry, and don't be afraid to remain silent if that is what an employee needs. Think carefully about any arbitrary action you might take and use pressure only when you think it is really necessary.

Counsel the site administrators to tolerate employees' behavioral reactions as long as they do not interfere with the students or the rest of the staff. Administrators should consider holding a staff debriefing for staff members affected by an incident. This could be led by a member of the CRT or someone outside the district. The format for such a debriefing follows closely that of the classroom debriefing outlined in Chapters 7 and 10.

After an incident, do not tell a staff member what to feel or not to feel. If the employee feels guilt, you can give assurance that the incident was not his or her fault, but you cannot tell the person not to feel guilt. If you can ease the pain by touch or comfort, then do so, but do not tell the employee not to hurt. Feelings are neither right nor wrong but they are very real.

This is not the time to critique the staff's performance, except to reassure them of a job well done. The following actions will help alleviate the stress:

- Share factual information about expected reactions. Alert employees to the potential for acute and delayed responses to crises.

- Explore support systems and suggest sources for additional help. This helps employees mobilize existing support and provides them with direction.

- Let staff members know that you will continue to be available to them.

Delayed Stress Response in Staff

Recovery from trauma often involves the gradual surfacing of feelings and thoughts that were suppressed during the incident. This is particularly true of teachers or administrators who had to perform their jobs and could not afford the luxury of fully responding emotionally at the time. Sometimes these thoughts and feelings interfere with normal functioning, and sometimes they work themselves out indirectly (see Figure 3-11).

Some of an employee's apparent job problems—such as irritability, substance use, morale problems, or excessive absences—may be misguided efforts to cope with the trauma. These problems may eventually become a management problem and can threaten job status. If they occur in the weeks and months following a school crisis, the administrator may wish to explore whether they are crisis-related.

CRT members may be asked to provide consultation in relation to delayed reactions during the recovery period. In dealing with a staff member recovering from a critical incident, supervisors should keep in mind that normal recovery can be a very long process and may include times when the individual looks and feels as if she or he is getting worse rather than better. This is because an individual is able to deal with more serious memories, thoughts, and feelings as she or he becomes stronger. Also, as the individual outgrows initial short-term coping mechanisms, she or he must develop new ones.

These periods of cycling through emotions should show gradual progress over time. If the employee seems to become "stuck" in a cycle of nonproductive, disruptive, or self-destructive

behavior, several approaches have proven helpful. CRT members may be able to counsel administrators to follow a modified version of the conference protocol suggested for students in Figure 5-7.

Chapters 8 and 9 review the areas of Self-Care and Cumulative Traumatic Stress. Both chapters provide valuable information for administrators and crisis team members to better understand staff reactions to crisis situations. Recent events seem to be multiplying, and old models of stress simply do not take the cumulative nature of staff stressors into account.

Suggestions for Community Mental Health and Crisis Response Teams

Particularly in liaison situations, it is critical for outside resources to schools to be aware of the unique territoriality of the school setting. Schools are organizationally complex, and part of this complexity lies in the matrix of authority inherent in the school. Apart from the frequently intense management-union tension is the certificated (teacher and administrator state credentialed) versus classified (noncredentialed) status. Territorial and status differences between these groups are not clear, and this can create power struggles and resentment.

In crisis contexts, all these forces collide. The changes and modifications that must be made in dealing with crisis situations, especially when outsiders are part of the equation, focus upon authority. This manifests in the issue of *face*. Face is the respect one expects in social situations based upon one's status or authority. When school functioning is unbalanced during crisis, multidisciplinary and territorial conflicts make face a critical issue.

School systems are top-down paramilitary organizations, from the Department of Education in Washington down through the subsystems to the local elementary school. At each level downward, a territorial wall exists where subtle and not so subtle differences define a

Responding to the Omagh Bomb

Elizabeth Capewell

On Saturday, 15 August 1998, at 3:10 on Carnival Day in the school summer holidays, a large car bomb exploded in the main street of Omagh, Northern Ireland, where, after an inaccurate warning, people had been evacuated. The death rose eventually to 29 plus unborn twins. Over 300 were injured, around 50 seriously, with burns and traumatic amputation. Half the dead were children and young people, half came from Omagh and the rest from villages around, except for three boys on a day out from Buncrana, County Donegal and two of their Spanish guests.

A close colleague, David Bolton, was Director of Community Care for that area. I had given seminars in Omagh on school crisis response four years earlier and I had trained school crisis management teams in Derry schools (in the same Education and Library Board district) over the previous three years. As the death toll mounted and the high involvement of children and young people emerged, I wanted to offer some help at least to the people I knew would be involved in the aftermath. I phoned to leave a message of support to David and his family.

Preparation

I began by collecting all the information I could about the bombing, noting key features such as the fact that an inaccurate warning caused people to be evacuated to the location of the bomb. As news of the dead emerged, I mapped where they came from. I knew the town of Buncrana and this drew me closer to the disaster. Then I began networking. I phoned my existing contacts in the Education Board, the Catholic Council of Maintained Schools (I had recently helped draft their draft management plan), and in Buncrana. This helped me gain information about the personnel who would be organizing the response to young people and to offer immediate help. I knew the staff were themselves shocked by the bombing— it signified a major break in the peace process and a massive loss of hope—so the help sent had to be reassuring, practical, and brief. I sent a simple "triage" method of assessment for school principals to have a systematic approach to work out the impact and its ripples through their school community.

The Situation on Arrival

- Schools were about to reopen after the summer vacation, and many school staff, Board Officers, and Advisors had only just returned from holiday. There was widespread distress, shock, and confusion among staff. Reactions ranged from retreat into the bureaucracy of the start of term to overwhelming involvement with the disaster.

- The names of the dead were known, but not the names of the injured. Schools were still unaware of the wider impact of the trauma on staff and pupils.

- There were no specific crisis management systems in place and information in the system about the impact of trauma and how to respond was minimal or not mobilized.

- I knew that over 80 schools and colleges were affected to varying degrees, as well as all the Youth Centres. The Omagh Library staff played a central role in the rescue of victims.

- I was given an office, car, and clerical staff to support our response to what was then still a very uncertain situation. Arrangements were made for two colleagues to join me in rotation.

The Response

- We worked at several levels simultaneously— personal, organizational, and community.

- By acutely observing, listening, sensing, and asking questions formally and informally, we set about learning as much as we could about the incident, personnel, organization, schools, and community. We aimed to identify resources, key agents of help, existing systems we could mobilize, group dynamics, cultural norms, areas of resistance, and boundaries.

- In all interactions, short or lengthy, we aimed to offer *information, support,* and *alternatives.* We focused on present needs but always with an eye to the future, using every opportunity to establish the foundations for the next step and to give a glimpse of the whole response process. In the immediate aftermath, while receptivity to new information was low, we made use of metaphor and images that could also be used in school assemblies and class discussions.

- Some blocks in the system were resolved but some major blocks needed more time and strategic management. Much of our time was spent in challenging taboos and some cultural norms by giving alternative frameworks that would allow people to gain "permission" to own their individual experience and seek the level of help they required. A "hierarchy of suffering" was rapidly being established along with the emergence of difference in attitudes, coping, and material benefits.

- We returned for another four days soon after the initial response. Our aim was to consolidate the work and put the embryonic systems onto a sound footing in preparation for the transition to the medium-term response.

- A great deal of time was spent giving information to senior personnel to allow them to make what is, for unprepared organizations, the difficult transition to the next stage of the response. This was a time when superficial restoration could be mistaken for real recovery and before the persistent nature of trauma was realized. We also noticed that key personnel were using their own coping styles as a yardstick for the state of others and concluded after six weeks that all schools were coping. Our contract with the Board ended at this point and work continued with individual schools and other authorities.

Longer-term work

- In one school this work involved two full days of processing the impact of the bomb on staff and managing differences in the staff team. This was followed by training for staff in responding to affected children and parents and review sessions for the Community Response team. A major spin-off for this work is the production of *Guidelines for School Crisis Management* by the Irish Teaching Unions.

- In another badly affected school, after many delays, a program was achieved allowing short intervention each term until the second anniversary of the bombing. The school situation was complex with a long history of trauma, other current stress, and several further fatal incidents after the bomb. The nature of the school and its circumstances has required a program of sensitive support, information giving, advocacy, and management of relationships. We have also supported the Board of Governors and parents and spent several days working with the children in order to model methods such as "Circle Time" to build up healthy coping in their pupils.

- Further work involved assisting the coordination and development of community-led responses, facilitating Review and Action Planning sessions for interagency groups, and continuing work with journalists and the producer of a TV documentary.

Elizabeth Capewell is the Director of the Centre for Crisis Management and Education in Newbury, Berkshire, U.K. Telephone and fax: 00 44 1635-30644. E-mail: capewell@which.net.

unique subsystem. Each subsystem, down to teacher cliques within schools, has its own history, its own culture, its own eccentricities, its own characters, conflicts, political divisions, and issues. Because of the way territoriality is linked with *face* in the schools, face runs in several directions: up, down, sideways, and through time. The two most obvious ways face affects outside mental health workers and crisis responders in schools are:

1. Internal teams must somehow gain input to administrative decision making and classroom autonomy. Dealing with issues of face is critical to this process. Both administrators and teachers must be dealt with constructively in ways which do not trigger loss of face or challenge the territorial authority of the various disciplinary and organizational groups involved.

2. Similarly, external teams must somehow gain input to the entire school, including the internal team, if one exists. Again, the greatest threats to this collaboration are issues of *face* and *territory*.

The quickest way to sabotage an intervention is from within, and it often results from boundary threats and anticipated loss of face. Working with schools presents a multitude of challenges to outside mental health and Crisis Response Team members.

Copy masters (Figures 4-1 to 4-3) for this chapter can be found on pages 177–179.

CHAPTER 4

Emergency Management

For the month following the shooting at Columbine High School, schools all over the country received bomb threats, phone calls from students and adults worried about suspicious behavior or comments made by others, and graffitied messages promising mayhem. Even the postincident anniversaries continue to trigger contagion effects. The shooting at Columbine High School in Littleton, Colorado, touched off hundreds of would-be copycats and thousands of reports. School officials struggled to balance prudent caution with panic avoidance and overreaction.

In a myriad of less broad-scale crises, issues of child safety versus institutional destabilization compete in cases of suicide, gang violence, and community instability in which school personnel must consider a variety of factors and possible consequences before they act. Just as teacher colleges cannot prepare teachers for the reality of the classroom, administrative training programs cannot possibly equip administrators for the complexity of crisis management. A good definition of crisis management might be this: sudden, consequential, high-stakes decision making under aggravated conditions of limited information, limited time, uncertain resources, and maximum vulnerability and duress.

Incident Command

The principal handles most crises. Any given number of support personnel may be assigned to help, some of whom may have special expertise such as crisis intervention or public relations. The majority of these situations require no extensive modifications to the existing role structure in the school. When the incident involves issues of public safety, consultation with law enforcement, fire agencies, public works, or other agencies may be appropriate.

In larger incidents where public safety issues predominate, the management of the incident may be turned over to one of those appropriate agencies, and the principal may direct school functions as an extension of overall incident management by that agency. Large incident management usually involves some form of Incident Command System (ICS).

The ICS breaks the management of large incidents into five functions: management, planning/intelligence, operations, logistics, and finance/administration (see sidebar "Five Functions of the Incident Command System for School Systems"). Schools are increasingly adopting some variant of the ICS for large-incident management (see sidebar "Care and Feeding of the Crisis Intervention Team"), and the use of such a system facilitates the transfer of incident management to other agencies if necessary. Also, in the event of a communitywide incident such as disaster, the school is better able to communicate with and integrate its actions with the municipal Emergency Operating Center if it is organized using an ICS structure.

As mentioned before, one service school Crisis Response Teams can provide is administrative consultation. This can take the form of helping the administrator determine what issues need consideration and which specialists can assist in situation assessment and planning. Taking the basic ICS role structure into account during incident consultation may bring greater clarity to management organization immediately and set the stage for smoother transition later.

This chapter and Chapter 6 provide suggestions for making a practical and rapid assessment of both overall school and individual crisis needs. This chapter deals with schoolwide considerations and gives direction to administrators and those who advise them in assessing

Five Functions of the Incident Command System for School Systems

Mary Schoenfeldt

The five basic Incident Command System functions are management, planning/intelligence, operations, logistics, and finance/administration. These functions are performed in any emergency response anywhere. A few people or many may be involved, depending on the size of the emergency and the human resources at hand.

Management: Responsible for overall policy and coordination

Incident Commander

Normally, the principal or his or her designee. The school incident commander works in conjunction with law enforcement or a fire incident commander.

Public Information Officer

One person is designated spokesperson for the school or district by the principal or superintendent.

Safety Officer

The job of overseeing campus security and making sure the working conditions are safe can be done by almost anyone, as long as that person is trained and understands his or her responsibilities.

Planning/Intelligence: Responsible for collecting, evaluating, and disseminating information; maintaining documentation; and evaluating incoming information to determine the potential situation in the not-too-distant future

Teachers or other staff can perform this function. These people must be able to use communications equipment, gather information in a timely manner, and weigh it for significance.

Operations: Responsible for actually performing the actions that make up the emergency response

This function can involve a number of teachers, facilities, and food service workers. It can

also involve the nurse, if she or he is on site. Various response teams are included under this function:

- First aid team
- Search and rescue team
- Site security team
- Damage assessment team
- Evacuation team
- Student release team

Logistics: Responsible for providing facilities, services, personnel, equipment, and materials

This function will utilize an administrator and other staff—anyone who knows how to procure what's needed.

Finance/Administration: Responsible for financial activities such as establishing contracts with vendors, keeping pay records, and accounting for expenditures

An administrator plus anyone who usually deals with buying things, paying bills, and balancing books is best suited to this function. Knowledge of procedures and personnel at the central office is very valuable.

The ICS structure is a modular one that starts at the top and can expand to address the needs of the situation—as need and personnel grow or shrink. Each box in the organization chart represents a function, not a person.

A school district can tailor the ICS to suit its own needs, as long as the five functions are somehow covered.

Material adapted from California OES document "The Little School That Could" and other sources, by Mary Schoenfeldt. She is a consultant to the California Department of Education and other school systems around the country. She can be reached at (425) 227-7442.

and managing large, ongoing situations. Chapter 6 provides direction for field assessment of individuals who have been impacted by crisis and may be in need of referral for specialized services.

Assessing Crisis Situations

Chapter 2 outlined broad goals and objectives for school crisis management. As indicated there, not all situations require any particular objective. The selection of objectives and strategies is situation-driven, in the sense that the characteristics of the particular emergency determine which objectives and which strategies might be appropriate. Administrators and crisis team personnel must assess several things prior to planning and must continually update their assessment in order to guide decision making.

The nature and scope of the incident will be a major determinant. Different types of incidents have different demand characteristics. Natural as opposed to human-caused disasters carry different meaning and create different effects. Further, as incidents run their course, their nature sometimes shifts. Looting may follow an earthquake, which can then precipitate law enforcement-community tension. The number of people affected by an incident can range from a single individual to the entire community, and the status of those impacted can vary widely.

The students or even the entire community may react positively or negatively to the situation, again shifting the demands on crisis responders. Incidents can take a political turn or create dissent among students. The actions of media and the effects of the type of coverage can play a large roll in determining what crisis response strategies are employed. Similarly, the extent and type of law enforcement or emergency agency involvement will affect the role of both administration and crisis responders.

These factors and more must be assessed rapidly, informally, continually. The checklist on pages 40–41 presents a model assessment form useful in guiding observations for use in

decision making, and Appendix II presents a Crisis Consultant's Checklist useful in determining, given the particular situation, just what strategies make sense.

Threat Assessment

In the midst of crisis, organizational and political issues vie with logistical and practical considerations. Pressing issues of liability, public relations, community expectations, organizational pressure, parental demands, and media pressure can eclipse the best interests of the children involved. For these reasons, administrators stand to benefit from counsel by specialists during crisis. Consultation with mental health professionals, law enforcement, or legal counsel can lend valuable perspective during the unfolding of critical events.

Threats to students or staff present an immediacy of risk for the entire school and community. In addition, assessment of risk has become sufficiently pressing and controversial as to warrant discussion separate from other crisis assessment. Thus threat assessment will be discussed here rather than in Chapter 6, "Rapid Assessment."

It is critical to assess whether an individual represents a threat to others. If it is judged that this is likely, action must be taken to ensure the safety of an intended victim. Crisis workers may be liable for not recognizing signs of danger if such recognition could reasonably be expected of professionals working in this capacity. If in doubt, act to ensure safety. Stabilize the individual, refer for further evaluation, and notify law enforcement officials immediately. Individuals judged to be at imminent risk for injuring others should not be left alone. Nor should they be referred for further evaluation unescorted. Law enforcement should be involved in all decision making (see sidebar "School Violence Prevention and Intervention: A New Application of Threat Assessment Technology").

Certain factors have been shown to indicate increased risk of violent behavior toward others. The majority of these factors have to do with background history. A history of violent

School Violence Prevention and Intervention: A New Application of Threat Assessment Technology

Kris Mohandie, Ph.D.

The concept of threat assessment may be defined as the process of assessing risks to a particular target, group of individuals, or individual and designing and implementing intervention and management strategies to reduce that risk or threat (Mohandie & Boles 1999). The discipline of threat assessment originated in the work of the Secret Service, which requires a methodology and technology for proactively maintaining the safety of its protectees. While this represents the formal beginnings of a technology for managing threats and risks, issues of safety and dangerousness have long fallen within the purview of psychology and psychiatry, and human beings have always been concerned about issues of this sort.

Within municipal law enforcement, threat assessment technologies were applied to the management of stalking cases, and in 1991 the LAPD developed the first unit, the Threat Management Unit (TMU), tasked with managing stalking and threat cases. As with many new developments, this innovation was in response to several tragedies, in particular the killing of actress Rebecca Shaeffer by an obsessed fan, Robert Bardo.

Since that time, similar units have been founded, and within the criminal justice system special entities for the prosecution of threat and stalking cases, such as San Diego County Stalking Strike Force, have been developed. In addition, a unique organization, the Association for Threat Assessment Professionals (ATAP)—a multidisciplinary association for those involved in addressing various types of threats within their span of control—was founded in 1992. The ATAP holds regular meetings where these issues are discussed and also sponsors a major training conference each summer, traditionally held at the Disneyland hotel and with a routine attendance of more than 500.

Since these developments, the technology and practice of threat assessment—previously concerned with those who may pose or actually have made threats—has been applied to protecting the safety of public figures and private citizens, to reducing the risk of workplace violence, and, most recently, to reducing the risk of school violence. With recent concerns about high-profile incidents on our school campuses, and, in particular, multiple-victim events, once again there is a need to apply and modify this technology, this time to the realm of school safety.

Towards that end, one particular strategy, the use of Threat Assessment Teams—also known as Incident Management Teams—has been applied successfully to this arena. It is introduced here, not as a substitute for comprehensive training in school violence prevention and intervention, but to familiarize the reader and offer reassurance that good work is being done in this arena.

Threat Assessment Teams are multidisciplinary teams often consisting of an educator (principal or assistant principal), mental health consultant, campus-based security or law enforcement officer, and school legal counsel. They convene when a problem is identified, and their task is to process and seek appropriate information and resources to manage a potential threat and bring it to a logical conclusion. This approach relies upon, among many other things, educating teachers, students, and staff about the early warning signs and where to report them. Thus the team members may review the information, apply their varied specialized expertise, advise decision makers, determine essential versus less essential information, and evaluate and recommend strategies, taking into consideration safety and individual rights. Many school districts, without realizing it, have perhaps been using this process in an ad hoc fashion already. The point is that core skills are being taught in districts throughout the nation and abroad, high-risk cases with high violence potential are being successfully addressed, and tragedies are being avoided.

Kris Mohandie, Ph.D, is Police Psychologist with the Los Angeles Police Department. This approach is the subject of A Practical Guide to School Violence Prevention and Intervention, *to be published in spring 2000 by STS Publications, (800) 848-1226, mohandie@mail.earthlink.net.*

Situation Assessment Checklist Status Update

Incident: **Date:**   **Time:**

Nature / Projected Course of Incident: Priority Issues:
Contact / Person Responsible:
Status:

Number of Students Directly Involved: Priority Issues:
Contact / Person Responsible:
Status:

Current Status of Those Students: Priority Issues:
Contact / Person Responsible:
Status:

Community / Political Sensitivity of Incident: Priority Issues:
Contact / Person Responsible:
Status:

Safety Issues: Priority Issues:
Contact / Person Responsible:
Status:

Situation Assessment Checklist Status Update

Incident: **Date:**   **Time:**

Behavior / Mood of Staff / Students / Parents: Priority Issues:
Contact / Person Responsible:
Status:

Current Media Involvement: Priority Issues:
Contact / Person Responsible:
Status:

Projected Course of Incident: Priority Issues:
Contact / Person Responsible:
Status:

Site / District / Community Resources Available: Priority Issues:
Contact / Person Responsible:
Status:

**Current Involvement of Law Enforcement /
Emergency Agencies:**   Priority Issues:
Contact / Person Responsible:
Status:

incidents, threats, conflicts and anger, impulse control problems, and emotional instability are considered risk factors. An important risk factor that is not historical, however, is the presence of a precipitating incident. Thus an incident such as a breakup, recent loss, job action, or harassment may be considered a risk factor, particularly in combination with significant background factors (see Figure 4-1).

It must be remembered, however, that the factors, signs, and protocols outlined here are general considerations, and there is always a danger of "false negatives"; that is, situations that do not fit the general patterns but are nevertheless lethal. It is imperative that situation managers and consultants take these considerations as starting points only. No one set of protocols can be considered comprehensive in situations involving high stakes.

Certain outward signs can be considered warnings of potential violence. These include actual threats made directly or reported by credible witnesses. There are two elements to be assessed regarding the expression of anger: the affect itself and its expression. The inappropriate expression of anger is a possible sign of potential violence, as is the expression of inappropriate anger. The expression of delusional or persecutory thoughts is also a possible sign, as is obsession with control or death. Records, notes, and writings expressing threat are problematic, as are plans or preparation that are specific and lethal (see Figure 4-2).

Again, this list is not to be construed as exhaustive; it is only a starting point for further inquiry. Significantly dangerous cases may not fit the profile.

It is critical to remember the limits of assessment in educational contexts. Following a threat assessment, if background factors and warning signs suggest that a situation may be dangerous, and if the situation is judged secure enough to discuss safely with the possible perpetrator, proceed to do so judiciously. The intent is to ascertain the existence of a specific and lethal plan. Figure 4-3 provides a general protocol to be followed. It is important to consider indirect signs prior to direct inquiry, and if the situation looks dangerous, involve police sooner rather than later. If there is any reason

to believe the individual might withhold information, do not proceed without first conferring with police.

"Automated" Threat Assessment Programs

While computer-assisted decision making is not new, its application in school crisis management and threat assessment is now beginning to emerge. Programmatic approaches to situation assessment cannot truly be automated, as situations are complex and subject to a great many influential variables. Crisis managers (and those liable for the consequences of their decisions) might like a black-box approach where, if enough data is entered, a clear remedial action plan is generated. This would take the "risk" out of risk assessment. Unfortunately, this is not possible. The best we can wish for from a programmatic approach is to structure our inquiry as comprehensively as possible. In the poet Rainer Maria Rilke's words, we must "live the questions."

The good news of programmed threat assessment is that it guides our questioning and thinking to ensure we consider all the salient factors that bear upon the situation. By structuring our thinking, the program helps us overcome the "tunnel vision" that emergencies tend to create and forces us to take into account perspectives we might otherwise ignore. We are thus able to utilize school and community resources in a more helpful manner. Further, because our thinking, inquiry, and decision making are done systematically, we are able to reconstruct, reconsider, and reassess our actions at each step.

The bad news is severalfold: Districts may be tempted to become "protocol-driven" rather than "inquiry-driven," relying upon the program to define the incident and limit the questioning. Districts that have not invested in personnel development, and have not orchestrated a multidisciplined assessment team, might be tempted to allow the expediency of incomplete and poorly collaborated answers to the program's questions. This could result in shoddy and dangerous assessment.

Computer programs can only associate prespecified text with response strategies. Thus, they can provide professional-looking documentation of unprofessional assessments: "Garbage in, garbage out." Worse, unscrupulous or incompetent school officials can, intentionally or unintentionally, misuse programmed assessments to substitute for effective threat assessment. This is of critical importance when lives of students or school personnel are at stake.

A balanced approach for responsible utilization of even the "ideal" system would be to assume that it is at best a heuristic device; that is, a tool to guide inquiry. The inquiry process itself would be informed by the logic of the program, but this logic would simply be the starting point for identifying and securing needed information. Threat assessment programs can inform the assessment process, just as the assessment process must inform incident management. Artificial intelligence can assist, but never supplant, the collective wisdom of trained professionals working together to protect children.

When considering adopting a programmed approach to threat assessment, ask the following questions:

- Is the existing team professionally diverse, competent, and experienced now? Is the adoption of this instrument a substitute for trained professional judgement?

- Will the instrument be used to enhance rather than supplant the team's skill? Is there any danger of the instrument being applied in a perfunctory manner, without supporting and collaborating professional judgement?

- Has there been satisfactory documentation of the instrument's effectiveness? Has that documentation been professionally reviewed commensurate with the stakes involved in its deployment?

- Are the choice of question items and the resulting weighting of the items' importance supported by empirical evidence? Are they based upon experts' opinions? If so, how broad a basis is it, what is the experi-

ential basis, is the opinion based upon a multidisciplinary group, and were educators included in the group?

- Does the instrument claim to predict dangerousness or simply assist professional decision making?

- Does the instrument provide direction to managing the situation?

- Does the instrument provide useful information for the vast majority of nonlethal school threats (such as drug-, turf-, or interpersonal-conflict-related issues) as opposed to high-profile threats (such as bombings or mass murder)?

- Does the system require some sort of user licensing to ensure professional application?

- What happens to the information? How are all interested parties' rights protected? How is information kept confidential?

- Are questions and interpretations culturally sensitive, and is the process fair? How do we know this?

- Are the questions, and the weightings of those questions, selected with regard to the developmental level of the person in question? The youngest active participant in a mass murder at school involving firearms was only 11. Is each of the questions as valid for an 11-year-old as for an adult?

- Does the instrument's supporting documentation honestly and responsibly address the issues of false positives (situations designated dangerous that turn out not to be) or, more seriously, false negative (situations judged not to be dangerous that turn out to be dangerous)?

- Does the instrument's supporting documentation honestly and responsibly address the issue of inter-rater reliability?

- If field tests were conducted on the instrument, were they completed in time for actual modifications to be done on the instrument to reflect the results of the test?

These questions must be asked critically of companies marketing such products, and the answers to those questions scrutinized carefully. While we may not be able to expect the rigorous scientific standards we are accustomed to for laboratory applications, we must nevertheless know the weaknesses of each instrument we use in the field. That way we can err on the side of caution. Threat assessment is a high-stakes endeavor.

There is a bottom line here. However valid the assessment protocol (in the sense of asking the right questions), and however valid the weighting of the questions, does the assessor possess the necessary skills and resources to adequately corroborate the answers to the questions and to translate the assessment information into constructive situation management? It is critical whenever assessing threats of danger—and when making decisions that affect the safety of students or staff—to utilize trained district personnel, law enforcement, outside mental health resources, and district legal counsel (see sidebar "Care and Feeding of the Crisis Intervention Team").

Situational Planning

Planning for situation management is not protocol-driven. There are simply too many factors to be considered. The complexity and political nature of the school context and the wide variety of possible crises tax the reserves of crisis planners. Each incident carries different meaning to the school community, and these meanings shade the planning process. Given this, planning must be driven by a flexible, principle-driven approach. The school crisis management goals and objectives provide the principles. Strategies used to forward those principles must be adopted and adapted to fit the individual situation in all its complexity and uniqueness.

Again, some generalities are possible. First, the threat can be at least temporarily removed; the law provides for the arrest—or, in some cases, temporary psychiatric hospitalization—of potential perpetrators. The rights of both victims and potential perpetrators must be taken into account when considering such strategies, and school personnel may be liable for protecting those rights. Law enforcement professionals and legal counsel can help determine whether this strategy is warranted, feasible, and legal.

Situational planning can also entail increasing campus security, monitoring potential threats, arranging psychological consultations, and issuing administrative or legal restraints. Notification of parents and potential victims can take place and may even be legally required. Background checks can be made for arrest records or a pattern of similar behavior in the past. Alert school staff members and keep them apprised of potential difficulties so they can respond intelligently in the event of difficulties. Again, consultation with law enforcement, emergency agencies, and legal counsel can assist in generating strategies and making informed decisions.

Decisions as to whether or not the school should remain open are difficult. On the one hand, the school has a responsibility for the safety of all students and staff. On the other, to disrupt the educational process is itself a cost and may lead to repeat cases. Again, no formula or protocol can substitute for responsible professional judgement in such situations. The very best approach is preplanning with other agencies and district-level administration, with simulation exercises covering possible situations. These exercises can help major players get used to working with one another jurisdictionally and personally.

Suggestions for Community Mental Health and Crisis Response Teams

While schools often resist outside assistance, once they accept help they sometimes treat the arrival of outside resources like that of the belated cavalry, expecting community mental health professionals or Crisis Response Teams to hold almost divine powers of insight and re-

Care and Feeding of the Crisis Intervention Team

Michael Pines, Ph.D.

Crisis teams for children require more than just training. Strong regional leadership can guide schools in the adoption of policies and procedures that pave the way to effective programs. To this end, the Los Angeles County Office of Education (LACOE), the nation's largest regional educational agency, through its Safe Schools Center, is able to provide training and technical assistance to the county's 81 school districts, and to other schools throughout the state, in many areas of school safety and school crisis intervention. In addition to basic training in technical skills (such as Critical Incident Stress Debriefing and Violence Threat Assessment Training), the center serves as a catalyst for interdisciplinary team building, collaboration with other schools, and linkages to community and governmental resources. Safety policies, procedures, and training are also articulated with other key emergency response agencies.

The Standardized Emergency Management System (SEMS) is employed throughout California. The roles of all emergency services and governmental agencies are clearly defined and facilitate the rapid deployment of resources when "the time comes." SEMS recognizes that the majority of emergency situations are resolved at the school site by available resources at the school. Every day school personnel either provide services on campus or summon outside emergency services with minimal disruption to the educational process. It is unusual that an event occurs that surpasses their ability to solve the problem.

In those critical situations, however, school personnel turn to their school's Comprehensive School Safety Plan to guide them. The Plan, required in California schools since 1998, contains the names and responsibilities of members of the Crisis Intervention Team and other specialized emergency teams. Also included in the plan are schedules for training, drills, meetings, and simulated events that include resources outside of the school, such as law enforcement, fire service and rescue, and the American Red Cross. The school-wide distribution of crisis procedures ensures that the procedures mobilizing Crisis Intervention Teams are well understood by all key administrators on campus.

Because the Safe Schools Center has trained hundreds of school-based and community-based professionals in crisis intervention, it plays a key role in linking schools with others who can assist if outside help is required. The center can help school officials identify others with training so that arrangements can be made for mutual assistance. Help can be obtained from nearby schools, community mental health agencies, and other community partners. These resources are also detailed in the School Safety Plan. In the aftermath of recent high-impact school shootings, the Safe School Center has been instrumental in helping schools organize multidisciplinary Threat Assessment Teams. These teams are convened when someone poses a threat to students or staff. Members include school administrators, school-based and community-based mental health practitioners, and law enforcement partners. The teams receive state-of-the-art technical training by law enforcement professionals who are experienced in assessing threats to schools, workplaces, and public officials. Technical assistance is provided to ensure that the school community and student confidentiality are both protected. Teams are also linked with other community agencies that are able to provide assistance when needed. These agencies include community mental health, children and family services, fire service arson investigators, and others. LACOE also arranges for team meetings so those districts can share their best practices and concerns.

With student safety the ultimate goal, school administrators in Los Angeles County can count on well-trained Crisis Intervention Teams to lead students through their recovery from traumatic events.

Dr. Michael Pines is Emergency Mental Health Consultant to the Safe Schools Center, Los Angeles County Office of Education, (562) 922-6391.

source and hoping to hand them problem cases for quick resolution.

A handoff of this sort is particularly likely when liability may be a possibility. Faced, for example, with a threat to self and others, schools can be quick to put the case into the hands of a community worker. This creates several problems, particularly since very few outside mental health professionals have any training in crisis management, much less threat assessment. Additionally, outside professionals normally have little or no ongoing contact with those whose behavior they are to assess, and hence have no sense of the individual baseline behavior.

It is a good rule not to attempt threat assessments alone. Work with school personnel and include law enforcement in decisions regarding situation assessment and management. School personnel can provide baseline data, while law enforcement can provide a community point of view and initiate community-based actions the school cannot.

Interpretation of these messages is always a judgement call on the part of those who best know the person making the threat; there is no exact science, no "correct formula" for assessing which individuals represent a real danger and which don't.

The Los Angeles Police Department Threat Management Unit, among other law enforcement agencies nationwide, has spent considerable time developing criteria for identifying dangerousness in threatening communications. While no hard and fast rules exist, some generalities can be drawn.

First, is the message organized or disorganized? The greater the consistency, coherence, and structure in the message, the more it is considered dangerous. Does the message follow a single theme, or does the thematic content wander? Similarly, is the threatened violence focused upon one target, or is it more general? Again, the more the message follows a single theme, and focuses upon a single target, the more dangerous it is presumed to be. Is there a sense of necessity implied in the message regarding either the action or the time? "I must act, there is no recourse, and I must act now!"

The greater the sense of action or time imperative, the greater the likelihood of the act taking place. Remember, however, that these are simply generalizations.

Again, threat assessment is not a science, and there have been a great number of unfortunate surprises. Different types of messages carry greater or lesser significance given different types of senders. Consequently, the predicative value of specific characteristics varies. The more that decisions regarding children's safety are shared between community agencies, the greater the likelihood that those decisions will be well considered and helpful.

Copy masters (Figures 5-1 to 5-8) for this chapter can be found on pages 180–187.

CHAPTER 5

Individual Intervention

Crisis events overwhelm us. They are disorienting and isolating. They leave us distrusting our ability to judge the world and our own experience. We tend to withdraw into our own confusion and assume there is something wrong with us. It helps greatly to relate to someone at this time. Crisis intervention provides that opportunity.

Crisis intervention is a natural human response. People have always sat down with others who have been through difficult experiences and talked about them. Some "talkings" are better than others, and the current protocol for crisis intervention is simply a structure that gives focus and direction to the talk. While the content of discussion varies between individual situations, the process pretty much follows a natural progression.

Individual crisis intervention remains the basic technique of school crisis management at the individual level and serves as an instructive paradigm for more advanced group practices. This chapter elaborates on this basic process. The past 10 years have seen the development of group crisis intervention approaches as well as classroom postincident strategies. These will be dealt with in separate chapters.

CRT Strategy 7: Individual Consultation and Assessment

Individual consultation and assessment can be conducted with anyone from administration to community members. It aims at assisting the person in understanding the situation, assessing him- or herself, and determining what needs to be done next. Depending upon the situation and personal reactions, individual consultation can utilize a formal crisis intervention format or simply be limited to a friendly conversation. The subject of the transaction can range from thinking through complex

An Open Letter to My Counselor

Dear Michelle:

Before I started seeing you, I was miserable. My Grandpa died, I had no real friends, and I had a freshly deceased rat. My social life was decrepit. My life started to suck mud.

I hated myself during those times. I cried at least once a day. I told myself (mindlessly) Grandpa was dead and that my feelings would never mend. Also, I dreaded school. All of this ruined my schoolwork and grades.

You showed me that I did have friends. You also showed me how to cope with Grandpa's death. I was happier then and I still am.

Now I am doing even better. Grandpa's death still brings back memories. I sometimes even cry. Mostly I have tears, but sometimes it's just dry sobs. I especially cry while listening to "Don't Want To Lose You Now" by the Backstreet Boys, like when I'm typing right now.

Thank you so much. You have helped me cope with the real world.

Love from,

Whitney Losh-Johnson

47

problems to dealing with personal reactions. In short, its content and process are dependent upon the demands of the situation and the individual's functioning level and responsibilities. Consultation may consist of helping the individual think over a wide variety of strategies for broad-range decision making, or it may narrowly focus upon the individual's ability to function independently.

It is important to assess the relative level of cognitive functioning and behavioral control to determine the individual's need for more concrete planning or even an imposed structure. In extreme cases, the individual consultation may require immediate referral to medical support (see Figure 5-1).

Crisis Intervention

Crisis intervention aims to help crisis victims absorb what has occurred, understand how they are reacting, and decide what they need to do next. Crisis intervention is not psychotherapy; its function is not to change long-standing traits or behavioral problems, nor does it seek to work through resistance or defense mechanisms. In fact, crisis intervention attempts to strengthen individuals' sagging defenses and marshal their preexisting habit patterns so they can meet the temporary but overwhelming stress of the current situation.

The purpose of crisis intervention is to

- restore the person to his or her previous level of functioning

- assist the person in planning what to do to cope with the situation

- mobilize whatever resources are necessary and available to meet the crisis

- assess the person's ability to function and refer the person to further assistance if necessary

Crisis intervention follows the general format outlined in Figure 5-2. First, communication must be established in order to build sufficient trust and rapport. Functioning capabilities are assessed initially and throughout the inter-

vention. Each person involved is given assistance in articulating and defining exactly what has occurred and how he or she is affected. This helps to define the problems to be faced within the immediate lifestyle, given the sudden change in circumstances. Then, the affected person has an opportunity to vent his or her reaction to both the incident and the anticipated changes it will cause. Resources necessary for meeting the situation are explored. Appropriate stress management techniques are developed. A plan of specific action for coping with the situation is formulated. If necessary, resources are contacted and mobilized.

The purpose of this general progression and outcome is to empower the person to move out of the position of victim and toward a position of survivor. Crisis intervention culminates by offering the individual suggestions and recommendations for the specific situation. How to assess the client's need for certain types of structure and suggestions on how to make these recommendations are discussed in Chapter 6. Figure 5-3 demonstrates a more elaborate crisis intervention adapted from the SAFER protocol used by the International Critical Incident Stress Foundation (Everly and Mitchell 1999).

Providing psychological first aid to students extends beyond the initial crisis intervention. It includes ongoing interaction between the child in crisis and each of the significant adults who work with the child. Normally, parents are the most influential adults in the child's life. Teachers possess the next level of influence. By the way they provide or withhold support, parents, teachers, and other significant adults can make a crucial difference in mediating the child's response to crisis. Crisis Response Team members can multiply the effects of their intervention by ensuring that significant adults in the child's life are aware of what they can do to help.

Holding conferences with supporting adults provides a good opportunity to provide them with pertinent information. Personal letters, newsletters, and handouts can be useful in this process. Even newspaper, radio, and television can be utilized in large-scale events.

When providing psychological support and first-aid information, make sure the approaches are geared to the child's developmental level. While a more specific breakdown is possible, dividing developmental levels into preschool/kindergarten, elementary, and secondary age spans is probably the most useful.

Preschool and Kindergarten

Children in this age range are wrestling with becoming autonomous in their functioning; therefore, the factors at risk are those related to maintaining independent functioning. Psychological first aid and support objectives for this age group should aim to reestablish trust and security, self-control, and autonomy (see Figure 5-4).

Intervention approaches providing this type of support focus on comfort and stability. Physical comforts—such as warm drinks, holding, food, and extra rest—are important and highly satisfying. Because daily routines are a major source of security, they should be reestablished as soon as possible. Spend the necessary time assuring the child of adult protection and demonstrate this with actions. Sometimes younger children will want to sleep in an adult's room following a crisis. Allow this to happen—children will want to reestablish their independence as quickly as possible; nevertheless, they need to test out whether it can be trusted. Help the child to draw, act out, discuss, or in any way communicate his or her experiences. Clarify what happened, dispelling misconceptions and misunderstandings as much as possible. Children at this age will look to adults' reactions to gauge the severity of the situation; therefore, be calm.

Elementary

For children in the elementary age range, the important developmental issues are the abilities to take initiative and establish productivity (see Figure 5-5). Establishing control over one's life is essential to self-esteem. Thus, for this age group the objectives of psychological first aid are to bolster self-esteem, relieve guilt, reestablish productivity, and continue assurances of personal safety. A less obvious objective is to help the child understand and make sense of the crisis event. Understanding is a necessary step toward empowerment.

The following approaches have proven useful in accomplishing these objectives. Elementary children should be provided opportunity and encouragement to express their thoughts and feelings about the incident, which is more important for this age group than for younger children. Their reactions need to be validated as normal, since this is vital to their sense of self-esteem. Temporarily lessening the requirements placed upon the child for optimal performance in schoolwork and home responsibilities reduces stress and provides positive learning experiences.

Although regressive behavior may be expected and should be tolerated, reinforce age-appropriate behavior in order to help save the child's self-esteem, which unnecessary regression is likely to compromise. Be sure to provide the level of structure and control that, through behavior, the child indicates he or she needs. In particular, look for the child's expression of feelings of responsibility and clarify any misperceptions the child may have. Talk directly about the child's dreams. Provide the child with opportunities for success.

Middle School and Senior High

The adolescent's world is wrapped up in concerns about peer status and identity (see Figure 5-6). At issue in this age group's reaction to crisis are isolation, depression, and impaired identity development. Intervention objectives include reassuring these youngsters of the normalcy of their reactions and inoculating them against secondary reactions. To counter any tendency toward maladaptive coping patterns, focus on stress management. Select tactics that facilitate and reinforce their identity development and reaffirm their life direction.

These objectives can be furthered by the following approaches. As with elementary-age students, encourage adolescents to express themselves through discussion and other means. Validate their reactions as normal, and temporarily lessen performance requirements. Unlike elementary students, adolescents will benefit from a problem-solving approach.

Teach general and individualized stress management techniques and provide opportunities for positive action to deal with the crisis. You may also find that it is useful to monitor student behavior and guide students who are coping with problems. Counselors should help provide an understanding of the incident, the reactions to it, and the current situation.

Older elementary, middle school, and senior high school students suffering from delayed stress reactions often act out their distress. This may take the form of behavior problems in school; the line between discipline and assistance can blur as you deal with the aftereffects of crisis. The following conferencing protocol is useful in handling behavior problems in such cases (see Figure 5-7) and may be especially helpful for classroom teachers:

- Provide the student with a clear description of the problem

- Inform the student of your concern that his or her behavior might be related to the incident

- Work out a set of mutually agreed upon expectations regarding minimally acceptable performance and behavior limits

- Focus on the problem, the issue, or the behavior, rather than on the person

- Work to maintain the student's self-confidence and self-esteem, as well as your own professional image

The intervention protocol and tactics discussed so far are primarily intended to be used on an individual basis. But schools also consist of groups. For groups impacted as groups, or for groups whose members have been impacted in ways that affect the entire group, a group intervention is the preferred modality. While group intervention follows the basic objectives of crisis intervention, its tactics differ. Classroom debriefing and several variations of group intervention are discussed in Chapter 7.

CRT Strategy 8: Parent Consultation

Parents often feel intense anxiety following crisis. Consultation can help them focus their concern, understand the situation, and determine what needs to be done next. Depending upon the situation and personal reactions, individual consultation can utilize a formal crisis intervention format or simply be limited to a friendly conversation. Of particular focus are the needs of the child. The consultation aims at assurance that the school is providing security and care for the child and identification of further assistance (see Figure 5-8).

Assessing parental function is important, as the family may need more structure than either they or the school can provide. Redirection to other resources may be necessary. It is also important to recognize the tendency of parents to displace their fears and anger onto the schools. Helping the parents clarify the sources of anger and fear can help redirect these feelings more productively.

Treating the parent consultation as a crisis intervention helps focus the discussion toward support, problem definition, and planning for meeting the child and family's needs. Observe carefully for the family's ability to meet the needs of the child.

Suggestions for Community Mental Health and Crisis Response Teams

Outside mental health professionals, community crisis responders, and clergy have special expertise in individual crisis consultation and intervention. They frequently have well-honed consultation skills and training in diagnosis and referral. Two things bear keeping in mind in working within the school setting in this regard.

First, remember the scope of practice of the school within the larger community. The school exists to educate and follows its own lines of procedure and authority. It is important to operate within those boundaries.

Second, a key difference between the school

and community has to do with the distinction between doing crisis intervention and doing therapy. Outside resources to schools sometimes feel as if they are being invited to conduct short-term psychotherapy. In many states and some foreign countries, psychotherapy is beyond the scope and practice of the schools. This is complicated by the fact that when school people say "counseling," they often mean "guidance" rather than clinical counseling and often hold an education model of counseling in their minds. For many of them, to "counsel a child about the use of alcohol," for instance, means to point out the negative consequences of its use.

Thus, it is important to take a conservative approach and interpret directives to "counsel" students to mean nonclinical intervention, at least until informed differently.

Some helpful distinctions might be that generally, while therapy aims at "emotional processing," counseling in schools aims to "teach about feelings and reactions." Crisis intervention may discuss feelings, but generally does not attempt to encourage expression of feelings in attempts at catharsis. For the most part, the primary process should be cognitive and the role of the counselor supportive and facilitative rather than confrontational.

Conclusion

Strategic individual intervention is a basic component of school crisis management. Students, staff, administrators, and parents can be helped to bring stability to the chaotic situation, thereby reinforcing the school's ability to meet all students' needs. This chapter has covered the general format and developmental considerations of individual intervention. Some greater specificity regarding assessment is necessary before proceeding to the discussion of group intervention or managing special problems.

Copy masters (Figures 6-1 to 6-9) for this chapter can be found on pages 188-196.

CHAPTER 6

Rapid Assessment

During crisis, there is no time for thorough, standardized assessment. Crisis situations demand rapid appraisal: school crisis managers must estimate the overall impact of the event and evaluate the status of staff and students who have been affected and establish appropriate intervention strategies. Then they must decide on the number of CRT members who will be needed. School crisis managers and CRT members must also determine which students and staff members will need further evaluation or follow-up services.

To accomplish these objectives within a pressing and fluid crisis context, the assessment methods must be

- practical

- appropriate to the context and to the individuals involved

- field-based

- within the CRTs scope of practice

- focused on CRT decision making

The results of these assessments provide the site leadership and the Crisis Response Team with the information needed to respond appropriately to the crisis at hand and to make appropriate referrals to outside resources.

Because of time and personnel constraints and because of the unique nature of crisis events, crisis assessment must be based on all available data. Sources of data regarding individuals or groups can include an individual's self-reports, ongoing observation of the individual during intervention by CRT or staff observers, reports from friends or family, and reports from school personnel (including preincident risk factors). Site leaders and CRT members must determine at the outset the information they need and how to obtain it quickly. They must also be aware that as the situation and the intervention unfold, need for new information will emerge. In larger incidents, it is helpful to have a central repository of assessment information, with one person in charge of organizing and accessing data so that it is available as needed.

Due to the restrictions imposed on assessment measures during crisis situations, assessment data must be treated as suggestive, not conclusive. In such environments, assessment must be (see Figure 6-1)

- informal

- approximate

- conservative

- unobtrusive

- tentative and ongoing

This chapter provides suggestions for making a practical and rapid assessment of individual student and staff crisis needs. It also provides direction for field assessment of individuals who have been impacted by crisis and may be in need of referral for specialized services. Areas covered include functioning level, potential for threat to self, level of family functioning, and configuration of social support.

Individual Functioning

An individual's overall functioning is the most general area for assessment. The issue at hand is simple: What kind of assistance does the individual need right now in order to ensure his or her safety? More precisely, can this person leave here unattended with reasonable assurance that he or she can get home, meet his or her daily needs, and solve whatever problems arise?

To make such an assessment, spend time observing the individual's actions and listening to the person's speech. Demand enough problem solving through the course of the intervention to gain a sense of several aspects of the person's functioning.

More specifically, crisis assessment for an individual must

1. Determine the individual's functioning level in order to make decisions regarding the nature of assistance needed

2. Determine whether or not the individual represents a threat to himself or herself

3. Determine whether the individual's family or social network can provide adequate support

4. Determine if there are medical considerations that need attention (including substance addictions)

5. Determine if there are others dependent on this person

6. Determine if there are other factors bearing on the individual's safety

The type of structure needed by an individual varies according to his or her current state of mind and ability to manage his or her situation and reactions (see Figure 6-2). An assessment should consider the extent to which the person is able to maintain internal control over his or her behavior. A person's degree of empowerment, or ability to make changes in the world, is vital to how the individual copes with crisis-related obstacles to everyday living. Similarly, he or she should have clear cognitive functioning.

Significant impairment in either empowerment or cognitive functioning must be noted and considered in the assessment of the external support the person will require. An individual's external resources—available through family, friends, or the wider community—will influence that person's ability to function. Finally, an assessment is needed of the individual's ability to tolerate ambiguity. This knowledge will help determine the best way to make suggestions and referrals to further assistance.

Moderately Impaired Functioning

After crisis, it is normal for individuals to be slightly disoriented and confused and to experience difficulties planning. Crying, anger, and quietness are also normal responses, as are excessive talking or laughter, restlessness, and frequent retelling of or not wanting to discuss the incident.

A checklist based on Figures 1-6 and 1-7 can be useful to document your impressions during crisis. For intervention several days or more after the incident, a general checklist can be made based on Figures 1-8 and 1-9 or more developmentally specific checklists can be constructed from Figures 1-18 through 1-24.

Reactions that essentially fall within the range outlined by Figures 1-6 through 1-9 and 1-18 through 1-24 represent moderate impairment in functioning. Referring the individual to further counseling or evaluation could be very helpful; a conservative response would be to make such a referral to resources either within or outside of the school system. If the individual is a minor, his or her parents should be notified of such observations.

Depressive reactions following a crisis can signify a particular problem. Like many other posttraumatic reactions, however, they can range from mild to severe. Appendix III illustrates the range of depressive reactions. While it can be used as a checklist, there is no set "scoring pattern" for determining exactly how many responses an individual can have in a given severity category that will warrant classifying the individual as such. The outline is offered only to illustrate the range of responses, and CRT members are again advised to take a conservative position in determining whether an individual requires additional assistance. When it comes to human need, it is far better to err on the side of overresponse than underresponse.

Seriously Impaired Functioning

The agitated and depressed forms of Acute Stress Response, as discussed in Chapter 1, represent seriously impaired functioning. Figure 1-18 provides a checklist of the symptoms of the two forms of ASR. While early intervention is very helpful in such cases, ASR needs follow-up care even when it appears that the individual's functioning is likely to be restored. Children showing signs of ASR should be referred as soon as possible for psychological evaluation.

Certain signs of psychological disturbance—which may occur during the incident itself or during the weeks or months following the incident—indicate that immediate referral is necessary to obtain a competent psychiatric assessment for possible medication and/or protective care. While these signs may or may not be symptoms of serious psychiatric disturbance, they are clear indications that the individual will have difficulty functioning normally and that the individual's personal safety is at issue.

Crisis creates cognitive, emotional, and behavioral disturbances, which should be expected and which for the most part are normal. As Chapter 1 indicated, most of these disturbances are transitory. Each sign of distress can, however, go to an extreme that impairs the individual's functioning. The following indicators for psychiatric referral are presented here, along with their less extreme "normal" counterparts.

Cognitive indicators

Critical incidents are normally disorienting because of their extreme conditions and overwhelming nature. But when slight disorientation becomes an inability to identify one's own name, the date, or a brief description of the event, psychiatric and functional impairment

must be suspected (see Figure 6-3).

Crisis events often create difficulties in prioritizing demands and actions. Keeping perspective is critical in order to allocate energy and resources to the most pressing needs. When an individual becomes preoccupied with one aspect of the situation, he or she loses this perspective. Exclusive preoccupation impedes functioning, implies impairment, and should be assessed.

Denying the severity of an incident is a normal survival mechanism. However, engaging in wholesale denial that the incident even occurred signifies a severe reaction. Similarly, flashbacks shortly after an incident can be expected; when flashbacks become hallucinations, however, it is time to assess psychiatric status. Self-doubt is also normal during crisis, but when self-doubt is so debilitating that it results in an inability to act, it requires psychiatric attention. Physical immobility and refusal to move without being led are examples of traumatic paralysis, and they require immediate care.

General cognitive unresponsiveness, or numbing, is one response to acute stress. This can take the extreme form of disconnection, where the individual does not recognize the incident as having an effect on or being related to him or her. While problems with planning are normal, the inability to perform the basic life tasks is not. Similarly, while confusion or misconceptions regarding the incident are normal, holding bizarre beliefs and then acting on those beliefs require psychiatric assessment.

Emotional indicators

As indicated in Chapter 1, emotional signs of distress will reflect either extreme overreactivity or underreactivity to the incident (see Figure 6-4). While crying, anxiety, and general upset are "normal," hysteria and panic are not. Anger and self-blame may be expected, but real threats to self and others are extreme and necessitate further assessment. A dulled, blunted emotional response is essentially normal; no emotional response at all, physical rigidity, and fetal positioning are serious indicators that assessment is critical.

Behavioral indicators

Behavioral signs follow a progression from essentially "normal" emergency reactions to their pathological counterparts (see Figure 6-5). However, they do not group into two extremes as emotional signs do. During emergencies behavior is typically undercontrolled or overcontrolled, but the signs of serious distress are simply measured in terms of an individual's ability to continue functioning independently. If the person's excessive talk or laughter goes from normal to crisis proportions or becomes uncontrolled, or if restlessness and excitement turn into unfocused agitation, then the person needs referral. Pacing, hand-wringing, and frequent retelling of the incident that become ritualistic and continual are also a concern. While withdrawal from others is a "normal" response to extreme situations, immobility and rigidity are causes for referral because they indicate possible psychic impairment. While a disheveled appearance is indicative of distress, the inability to take care of personal needs is a clear sign for referral.

Each community differs in its available psychiatric resources, and each school district has its own policies and procedures for such referrals. It is important to review the adequacy of these policies in view of disaster or large-scale crisis projections and to consider whether the policies are realistic given the available resources.

Threat to Self

Crisis response personnel have the responsibility to assess an individual's potential for suicidal behavior. Grounds for concern can include background and risk factors, statements by and certain behavior of the individual, or reports made by others. Site personnel can be invaluable if they can provide relevant background information to help identify students currently at risk and those previously identified as being at risk.

Be aware of background factors that increase an individual's risk of suicidal behavior. These include prior attempts, particularly those occurring recently; recent losses and prior traumatic events; isolation or withdrawal; and destructive coping styles such as substance abuse (see Figure 6-6). Cognitive disorientation lowers a person's coping ability, as does inadequate social support. The presence of any of these factors should be considered as indirect indicators of increased risk.

Specific signs of suicidal behavior include actual threats of suicide and preoccupation with death or another's suicidal actions (see Figure 6-7). Making final arrangements, giving away personal possessions, and excessive risk taking are also suicide indicators. Changes in personality, attitudes, appearance, performance, or the level of substance use should be considered "red flags": they do not necessarily mean that suicide is likely, but they do mean that a more formal assessment is necessary.

Assessing suicidal risk follows a general protocol (see Figure 6-8). After establishing contact and rapport, the intervener should express any concerns raised by his or her observations of the individual's risk factors and signs. Ask the person directly if he or she has been thinking of suicide. Through discussion, try to determine whether the individual has a suicide plan. To the extent the plan is specific as to method, time, and place, to the extent it is imminent, and to the extent the means are available and lethal, the individual is at greater risk of completing the plan and attempting to commit suicide.

As with the threat of risks to others, remember that the factors, signs, and protocols outlined here are general considerations, and there is always a danger of "false negatives"; that is, situations that do not fit the general patterns but are nevertheless lethal. It is imperative that situation managers and consultants take these considerations as starting points only. No one set of protocols can be considered comprehensive in situations involving high stakes.

Appendix IV details more specific assessment issues that can be used to determine whether the risk of completion is low, moderate, or high. A single factor may determine the extent of the risk. For instance, suicidal ideation alone may be enough to classify an individual as low risk as opposed to no risk. Given what is involved, a safe approach to risk assessment is critical. If the overall configuration of factors is hard to categorize as low versus moderate, assume the risk is moderate and act accordingly.

Again, these lists are not to be construed as exhaustive; they are only starting points for further inquiry. Significantly dangerous cases may not fit these profiles. It is important to consider indirect signs prior to direct inquiry, and if the situation might be dangerous, involve a psychiatric assessment team or police sooner rather than later.

High-risk individuals should not be left alone, nor should they be referred to further help unescorted. If the student (or adult) is assessed as high risk, then that person cannot be trusted to follow recommendations to take care of himself or herself. Similarly, moderate-risk individuals should not be trusted to be alone unless you are certain that they will not attempt suicide. Before releasing any person at moderate risk of suicide, ask yourself whether such a decision would be justifiable to a court of law, your professional licensing body, your school administration, and your own conscience.

In cases involving the assessment of threats to either self or others, it is better to err on the side of caution. Document the reasons prompting action and then act to protect life. Notify and utilize police and psychiatric assessment teams whenever in doubt.

Families

Family conditions can strengthen or weaken a person's resistance to external crises. Families can provide nurture and support, resources and assistance. They can also increase a person's stress, undermine self-worth, and create greater need. Several factors can make families a source of pain and complication during crisis:

Dysfunctional Family Member or Members. Specific dysfunctions include substance abuse, mental illness, compulsive behaviors,

and physical illness. When one member is dysfunctional, the others may develop compensatory behaviors including overachievement, acting out, getting trapped in rigid roles, and hiding family secrets, and they may have difficulty adapting to changing circumstances. These limit the family's capacity to respond effectively to crisis, and a school or community crisis may, in turn, trigger a secondary family crisis that ends up being more severe than the primary incident.

Abuse. Families in which physical, emotional, or sexual abuse or neglect are a normal part of life present two problems for CRT members. First, the effects of the crisis are likely to be greater and less predictable. Second, the abuse must be reported and dealt with as a separate issue.

Codependency. Families in which one or both parents grew up in dysfunctional families are often characterized by overcontrol or undercontrol, resentment, indirect expression of feelings, pressure to conform or achieve, denial, shame, and addictive or compulsive behavior. Honesty, balance, communication, and effective problem solving are scarce. Because successful adjustment to crisis requires all of these, codependent families are at risk.

Recovery. Families who are in recovery from addiction or compulsive behavior are at risk of relapse following crisis. Recovery challenges families to work out new forms of interaction, and crisis conditions place stress on these newfound and unfamiliar coping systems.

Assessing Critical Factors

Certain crises that can occur within families can have a profound effect on children and adults and may require crisis intervention. They are

- separation

- substance abuse

- violence binge

- death in family

- loss of job or residence

- medical crisis

- transition

During assessment, CRT members must inquire about family resources and conditions. Information and clues about family functioning are usually received during discussion of other subjects. A sensitive interviewer will notice any indications of family vulnerability factors and specific family crises. Further inquiry into these "red flag" areas may uncover family information essential to planning intervention. A three-fold questioning process is helpful in following leads regarding vulnerability factors or specific family crises:

First, begin with general, suggestive questions. For example, if the interviewee makes reference to one parent living at another residence, this can indicate a family separation. The interviewer might ask, "Are your folks living together?" or even more generally, "Did I hear you say that he (or she) lived in —— ?"

Second, if the first suggestion is substantiated, then pointed questions can be asked to clarify the situation. In the above example, it would be important to find out when the separation took place. You could ask, "Are your parents divorced?" or "Is this recent? Did it just happen?"

Finally, you can ask specific questions that will help with intervention planning. "Can you rely on your father to help you?" "Can you talk to your mother?" "Who can you count on?" "Can your mom give you that?"

This sort of questioning does not need to be done for each vulnerability factor or possible family crisis. Explore only those areas that come up in more general discussion and pursue only those areas that yield a positive response. Integrate this questioning protocol into your own personal style.

Assessing Support

In assessing family support, it is important to remember two things. First, assessments are relative; the goal is not "objective" facts but rather to determine the degree of support perceived by the affected individual. If support is not perceived, it is not experienced. Second, if the individual is a minor, and if abuse or neglect is disclosed, CRT members are obligated by conscience and probably by law to report their suspicion to the proper authorities. In such cases it is important to be aware of and comply with relevant state laws and district policies and procedures.

Consider several factors when assessing family support: the composition of the family, the basic dynamics of interaction between family members, past events that could compound the effects of the crisis, and current factors (such as family dysfunctions) that could affect the ability of family members to provide support to the individual.

It is important to begin by determining who the family consists of, their ages, and general roles. This includes siblings, extended family if local, and any other persons who play an ongoing role in the family.

Understanding the basic family dynamics is essential. It is useful to know who is the most powerful and influential person in the family and makes major policy decisions. It is equally important to know who makes the majority of the day-to-day decisions and conducts family business. They are often not the same person. Political divisions within the family may prove telling. It is good to know who provides most of the emotional support and to what extent family members are critical and judgemental. Inquire as to whether or not the individual can ask for support and expect to get it. Finally, the way the family is affected by the current crisis provides useful information for planning.

It is especially important to find out whether the family or individual family members have experienced difficult events in the past that could compound their experience of the present crisis. Particularly important are incidents that have parallel themes (for example, loss or victimization). The benefits of prior experience in helping them cope successfully must be weighed against the cumulative effect of retraumatization.

Current factors in the life of the family could diminish the support available. If another family member is sick, if the family recently suffered a financial setback, if the family just moved, or if any number of situations exist that increase family stress, the family may be less able to respond to the needs of the individual. Similarly, if the family is generally inadequate, suffers from some dysfunction such as alcoholism or marital schism, or holds values that run counter to the individual's interest, the family may be unable to provide the support an individual needs to deal with crisis.

Moderate impairment in family support includes those cases where the individual's unusual emotional or physical needs caused by the extra stress of the crisis cannot be met by the family. In such cases you must attempt to arrange supplementary support from extended family or community. Referral for additional assessment is also advisable.

Serious impairment in family support includes those cases where an individual's basic needs cannot be met or where he or she will be neglected or hurt by remaining with the family. If the individual is an adult, referral for additional assistance is necessary. If the individual is a minor, the child must be evaluated for protective care and the proper authorities notified.

Family Mapping

The family map is a useful tool for recording observations. In this technique, the family of the individual in crisis is described using a spatial metaphor. Often individuals, particularly children, are unable to conceptualize their family dynamics verbally. Getting them to describe these abstract relationships in concrete, spatial, nonverbal ways may help in obtaining useful information about the family's composition and basic dynamics. In addition, the process may open communication about family history and functioning.

With the assistance of the intervener, the individual draws family members as circles arranged in a way that best portrays the relationships between them (Appendix V). The individual can be asked to portray the relative power of each member by the size of the circle and to arrange the circles so that their closeness on paper reflects emotional closeness. Affiliation among family members is represented by groupings on paper.

Dynamic dimensions of family life such as communication, authority, decision making, and quality of relationship can be expressed by various coding systems. One such system, as illustrated in Appendix V, consists of lines drawn between members. A solid line indicates a solid relationship or solid communication. A broken line denotes a relationship with both good and bad aspects or communication that is good at times and breaks down at times. A "lightning bolt" between two members could represent antagonism or chronic fighting. A severed line could be used to indicate a severed relationship. The symbols used can be indicated in a key on the map.

Space around the map itself can be devoted to particular content issues. Specific questions could be written on the map or in boxes that are used in ways that the individual and interviewer decide. Some important questions include:

- Has your family gone through difficulties like this in the past?

- If so, what happened, how did family members handle it, and how did things work out?

- How much do the people in your family like one another?

- Do you have difficulties with any particular members of your family?

- Are there any particular arguments or hard feelings that might make things more difficult?

- Which people in your family can you rely on for help?

- Are there things going on in your family that worry you?

It should be stressed that family mapping is subjective and limited to the perspective of the individual who is being assessed.

Social Support

No one stands alone. We each exist within networks of mutual assistance, support, and obligation. While self-reliance is a worthy aim, the reality remains that we are all interconnected for meeting our basic needs. Even the boundaries of our community have expanded, so that we are now directly affected by what goes on daily just about anywhere in the world.

As our support needs vary, so do the sources through which we get support. The most important source continues to be one's family, including extended family. Close friends and neighbors are the next most important source. Coworkers or business-related associates come next, and local professionals and service providers follow. Finally, public agencies may offer various forms of support.

In crisis, old sources of support may be disrupted, while new needs for support emerge. If the crisis impacts one sphere of support (for example, job or family), other sources must be developed. During communitywide disaster, many spheres may be impacted. An earthquake, for instance, may destroy the family home, injure family members, and also lay waste to the workplace and source of income. Further, the need for relocation may sever neighborhood support systems and cut off the family from community resources.

Intervention involves determining what support is necessary and what alternative sources are available; crisis assessment involves taking inventory of these support needs and sources. Figure 6-9 provides one possible format for assessing social support. The horizontal dimension lists potential sources of support—old sources as well as new ones— and the vertical dimension lists each type of support needed. In general, the more needs listed on the left side of the page, the more the individual is at risk and requires assistance in getting support.

Other Issues

Three other issues need to be addressed in crisis assessment: medical considerations, the possible dependency of others on the individual's functioning, and other safety factors.

First, determine if there are medical considerations that need attention. If the individual is under a physician's care for an illness or chronic condition, the nature of the condition and the need for medical supervision must be assessed. For example, someone with a cardiac condition may be at high risk during a crisis because of the extra physical and emotional demands of the situation. Of particular concern during a disaster or large-scale crisis are those who require prescription drugs such as insulin. Accessibility to medication might be disrupted, causing a medical emergency. Similarly, illicit drug dependence, whether on alcohol, stimulants, depressants, or opiates, can present medical or behavioral emergencies if supply is restricted. These situations may require medical intervention.

Are there others dependent on the person in crisis? Adults in crisis, and often even older children, may have others who depend on them. Children, the elderly, or those with medical conditions often require ongoing assistance for their well-being. If the person who provides that assistance is functionally impaired, dependents can suffer. Assessment should determine whether such a situation exists and how responsibility can be shifted if necessary.

Other factors may bear on the individual's safety. Many unforeseen circumstances may put a person in jeopardy if he or she is functionally impaired or if crisis-related circumstances have changed his or her living environment significantly. It is critical to be open to such factors and be willing to explore them if the need arises.

Suggestions for Community Mental Health and Crisis Response Teams

Educators may project their needs for absolute answers upon outside resources in the form of expectations for impossible insight, magical thinking, and ability to foretell the future.

While it is tempting to reinforce this perception in order to relieve their anxiety or gain voice in decision making, to do so is to invite a sense of betrayal later.

While less glamorous, it is more productive to stress the positive differences in background training and perspective. While not mind readers, mental health professionals do possess a strong theoretical base of understanding individual's reactions to stress and trauma and can often predict likely courses of dysfunctional response. They can also think strategically in terms of intervention options from the individual perspective and often have a broad range of experience to draw from in dealing with families.

Outside personnel bring an outsider's perspective to a situation that may be bound by insider's limitations. Fresh ideas may be obvious to outsiders but hard to generate from within a system. From these broadened perspectives can come new intervention strategies.

Mental health professionals may be better able to pick up on subtle, indirect signs of child abuse, family dysfunction, or psychopathology that may be affecting the crisis situation and that may call for different, nonstandard approaches.

Finally, outside personnel may be knowledgeable about outside resources useful to the school, individuals, or their families and may be able to refer accordingly.

It must be pointed out, however, that just as outsiders to the system have certain strengths and limitations, so do insiders. Assessment always benefits from a grasp of baseline norms, for the individual and the group. School personnel are in an excellent position to have this grasp, as the school is a naturalistic setting where the child or group is observed for six to seven hours a day, day in and day out. Thus, outside resource personnel do well by conferring closely with school personnel when assessing students or staff.

School personnel are also in the position of knowing more about preceding changes in the life of the child or precipitating incidents. Schools often have extensive school and health records that may assist assessment.

School-community partnerships open vast resources for children but can only work in an environment of cooperation and mutual respect. The more outside resources can learn about school functioning and territoriality prior to emergencies, the more productive that partnership can be.

Conclusion

Until you determine that the individual in crisis is functioning independently—does not represent a threat to self or others, has at least minimal support from family and community, is free from undue medical constraints, has no responsibilities for others' well-being that he or she cannot fulfill, and is relatively safe—you cannot make assumptions about that individual's welfare. Assessment strategies used to determine these conditions must be rapid, practical, approved by the school's administration, and within the scope of the CRTs functioning.

Copy masters (Figures 7-1 to 7-9) for this chapter can be found on pages 197-205.

CHAPTER 7

Group Intervention

During the summer of 1991, a Southern California town was threatened by a large brushfire. Over 30 homes were destroyed as the fire, blown by erratic high winds, spread rapidly. Following the fire, it was discovered that at least half of the more than 900 students at the nearest elementary school lived either within or immediately adjacent to the fire zone. Teachers began reporting high absentee rates, irritability, distractibility, and acting out among the students. An intervention was coordinated by the county mental health Crisis Response Team. Most of the contact between CRT members and students took place within the classrooms. Depending on the grade level, the team utilized discussion, art activities, teaching, and staff consultation to assist students in overcoming their fire-related anxieties and fears. As a result, staff members reported a quicker return than expected to normal school routine and productivity. At the time, this was a state of the art intervention.

Since then, the frequency, scale, and type of crises have escalated. School shootings—and mass murder in particular—command news reporters' attention, and graphic pictures horrify viewers with what has turned into a symbol of the new millennium: a breakdown of the social fabric. While reporting on the latest atrocity, reporters also mention that "counselors are now going into the school to talk to students about their reactions." Horror is becoming commonplace, but a reasoned and orchestrated response to the horror is becoming more routine.

A school consists of individuals functioning in groups; classrooms, homerooms, resource lab groups, peer groups, departments, lunchrooms, and office staffs are all groups of people. The school day is punctuated by ringing bells, signaling groups to break up and recombine into other groups. Crises affecting schools affect groups; in order for interventions to be effective in school settings, they must be tailored to these groups.

Crisis intervention aims at restoring individuals to their previous level of functioning. This may mean substantial changes in behavior, however, if the postcrisis environment is significantly altered for the individual. If we regard life as an ongoing series of struggles, then crisis is an interruption and crisis intervention attempts to get the individual back into the series, adequately confronting his or her struggles.

Group crisis intervention aims to help the group regain its previous level of cohesion. The impact of crisis over time will usually increase or decrease the level of a group's organization, depending on how the crisis is met. Thus, the long-range goal of group crisis intervention is really greater organizational solidarity.

There are many kinds of group intervention, ranging from simple classroom discussions, to more technical defusings and debriefings, to large-scale assemblies, to classroom follow-up activities.

CRT Strategy 9: Classroom Discussion, Defusing, Debriefing

Schools naturally group students, and students expect to work in groups. Less than five percent of their working day is spent on one-on-one activity, so group intervention fits smoothly into their expectational set. Furthermore, group discussion regarding current events is the norm, as is discussion regarding the students' understanding, interpretation, and reactions to those events (see Figure 7-1). Building upon this foundation, then, postcrisis group intervention simply extends the culture of learning to include critical incidents that are more unusual and distressing. The manner of the group discussion can range from informal and spontaneous to more structured and formal.

Discussion and Defusing

Group discussions are the simplest and most natural group intervention following a crisis. In general, they should follow similar guidelines for individual conferencing, taking into account the social dimensions of the situation. Students can be vulnerable to harassment following group discussions if they disclose sensitive information to an unappreciative audience. Their well-being must be protected. The following are some guidelines for conducting classroom discussions following critical incidents (see Figure 7-2):

- Conduct discussion in a comfortable place, away from crisis-related stimuli such as visual or auditory reminders, TV or radio announcements, or emergency vehicle traffic.

- Maintain calm, personally and within the group. The leader's calm demeanor models that behavior for students and encourages trust. The implicit message is, "It's OK."

- Be aware of personal reactions and limits. If the discussion leader is unable to handle the situation, someone else should take over.

- Observe behavior for congruency with speech. While a child is saying one thing, body language may be saying something more important.

- Validate students' feelings. While strong feelings often lie just below the surface, and while students should not be encour-

aged to act them out during a discussion, those feelings should be acknowledged. Convey the message, "It's normal to have unusual and strong feelings during times like this."

- Listen with attention, focus, and empathy. Use gentle probes for elaboration, and use increasingly focused questions when necessary. Maintain good eye contact, and be aware of the messages posture can send out.

- Show confidence, trust, and faith that the student is telling the truth as he or she sees it. Do not seek to place blame.

- Look for misplaced blame or responsibility children may place upon themselves for things that happened during the crisis. Help clarify what happened and dispel fault.

- Find the balance between support and overcontrol regarding the expression of anxiety. Without creating contagious hysteria, assist students in exploring their fears. Provide reality checks and assurance as appropriate. Observe different students' reactions and keep the discussion itself from becoming hurtful.

- Provide clear, accurate, and understandable information when possible. Don't contradict feelings, but help students to understand the situation.

- Sometimes situations require changes in routine. When such changes are fairly certain, explain what is to happen to students and help them walk through the process.

- Point out available resources at school and in the community, and pass out fact sheets so students can take the information home, as they may not remember it.

- Help students link up in natural support groupings. Networking for mutual support is very helpful.

- Let students know you are available if they need to talk to you after the meeting or at a later time.

Response to the Columbine High School Shooting by the Jefferson Center for Mental Health

Jo Anne Doherty

The shootings at Columbine High School (CHS) on April 20, 1999, by two CHS students resulted in twelve students and one teacher killed, and additional students and adults injured. The adolescent perpetrators then killed themselves, bringing the total death count to fifteen. This was the largest school shooting in U.S. history, requiring a massive community and school-based response.

The Jefferson Center for Mental Health—the private nonprofit community mental health center serving the area in which the school is located—assisted the school district and the community in this response. JCMH staff responded on site within two hours of the shootings. On that day, over 165 hours of mental health crisis services were provided at three locations. The main site was an elementary school just a few blocks away from CHS, where families waited to see if their loved ones were alive and where many emotionally charged reunions occurred.

Due to the massive destruction, loss of lives, and injuries, CHS did not resume school for ten days. This resulted in an immediate community-based approach to providing mental health services. Two local churches opened their doors to the youth and their families, providing a safe haven and sites in which mental health staff could provide counseling and support services. Many other organizations provided similar support. Schools throughout the Jefferson County school district were significantly impacted—fear was widespread, and there were several bomb threats at various schools in the weeks that followed. In the first 10 days after the tragedy, mental health staff provided over 3,000 hours of services at over 25 sites. These services included staffing the safe havens, as well as providing crisis intervention and debriefing to students who had witnessed their friends being killed by their peers and to parents who had waited for hours not knowing if their child was alive or dead. Counselors were on site at numerous local schools, debriefing students and staff, and formal debriefings were provided to local community organizations that were impacted.

School resumed 10 days after the shootings at a neighboring high school (Chatfield High School). Over 3,000 Columbine High School parents attended a school-sponsored meeting prior to school starting. National and local speakers on mental health and school staff addressed parent concerns. It is notable that the first question asked was how the mental health needs of their kids would be provided for. Seven additional mental health counselors joined the seven CHS school counseling and social work staff in providing crisis intervention services. Twenty-three additional counselors provided mental health services at area schools.

A cornerstone of the community response was the opening of a "one-stop resource center," Columbine Connections, and a youth drop-in center, SHOUTS. Columbine Connections is a multi-agency collaborative effort representing the Jefferson County Sheriff's Office, Victims Assistance, Jefferson Center for Mental Health, Foothills Parks and Recreation, and PACCT. Columbine Connections provides crisis and outreach mental health services, victims' assistance, and outreach and referral services. Individuals receiving services ranged from someone needing assistance in applying for victims' compensation, to an acutely suicidal child, to a parent seeking help for a child who had become so fearful he would not leave home. A multidisciplinary team of four outreach staff, one creative arts therapist, two mental health clinicians, and one community education and outreach coordinator work collaboratively with other partners including victims' assistance staff in providing services to the community. At the time of this writing, SHOUTS is open four evenings a week with an average attendance of about 25 youths a day. Students gather to drink coffee in the coffeehouse, write poetry, play pool, watch the big screen TV, join discussion groups, or get support from two peer mentors.

Jo Anne Doherty, MS, RN, CNS, is Vice President of Clinical Services and Chief Operating Officer of the Jefferson Center for Mental Health.

While crisis intervention is usually done on an individual level, children are often found in groups and are sometimes traumatized in groups at school. Accordingly, group crisis intervention is sometimes the preferred mode and sometimes the only mode possible given the exigencies of the situation. Group crisis intervention is possible in small groups or in large classes. In most situations group discussion following the above guidelines is the best.

In some situations, however, the upset is too fresh and the reactions too severe to conduct business as usual. In the immediate aftermath of a crisis, and in situations where there are simply too many unknowns to rely upon unstructured group discussion, classroom defusing presents an alternative.

Classroom defusings are typically conducted with intact groups such as classes or smaller groups of children who have been impacted together by a critical incident. A defusing is provided when the critical incident is over and before students leave for home. It is a small group meeting that demarks the event as serious, allows the supervising adult (such as the teacher) to maintain classroom control, and sets the stage for future group processing of the event. The defusing protocol is adapted from George Everly and Jeffrey Mitchell (1999), elaborated in Johnson et al. (1999).

Classroom defusings aim at reestablishing classroom control by opening a brief, structured discussion of the event within the group. Additional goals are to approximate the aims of individual crisis intervention, assess students' need for further intervention, and reduce the level of reaction to the incident on both the individual and group levels (see Figure 7-3).

In the **introduction** phase, after clearly stating the purpose and format of the discussion, the leader sets forth several simple rules. These include: Let each other speak; don't interrupt; tell what happened if you wish, but you can just listen to others if you choose; don't criticize; and keep what's said in the room.

During the **exploration** phase, the leader asks students to describe what happened and works toward pulling together a consistency of shared group experience. Included in this phase is the sharing of initial reactions to the extent students are comfortable doing so.

In the **information** phase, the leader summarizes the students' perceptions, clarifies misconceptions, and normalizes the students' experiences and reactions with statements such as, "What you have told me are normal reactions for kids who have gone through experiences like this." The leader also provides additional information as appropriate, outlines what students can expect next, and makes suggestions about stress management.

Classroom Debriefing

Classroom debriefings are more structured group interventions that take place a day or more following an incident. These debriefings provide a time-out from normal classroom routine, a time when class members can explore their own processes following a crisis. Individuals can air their perceptions of the event, their reactions to it, and their concerns for the future in a structured, supportive context. The exchange is therapeutic for the individuals and for the group as a whole.

If the event impacted a substantial number of class members, it is preferable to include the whole class in a debriefing. Classroom debriefings can be conducted with almost any size class, up to 40 students; they can take up to several hours, depending on the extent of impact, the developmental level of students, and the climate of the particular classroom. The basic rule is to take as long as it takes.

The form of the debriefing is quite basic. Under the guidance of the leader, the class discusses what occurred, the role each student took, the reactions experienced at the time of the incident and later, how each one currently feels, what can be expected in the future, and what it all means. With older children and adolescents, this can be a straightforward discussion. With younger children, the process might work best within some activity, such as an art project.

The rules are simple: The leader gets to lead. No one has to say anything, but everyone must listen when another is speaking. Most im-

Crisis Intervention Following
A Collective Traumatic Event

Dr. Ofra Ayalon

Children exposed to wars, shelling from across the border, and terrorist attack on civilian populations are not only physically threatened but may be badly damaged psychologically. A stress and trauma preventive program called COPE (Community-Oriented Preventive Education), geared for enhancing coping skills in school-age children, has been implemented in the Israeli school system with remarkable results (Ayalon 1979). This program integrates six major coping strategies: physical, cognitive, affective, imaginative, spiritual (belief systems), and social support (Ayalon 1993; Lahad 1997). It is usually practiced by stressing the benefits of proximity to the impact area, immediacy to the event, and expectancy for recuperation. COPE has been translated into different languages and employed in the wake of natural as well as in human-made disasters (Ayalon 1992, 1997, 1998; Ayalon et al. 1998, 1999).

I would like to share with you a very moving experience of a crisis intervention with a group of junior high school students, who were exposed to a gory terrorist attack on their neighbors. The terrorists arrived from Lebanon in a rubber boat after midnight and raided an apartment house on the beach in an Israeli resort town. They managed to abduct by gunpoint a young man and his five-year-old daughter and cruelly murdered them. The two-year-old daughter hiding with the mother in a small attic was suffocated to death. During the raid other residents of the immediate vicinity tried to barricade their homes or fled in the darkness to a safer area.

The next morning our Emergency Stress Prevention Team arrived in the schools to help teachers debrief their students and identify those who were near-miss and high-risk. Fifty-four of those children were found still hiding in their homes, barely fit to join their classes. They were escorted to school and put in small groups facilitated by team members. The list of complaints these children reported included acute anxiety states, reawakening of early frightening fantasies, fear of the dark, and fear of noises and of the beach (the scene of the crime). The children in this high-risk group were haunted by images of the murdered father and daughter and the tragic death of the little one. They found concentration impossible and were given to crying spells, headaches, and

stomachaches. At home, some suffered from sleeplessness and tended to cling to parents.

These reactions are consistent with Posttraumatic Stress Disorder (American Psychiatric Association 1994). The treatment, however, was unique and prompt. All the children (12–14 years old) were grouped according to age, to be observed and treated for the duration of the crisis (which at that time was unknown to us). As it turned out, each small group was conducted by a member of the crisis team for five consecutive days, four hours each day, within the school setting. We used our holistic COPE methods of dealing with trauma, including verbal and nonverbal modes of expression, peer support, empowerment, and enhancing coping skills (Ayalon 1992).

Initial ventilation of feelings and aggression channeling

The first stage was marked by a diffuse expression of the children's fear and anger, both verbal and nonverbal (in drawing and finger painting). Sighs and crying and feelings of misery and grief were dominant. Some children seemed flooded with frightening images of past and present experiences. All expressions, even the most idiosyncratic, were granted full legitimization by the therapists and explained as "normal" for this stage of mourning.

As violent emotions surged, they channeled themselves into scenarios of vengeance and retaliation against the aggressors. When these became too frightening, the children turned to make-believe games of rescue, in which they themselves were the rescuers.

Gradual in vivo exposure

Startle reactions to noises were desensitized by gradual exposure to noises in a state of relaxation. The extinction of the "beach phobia" was conducted in vivo—by parents and therapists taking the kids out to the seashore, bestowing love and confidence during the experience. One girl wrote later, "My father took me to the shore. I saw the terrorists' boat, the rocks on which they smashed the head of the little girl. I regret having seen the boat. It haunts me in my dreams. But I am not afraid of the sea any longer." *(continued)*

Cognitive reappraisal and working through

As the hours and days proceeded, new patterns of coping emerged. Having vented out fear and anger, the children regained their grasp on reality.

A lot of verbal sharing of the experience appeared, some of it in written form. Some wrote poems as a way to master their stormy reflections. The healing power of writing became evident in a poetic dialogue between those who praised God on their own rescue and those who defied God for neglecting to protect the victims. One girl wrote:

If there is a God
and yes, many claim there is
then how does it happen
that little kids are killed?

Provided with all the information about the event, participants engaged in suggestions for future encounters with threat and danger. The feelings that had been expressed in earlier phases were now channeled into a problem-solving mode designed to consider what could be done differently in future stressful events. By focusing on working through their feelings about both the past traumas and the present and future eventualities, the children slowly came to terms with the stress of being near-miss victims.

Erecting memorials signified the beginning of acceptance of the bereavement. Out of broken glass, drawings, and emotional epitaphs, the group as a whole created a "memorial hand." The inscription said, "This is how life was broken / In their death they commanded us to live."

During this period families were counseled in how to respond to their agitated children. The parents were encouraged to share their own feelings with their children and work together through the difficult period of recuperation. Most posttraumatic reactions subsided gradually, and the children resumed their daily activities. The follow-up surveys, eight months and then sixteen months later, found no perseverance of symptoms, with a few exceptions in children for whom treatment was resumed.

Dr. Ofra Ayalon works for the NORD International Trauma Consultancy at POB 76, Tivon, Israel 36000. Telephone: 9724-9832144; fax: 9724-9534963.

portantly, what is said in the room must stay in the room. These are rules common to many affective education group formats, such as Magic Circle.

Sometimes a group takes off by itself. The group needs little structure to process the critical incident and the leader participates as much as guides. This is an ideal scenario—the way things ought to be—but it is also unusual. Group functioning is often impaired by crisis; during these times groups usually rely more on leadership. This is particularly the case during the initial moments of a debriefing, when the group comes together for the express purpose of dealing with the recent events. At this time, a structured process, defined and followed by the group leader, is especially helpful.

The following formal debriefing structure is adapted from George Everly and Jeffrey Mitchell (1999), elaborated in Johnson et al. (1999) (see figure 7-4). Modifications of this structure for use with younger students will follow.

Introductory Phase

The first stage sets the tone of the meeting and defines the expectations of the leader and participants. You can assuage the concerns and anxieties of the group by giving a clear description of what is going to happen during the meeting, the leader's expectations, and the ground rules for participation. Rules provide people with security. Talking about disturbing events is difficult; therefore, having a clear format spells out what the student can expect in terms of the sequence of events, confidentiality, what others will talk about, and whether or not feelings will be heard and respected. Much of a successful intervention is at risk if the expression of feelings is not protected.

Fact Phase

Facts about a crisis confuse the issue in two ways. First, students tend to talk among themselves to try to understand what really happened and what it all meant. This makes for rumors and false information. Alternately, they may not talk at all, which increases their sense of overwhelming isolation. In either case, it is essential to the debriefing process that the facts of the situation be shared up front and as openly as possible. It is the leader's responsibility to bring as much objectivity as possible to the discussion at this point. It is also the leader's responsibility to recognize the subjectivity of crisis, by allowing each person the opportunity to share his or her own experience of the event. During this phase students explore and work toward agreement on the sequence of events and the role each of them played in the incident.

Each student must be given several opportunities to describe each major phase of the incident from his or her perspective. One technique is to allow students to speak in the order of their temporal involvement in the incident. Those who arrived first speak first. This helps recreate the incident as it unfolded.

In a specialized technique termed *sensory unpacking,* participants go round-robin, sharing impressions from each sensory modality. A good progression for this is to begin with sights, progress to sounds, and then to touch. Asking students how their body felt is often useful, but this should not be done in a group if the disclosure might in any way cause embarrassment. Sensory unpacking can be very powerful; therefore, it should not be used by non-clinicians, in debriefings where there is just one leader, in contexts where students are deeply affected, or in situations where the community or staff is suspicious about the intervention process.

Finally, students can be asked to share what they did during the incident. By the time this is done thoroughly, the events will be clearer for each student, and each student will have gained some realizations that she or he was not alone and that others were similarly affected. Further, a shared perspective of the incident begins to emerge.

Thought Phase

In the thought phase, students are asked what they were thinking at the time of the incident. This helps them draw the connection between the interpretations they made and the feelings they felt. It also helps them put their thoughts into the context of those of others and opens the possibility of alternative interpretation.

The leader then shifts to the present, asking, "Now that it's over, what are you thinking about it?" By sharing their thoughts and reflections in retrospect, students can further reinterpret—and eventually integrate—the experience.

At the same time, the leader is able to assess the student's functioning level and ability to reflect upon his or her experience. Troubling misconceptions can be targeted for future clarification. Groundwork can be laid at this point for the construction of a more adaptive shared group interpretation of the event and subsequent challenges, and this groundwork can be reinforced in the later teaching phase.

Reaction Phase

The reactions experienced during and following a crisis are frequently intense. Understandably, students are likely to be reluctant to bring those feelings to the surface again. Yet to do so directly or vicariously through listening to another is important in order to relieve the sense of isolation, the individual intensity, and the crippling feelings of personal limitation that can result from a crisis experience. By bringing these reactions to the surface, students are better able to cope with them.

The object of the reaction stage of classroom debriefing is to provide students with the opportunity to explore and share what they felt during the incident and how they are reacting now. The best way to allow that expression is to maintain the direction, tone, and style of the fact stage while channeling the discussion toward current issues. If the round-robin approach was used in the fact stage, followed by a discussion of the sensory modalities of sight, sound, and touch, it is quite natural to continue by asking, "And how are you reacting now?" or "How does your body feel?"

Within this format, students can explore reactions to the incident in a supportive context.

Those who volunteer information receive validation and encouragement for sharing, while those who choose not to speak openly learn more about the commonality of their reactions and vicariously experience the support given to the more vocal students.

It is important to emphasize that every student be given several opportunities to share, but that no student should have to share. To be coerced to do so amounts to another victimization. Also, feelings are neither right nor wrong; they just are. For example, if a student expresses feelings of guilt and shame for something over which he had no control, it is important to honor the feeling as well as to provide a reality check. A supportive response might be, "Of course, you feel responsible for that happening. Anyone who cares and wants to help would feel that. But tell me, what could you really have done differently? How?"

During this stage, reactions experienced after the crisis is "over"—such as having nightmares or trouble sleeping, feeling upset, and having other delayed stress reactions—can also be shared and supported. Class members need to hear that such reactions are expected, normal, and a residual part of the crisis experience. The leader can initiate this type of discussion with questions such as, "Has anyone been having bad dreams, stomachaches, or other sorts of things since then?" Alternately, a less direct approach might be a generalization: "After something like this, a lot of kids have unusual things like headaches, bad dreams, or being scared. How are you all doing?"

Overall, the tone should be that of "talking about" reactions rather than processing reactions emotionally. Students should not be discouraged from expressing feelings, but neither should they be made to think that emotional expression is expected. Debriefing is not a form of psychotherapy, and the school is not a clinic. If the leader suspects that a child needs to work on emotional expression with a therapist, then appropriate referral should be made.

Teaching Phase

Following the reactions phase, the group leader becomes more active. The leader can summarize the salient facts of the incident—enriched now with the combined experiences of the group members—to clarify the event. The leader should also clear up misconceptions regarding the incident or its effects. A skillful leader can do much at this point in suggesting more adaptive narratives in which constructive and healing interpretations are imbedded. In addition, the leader should share any information on what group members can expect in terms of the near future and explain facts about normal reactions to crisis, with particular emphasis on validating individual experiences. The leader should detail on-scene reactions and delayed reactions, including cognitive, emotional, physical, and behavioral symptoms, taking note of reactions that are more serious and deserve professional attention. The leader should also spend time on alternative and creative ways to deal with common problems and, finally, should share available resources and point out where to get help.

Closure Phase

The debriefing experience affirms group cohesiveness and the value of the group to its members. This is a good theme for the closure phase. Summarize the individual experiences of the incident, emphasizing the commonalities among individuals. Review the predominant feelings, stressing the ways class members can help one another. A group activity that allows the group to take some tangible action to help make sense of the event is very important. During the closure phase, the group can discuss such an activity, although at this point the actual activity does not need to be decided upon.

As the above discussion indicates, group intervention can and should be more than "just sitting down and talking about it with the kids." Debriefings provide a specific structure that allows the intervention to address issues without sacrificing much-needed security and control.

Red Flags and Warning Signs

Several signs indicate that group intervention is not appropriate with certain individuals or the entire group. If any individual is showing signs of Acute Stress Response, classroom debriefing is inappropriate and the child should be referred immediately to mental health screening. If the class or group is nonsupportive, if the needs of students vary widely, if the class is highly politicized (including having gang affiliations), or if families involved are highly impacted by the event, classroom debriefings are inappropriate and interventions should proceed at an individual level (see Figure 7-5).

Developmental Differences in Group Interventions

Following a major disaster in Southern California, one district attempted "group counseling" sessions for each classroom at one site. An outside mental health professional scheduled back-to-back sessions, each exactly 47 minutes long, from kindergarten through sixth grade, all day. She invited each group to come in and "talk about your reaction." At the end of the day, she was exhausted and emotionally drained. She reported great frustration with the youngest children, whose attention she could not hold, and with the older children, who took a long time getting started only to be reluctant to leave.

This case illustrates several strategic issues: developmental level of the students, length of the sessions, leadership, activities, and protection against leader burnout. This section addresses the strategy issues of conducting an intervention; the issue of self-care will be addressed in Chapter 9.

As Figure 7-6 illustrates, duration, leadership responsibility, and activity needs vary according to developmental level. A debriefing session should take as long as it takes to get the job done. However, preschool and kindergarten groups can rarely last longer than 15 to 30 minutes on any task they themselves have not initiated. This is particularly true if the children are anxious and distraught or if the subject of the activity makes them uncomfortable. Elementary school children can last up to an hour, if

the pace and activities of the session vary. Secondary students, often taking longer to warm up to a discussion, can sustain their attention span up to two hours or more, particularly if the subject matter personally troubles them.

Leadership needs vary as well. Preschool and kindergarten children see their teachers as a source of security and order. For an outsider to come in and remind them of an incident they are trying to forget simply compounds their anxiety. Alternately, high school students typically have much less of a bond with any of the five to eight teachers they deal with daily. Usually, students of this age have a greater respect for outside specialists and appreciate the change of authority status. For these reasons, when possible, debriefings with younger children should be led by their teacher with the specialist observing. Conversely, high school debriefings should be led by the outside specialist with the school staff playing a secondary, observational role.

In a high school situation, the leader conducts the debriefing and most of the interaction with the students. The observer watches for significant interaction and any nonverbal expression that the leader may miss, draws attention to issues and individuals as needed, escorts students out if needed, and goes to counseling with students who appear to be in distress. Most importantly, the observer provides a second set of eyes and ears to help assess if follow-up services seem to be needed.

Finally, the use and types of activity in the session are partly determined by developmental level. Activities can serve various functions. They can warm up the group process, enhance communication, diffuse anxiety, and focus attention on a particular issue. They can build intimacy and trust, deepen exploration of sensitive issues, and facilitate personal expression.

In general, the younger the participants, the greater the role of activity in the debriefing. With preschoolers and kindergartners, art activities may comprise 95 percent of the time spent with them. The teacher and observers may simply circulate, providing assistance and asking about pictures. Conversation may be kept to a minimum. With high school students, activities may be little more than a warm-up. Time spent away from group discussion may be viewed as an obstruction. Figure 7-6 illustrates a suggested balance, by grade level, of activity and discussion.

CRT Strategy 10: Classroom Follow-up Activities

As indicated in the previous section, discussion is the primary debriefing process for older children, while activities form the basis for debriefing younger students. Activities may also be used as prompts, warm-ups, and deepening experiences with older students. The types of activities selected should reflect the developmental level and skill level of the students, as well as the purpose of the activity.

There are three basic types of activities useful in postcrisis group work: art, writing, and enactment. Activities can vary according to the structure provided by the leader and the extent to which they are used individually within the class or form the basis for group process. They also vary in relation to the power and impact with which students reexperience or express their reactions to the incident. For the sake of simplicity, the word "debriefing" will be used in this section and the next to refer to all group interventions.

Activities are useful when

- The group or class would benefit from structure

- Students are feeling isolated and need assistance in sharing about the incident

- Discussion would benefit from impetus, direction, and context

- They are used with consideration toward student sensitivities

Choose activities that will stimulate reflection and communication without overwhelming students' ability to cope. Remember, a primary objective of school intervention is to bolster, not subvert, psychological defenses. See Figures 7-7 through 7-9.

Students who exhibit signs of Acute Stress Response or who indicate the need for immediate referral should not participate in either debriefings or follow-up class activities that address crisis issues until they are properly screened by mental health professionals competent to evaluate postcrisis functioning. Similarly, certain group conditions indicate that groups or classes should not use such activities. Group warning signs include

- the group or class has a history of being nonsupportive, hurtful, or divisive

- the group's needs relative to the crisis are polarized (that is, some are deeply affected while some are untouched; the incident represents loss for some, while it creates opportunities for others)

- some class members are highly traumatized or have suffered serious loss

In general, most activities—art, writing, or enactment—can be modified to change their impact. The impact of activities can be softened when prompts require

- individual rather than group activity

- cognitive rather than affective responses

- general rather than specific responses

- universal rather than personal responses

- principles rather than consequences

- problem solving rather than dwelling on the impact

- global impressions rather than sensory images

- writing rather than art activities

- art rather than enactment activities

Using Art

School intervention teams frequently use art activities, particularly with younger students. A wide variety of media can be used: crayons, markers, collage, paint, even clay. It is useful, but not essential, to have color materials available. Simpler materials, however, such as markers and paper, are probably best. Emphasize to students that they spend their time and energy on expression, rather than mastering a complex art project.

In a standard approach, the leader begins by setting the stage, bringing up the incident, and beginning initial discussion in a manner similar to a regular classroom debriefing. The leader then passes out the materials and students are invited to draw (paint, collage, or sculpt) anything they wish. CRT members or teachers circulate among the students, engaging them in conversation about their work. The class then reconvenes for summary, drawing attention to many of the themes that emerged. Teaching and closure stages proceed in a manner similar to standard debriefings.

A variation of this technique utilizes one common project, such as a mural, in which students confer as they jointly produce a rendition of what happened. This is obviously a group process; leadership of such a group requires flexibility in style, structure, and pacing. One issue to consider is how participation by all can be encouraged.

Another variation is to provide students with specific drawing themes or tasks designed to focus attention on predetermined elements of the situation or on their own reactions. The point of focus can then be explored with the whole group, in the form of either open discussion or didactic lesson, depending on students' needs.

Enactment

The theater is alive and well after thousands of years and has survived—even thrived—the onslaught of electronic home entertainment centers. The stage captivates the audience and beckons even the most passive and inhibited. Enactment allows for "right brain," concrete, immediate processing of subtle and complex material that might be abstracted or lost on the written page or in discussion. If it can be said that we are playing out our inner dramas on the stage of life, then the dramatic stage, whether in the theater or the classroom, provides a distilled focus for dealing with crisis.

Psychotherapists have used enactments to heal the injured just as playwrights have used the insights of psychology to enrich their plays. Psychodramatic therapies utilize enactment to help patients safely act out, verbalize, and experiment with the parts of their lives that are troublesome. Similarly, educators have long used plays, skits, dramatic readings, musicals, and, more recently, readers' theater and simulation games in the service of education.

Educational use of enactment following a crisis includes several applications, each with many adaptations. These can be tailored to the developmental and cohesiveness levels of the group.

Reconstruction. The group can work together to reconstruct what occurred during the crisis. By actually walking through the incident again, participants must work together to gain consensus about sequence, participation, and roles. They can share observations and serve as reality checks for one another. Crisis tends to tunnel perception; memory gaps often leave unanswered questions. During these sessions, details tend to emerge that can set to rest the students' concerns about the severity of the incident, personal performance, and adequacy. Group reconstruction often relieves the pervasive sense of isolation engendered by crisis.

Sculpting. The relationships and dynamics of some situations are complex enough to defy succinct explanation. Sometimes this type of situation can be quickly illustrated through sculpting. Utilizing a predetermined set of coordinates (for example, proximity = closeness, centrality = importance, height = power, posture = attitude), each participant illustrates the interpersonal situation by physically arranging other participants as stand-ins. The resulting tableau emerges as a basis for further explanation and exploration.

Role-play. Role-play can be used to act out situations as they were experienced or to explore and rehearse possible solutions to problems created by the crisis. Students can try out different responses or even demonstrate how they would do things differently if the opportunity arose.

Puppets. Puppets can be used with younger children to reconstruct or role-play the incident, as above. Puppets provide an intrinsically interesting medium for children who are capable of enough detachment. They can enter into activities and learn without being threatened or overwhelmed.

Revisiting. The incident location may hold special significance for students and staff. It may have become mystified or may stimulate such unexpected associations that participants avoid the location or are troubled in its presence. By revisiting the location with the group, students can gain a sense of comfort that may help defuse some of the feelings and associations. Visits can be facilitated by a modified debriefing structure while on scene. Extra leaders and support team members, including clinicians, should accompany the group, as students' reactions on scene can become unexpectedly intense.

Of the three activities discussed (art, writing, and enactment), enactment is easily the most volatile and powerful. It should be used carefully, appropriately, and with adequate CRT personnel to deal individually with participants if necessary. The difference between therapeutic and educational use of enactment is important to keep in mind, and CRT members are advised to use enactment only within their scope of practice and district and team policy.

Writing

By nature, writing is a more solitary activity than either art or enactment. Writing becomes public only when the product is shared with others. As such, expressing reactions in words can be much less threatening than other activities, as long as the student is not intimidated by the writing process. Nonwriters, on the other hand, are likely to be hampered by this approach. In situations with students or groups who appear to be volatile or barely coping, writing offers the leader more control over elements of group work that might otherwise be less manageable. These can include

- level of confrontation

- level of group intensity

- extent of group emotional contagion

- expressed emotions

- details of incident revealed

Writing activities tend to be cognitive; they empower students through controlled clarification of feelings, organization of experience, and renewed perspective. As writing is a basic school skill, it is less disruptive to the normal school day than art or enactment and reinforces routine.

Writing activities can include "quickwrites" (short, impromptu paragraphs in response to specific prompts), short answers to specific questions, longer narratives, filling out checklists or missing words, guided poetry writing, or letter writing.

You can use writing solely as a warm-up exercise or as the major activity of the intervention. Such material can be voluntarily shared with the group, put up on a board, arranged with others' contributions in linear time sequence, or compiled into a collected volume. The use of writing in intervention is limited only by the imagination and creativity of the intervention team. Remember, however, that the approach needs to be tempered by those general rules that apply to any intervention within school settings.

Whichever structure or format is adopted, one essential objective of group intervention is to identify individual students and staff members who need further individual assessment and follow-up. The writing procedures chosen must allow for this screening process, however informal.

The variations of group intervention discussed in this chapter should be chosen with due consideration to the issues discussed in the next chapter and in Chapter 11.

Suggestions for Community Mental Health and Crisis Response Teams

Sometimes teachers are uncomfortable talking about crisis events with children, and sometimes they are so emotionally involved that they are unable to do so. As an outside resource, you may be placed in the position of talking to students in groups as large as a class; the school may even ask you to address an entire assembly. In general, unless you are accustomed to presenting to large crowds of young people, this is not a good context to start, as postcrisis reactions could make a normally difficult situation untenable. Consider suggesting that you go around to select classes to deal with issues, which provides a greater opportunity to engage in dialogue. If you absolutely must address an assembly, do it quickly and forcefully, use vivid, verbal illustrations, make a few general points and gloss over details, and don't attempt to take questions from the audience. "Speaker baiting" is tempting enough without the added incentive of postcrisis anxiety and denial. Put detail and nuances into handouts or save them for classroom follow-up discussion.

In this chapter several group intervention strategies were discussed. In general, classroom discussion will be the appropriate mode for most situations. If you are called upon to speak to a group of students soon after the incident, when you expect reactions to be running high, use the classroom defusing format. If the situation then allows it, you can loosen the format into a more freewheeling discussion.

If it has been a day or more since the incident, find out more about the particular class or group. Are they not talking about what happened? Who asked for the intervention, and what are their observations about why it is needed? Consider a classroom debriefing format if the group is not talking much about the event, or if they seem to be impacted by it.

If it has been a while since the incident, consider using activities as discussed above. With middle school or high school students, have them do a brief writing exercise before beginning other activities: ten minutes at most.

Use this as a warm-up, but don't make it mandatory that students share what they have written.

Most importantly, do your homework beforehand and find out more about that particular group's experience, the preincident sense of group solidarity versus conflict, and the group members' postcrisis behavior. Follow the suggestions in this chapter, and observe the red flags for individuals and groups, which are counterindicative of group process.

CHAPTER 8

Special Problems

This chapter outlines general strategies for dealing with special circumstances. These strategies are offered as starting points only. Each crisis is unique and has its own configuration of background factors and moderating conditions. Each crisis must be dealt with on its own terms, given the resources available and the administrative and political restraints. Therefore, these strategies are generic preliminary organizers for planning specific approaches.

Certain incidents—such as suicide, murder, sudden loss, large-scale incidents, and staff trauma—present unique challenges to Crisis Response Teams. They create more than a normal amount of stress, because of either their scope, their inherent unmanageability, or the manner in which they raise personal issues for CRT members. Such circumstances may require unique knowledge, strategies, or skills, and they often test the Crisis Response Team's ability to perform under unusual conditions.

Staff trauma was discussed in Chapter 3, although each of the special problems mentioned here is likely to disrupt and possibly traumatize staff. Staff consultation will probably be required in all the situations discussed in this chapter.

Recent mass murder incidents on campuses throughout the United States highlight the need for "worst case scenario" planning, and considerations for managing such incidents are included in this chapter. It should be remembered, however, that the vast bulk of school crisis management work will consist of smaller incidents, which are still just as serious as they ever were.

Presuicide

Crisis team members are sometimes called on scene to intervene with students identified as at risk for suicide. Like any crisis situation, presuicide intervention is unscheduled, abrupt, and time consuming. Unlike most crisis management, however, human life is at stake. CRT members may find themselves confronted with a situation in which whatever they say and do may be measured in an immediate outcome.

Assessing the individual is critical in such situations. It is essential to consult with the staff or students who initially identified the possible suicide, those who know the person and his or her situation, those who possess background information, family members, and outside professionals involved with the potential suicide. (Chapter 6 discusses suicide assessment in depth.)

Assessment provides you with a rough estimate of the individual's risk for completing the suicide. Apart from the person's background and situational factors and his or her behavioral signs, the most critical factor for assessing risk is the suicide plan. The first rule of thumb is: *The more detailed, workable, lethal, and imminent the plan and the greater the person's psychological and physiological disturbance, the greater the risk of completing suicide* (see Figure 8-1).

Just as the assessment of risk is only approximate, there is no "right way" of intervening in a possible suicide. Because of the individual's personal, situational, and social factors, and because of the individual style of the intervener, there is no precise protocol for intervention.

It must be stressed that while assessment may provide an estimate of the degree of risk, how to interpret that risk in terms of intervention must be approached very conservatively. The second rule of thumb is: *Take all threats seriously.*

If assessment indicates that there is any risk at all, the following steps should be considered minimal intervention (see Figure 8-2):

- Alert the staff

- Notify an outside agency (for example, a crisis center)

- Contact the parents

- Counsel the student

Counseling should work toward determining the precipitating event and its meaning to the student. Attempt to defuse the despair and empower cognitive controls. Identify "triggers" that elicit suicidal impulses in the individual, and teach the person coping strategies. Explore new perspectives. Incorporate the family and outside resources into problem solving and planning. Refer the student to outside support.

While many of these precautions may prove to be superfluous, the stakes involved warrant erring on the side of overreaction. Crisis intervention must serve as an opening for later help, and that help must be a sure thing. If professionals later determine that the risk was overestimated, they can revise their treatment at that time.

Follow a similarly cautious approach when intervening in higher-risk cases. To the extent the risk is estimated to be serious, the intervener should take the following actions (see Figure 8-3):

- Do not allow the individual to leave. Assign a staff member for supervision and maintain visual contact at all times.

- Notify the police and an appropriate agency for professional evaluation.

- Notify the parents of the individual and include them in decision making as soon as possible. If there are disagreements with parents about what should be done, if a deadlock has been reached and you feel that the safety of the child is at stake, turn the situation over to the site administrator and police, giving them a full account of your concerns. Communicate your concerns to the coordinator of the CRT and proper district-level administrators. Document your concerns and actions.

- Inform the student about what actions have been taken.

- Facilitate the intervention transition to the police or to a hospital.

- Follow up on the individual's release: consider making a "no-suicide pact" with the person, help the person build a peer support network, and coordinate with outside therapy if it is available.

Intervention in such cases is likely to be very stressful; support for interveners should be mandatory. Even when things go well, the real responsibility, the legal and organizational liability, and the intensity of the intervention combine to put the intervener at risk of exhaustion or even trauma. Support for interveners should include debriefings, consultation, and time off.

Threat Assessment Teams

Until recently, school Crisis Response Teams focused primarily on response to traumatic incidents after they had occurred. Now, they are also assisting school staff in crisis and disaster planning, staff training, and consultation to administrators in incident assessment and planning.

In this latter capacity, threat assessment—a relatively new strategy—is emerging. The assessment of threats to the school, its staff, and its students assists the administrator in determining appropriate strategies to mitigate the risk. Because the crisis consultants are frequently school personnel, or sometimes community mental health professionals without special training in risk assessment, such planning often lacks experiential depth or specialized training.

Development of Threat Assessment Teams

Over the past several years law enforcement agencies have refined their techniques of assessing threats and determining the probability of threatened assaults taking place. Police once looked at the demographics of potential killers and then psychological factors; they are now adopting a multifactored system of weighing risk factors against stabilizing factors within a decision-making matrix to determine appropriate response strategies. The Threat Management Unit of the Los Angeles Police Department is setting the trend nationally in this regard (see sidebar "School Violence Prevention and Intervention" in Chapter 4). In an unusual and potentially powerful collaborative effort, the Los Angeles County Office of Education is coordinating the development of four-person district-level interdisciplinary Threat Assessment Teams in the county, consisting of school administrators, police, community mental health personnel, and legal counsel. These teams are designed to coordinate community resources in responding to threats to schools (see sidebar "Care and Feeding of the Crisis Intervention Team" in Chapter 4).

Threat Assessment and School Crisis Response Teams

The development of threat assessment technology represents a great step forward for school crisis management, and yet creates some potential problems of role and function. Although they serve the same general purpose—stabilization of school crisis—school Crisis Response Teams have a larger role than Threat Assessment Teams: the mitigation of detrimental effects of crisis beyond the purview of threat per se. While the Threat Assessment Team has much to offer the school, and much to offer the school Crisis Response Team, its function is likely to be maximized if it is indirectly linked to the school CRT. Organizationally, the Threat Assessment Team might be either a subcommittee of or a parallel team to the school Crisis Response Team. Because they are involved in the same incidents, are likely to use some of the same members, and serve the same school administrator, the linkage and communication between—and the coordination of—the two teams is imperative.

Postsuicide or Postmurder

A completed suicide or murder presents a very different picture from a presuicidal situation. You are concerned less with trying to save a life than trying to cope with its loss. With the exception of one factor, the mood is no longer one of emergency but rather of healing.

Notably, one of the concerns that plagues decision making following either suicide or murder is the possibility of more tragedy. The specter of serial suicides or revenge killings haunts administrators, parents, and Crisis Response Team personnel. One argument often made following suicide or murder is that any institutional acknowledgment—be it memorials, tributes, or interventions—encourages repeats. In the case of suicide, we fear that recognition of the loss may be construed as condoning or glorifying the action. There is, however, little empirical support for this. The faulty assumption underlying such a fear is that the institution could actually protect its young people from the facts of the situation or the issues it raises. Peer culture quickly responds to the news of a suicide or murder; the school's silence about it will only drive the ensuing discussion underground. Advise administrators, staff, and parents to assist young people as they work through their questions, fears, and reactions.

Murder or suicide in the presence of other students, whether on or off campus, creates issues of trauma, not just loss. If students or staff members happened upon the suicide scene or were witnesses to the killing, the sensory impact or personal threat may well traumatize them. Those students or staff members should be treated separately from others in a debriefing/crisis-intervention modality.

Similarly, students or staff members particularly close to the deceased should be seen apart from their normal groupings. This is especially the case with siblings, best friends, or a boyfriend or girlfriend. The impact is likely to be far more serious with close associates of the deceased; processing with a less-impacted group could serve to compound their isolation and pain.

Several factors and components should be considered when designing postsuicide and postmurder interventions (see Figure 8-4):

- Put one person in charge, following normal CRT operational protocol

- Get outside help to keep perspective on organizational and interpersonal issues

- Designate a spokesperson for media or other off-site communications

- Provide staff briefing
  — consider the facts of the situation
  — plan for school response
  — plan for student meetings
  — assess staff members for their role in meetings and for the intensity of their reactions
  — introduce outside resources into the intervention and explain their roles

- Provide classroom debriefings to affected classes

- Send notifications and educational materials home

- Provide staff debriefings and consultations as appropriate and necessary

- Coordinate follow-up student services and interventions as appropriate

- Assist the school in planning a memorial

Intervention following a suicide or murder can be difficult for CRT members themselves. Many personal issues that arise for survivors also arise for CRT interveners. Personal feelings about suicide, including low-level attraction to it, can become problematic. Suicide represents a wholesale rejection of the world that is difficult not to take personally. Murder can intensify the fear for one's own and one's family's safety, as well as a general despair over human nature and the state of the world.

When dealing with either suicide or murder, the major emphasis on the day of the incident should be maintaining and reinforcing normal school structure and routine and dealing individually with impacted classmates and staff. During the days following the incident, proceed with special activities such as classroom debriefings and memorials. The principles of self-care found in Chapter 9 are particularly important when dealing with suicide and murder.

Situational Assessment

Consider the following factors in the initial assessment of the situation following shootings or murders involving students in or out of school. Both administrators and Crisis Response Teams will find the answers to these questions useful.

- Are rival groups at school involved?
- Is crowd management or discipline likely to be a problem?
- Who witnessed the incident?
- Were witnesses likely to be traumatized?
- Which groups are likely to be impacted?
- Are there particular historical, social, or cultural factors that affect the situation?
- Will the school be safe and secure if students remain?
- Are particular classes likely to be impacted?
- Are particular staff members likely to be impacted?

- Is there likely to be a police investigation that will interfere with crisis intervention with participants or witnesses?

- Are there legal issues that would affect the Crisis Response Team or the school?

Sudden Loss

Crisis Response Teams are called upon to deal with issues of loss either in conjunction with a traumatic incident or because the incident itself is a loss. Because of their nature, many crises are predicated upon loss rather than trauma, although traumatic violence, civil disorder, and natural disasters usually also cause extensive loss. Reactions to loss can be a part of other crises or they can be the primary focus of the crisis experience. Sudden, overwhelming loss can itself be traumatic. Instead of the disturbing or overwhelming images of violent or destructive trauma that elicit fear and avoidance, loss presents a special set of grief reactions.

Most people, including children, react to loss in a stereotypical pattern. Specialists agree that for the most part people adapt to loss in a step-by-step manner, but many experts differ as to the nature of the particular stages. Most theories hold a core pattern similar to that presented by Elizabeth Kübler-Ross, who, in her book *On Death and Dying,* puts forth a five-step process of denial, anger, bargaining, depression, and acceptance. Other theories include stages of guilt, fear of the future, sadness, and renewal. Most theories acknowledge that sudden loss comes as a shock that is not immediately assimilated.

For the most part, younger children follow a pattern similar to that of adults; however, children's level of cognitive development limits their initial understanding, and they are more vulnerable to sudden changes in their routine. While adults utilize complex psychological maneuvering tactics to avoid accepting the loss, children tend to move cyclically between three basic postures: distress, "closing down" their awareness and responses, and resuming nor-

mal activity while seemingly oblivious to the loss. Children do as adults do: They accept as much as they can process—cognitively and emotionally—and hold off on the rest until they can accommodate it.

Adults attempting to talk to children about the death of someone close meet mixed responses. While sometimes such efforts are well received, more often they are ignored or scarcely tolerated. Children may look or walk away, change the subject, or act out. They may appear to be in denial when in fact they are simply baffled by surrounding adult behavior, parental absence (due to death or preoccupation with grieving), and changes in routine.

Younger children tend to exhibit clinging behavior and separation anxiety following traumatic loss. By asking incessant, blunt questions about where a lost loved one has gone and what to expect next, children frequently exasperate parents and teachers who try to protect them from such intense feelings and premature introduction to the concepts of finality and loss. Children sometimes approach the loss as they would an unsolvable but irresistible puzzle, making repeated attempts to fathom its meaning.

Mid-childhood-age children have a better grasp of the permanency and meaning of loss. Consequently, they tend to show distress more directly, going through periods of more obvious suffering. If the pain is too great, they may withdraw and deny the emotional reality of the loss to others or even to themselves. Their feelings often appear blunted, and when they discuss the loss, they tend to do so in a detached manner. They "play out" their distress through games, fantasy, acting-out behavior, and rumination.

Adolescents often talk about the loss in a straightforward manner; they express immediate emotions overtly but show deeper feelings indirectly and often in self-destructive ways. Their reactions parallel those of adults, with the exception that they reflect adolescent developmental issues of individuation, independence, adequacy, and social acceptability. One minute they may discuss the loss with appropriate expression of feelings, the next they may act out in a clearly childish manner, and in a third they may make permanent life decisions more appropriate to a 40-year-old. One moment they may want to be near their parents, another moment they may be caught up in a paroxysm of peer-group hysteria.

At each developmental stage, regression is a common response to loss. Four-year-olds may lose toileting abilities and need to be fed, eight-year-olds may need to be bathed and want to play with dolls, and thirteen-year-olds may throw crying tantrums when things go wrong.

The more serious and sudden the loss, the more the child's cycle of distress, withdrawal, and normalization resembles traumatic stress. Such reactions are a form of Acute Stress Response.

Sudden Loss Intervention

Sudden loss intervention (SLI) is similar in format to crisis intervention in that SLI seeks to assess and restore the individual's functioning, assist in planning, mobilize resources, and provide referral if appropriate. In addition, and depending on the circumstances, SLI may also provide the context in which to notify the children: Children can vent initial reactions, and you can provide education about the grief process and begin preparation for grief work.

Also, like crisis intervention, SLI can take place in both individual and group contexts as appropriate. The general protocols for crisis intervention (Chapter 5) and classroom debriefing (Chapter 7) provide useful models for loss intervention. Deviation from these models can be made to allow for situational variables (such as the need to assist a parent in notifying a child about a death or newly emerging information during the intervention that changes the picture significantly).

Several things are useful to keep in mind when discussing loss with children (see Figure 8-5):

- Remember ages and stages; consider the implications of conceptual development in making sense of the particular situation

- Start by asking, not telling; determine the child's

— knowledge of the situation

— understanding of the facts

— misconceptions about the situation, death, or loss in general

— personal background and issues

- Keep it simple

- Minimize the theorizing

- Give hope, but avoid minimizing pain by making unrealistic promises or imposing personal belief

Acute Grief Reaction (AGR) refers to an extreme response to sudden loss that incapacitates the individual. That extreme response is a form of Acute Stress Response and will manifest similar signs. As in ASR, AGR can have an agitated or a depressed form. AGR intervention utilizes similar strategies as ASR intervention: Assess the individual's functioning ability and safety needs as discussed in Chapter 6 and mobilize the necessary assistance and structure.

Family Crisis

Crisis Response Teams are not normally contacted as a team for family crises, although a team member may deal with such situations in the course of normal duties. In addition, during school interventions, students or staff who are involved in a crisis may be simultaneously involved in their own family crisis. Stressful family situations render crisis victims at greater risk for psychological distress and present complications for crisis management. Not only may family support be impaired, family issues may be part of the problem. Closely assess the individual's support needs and figure external resources more heavily in planning to meet them.

Chapter 6 detailed how to assess family support. On the basis of this assessment, you can estimate the family's contribution to the problem and its ability to be part of the solution. Intervention must reflect the family's strength, utilizing family resources or compensating for their lack. Planning strategies for facilitating family support vary accordingly and include the following:

- Assist the child or staff member to communicate her or his needs to the family

- Facilitate communication with the family

- Link with a care provider in extended family or social network

- Refer the individual for further assessment (medical, psychological, social)

- If there is concern for the individual's safety, refer the adult or child to an appropriate agency to assess the need for shelter or supervision

Disaster and Large-Scale Crisis

Natural disasters or large-scale crises, such as mass murder on campus, bombings, nuclear incidents, transportation or industrial accidents, or civil disorder, may present unprecedented challenges to Crisis Response Teams. This section discusses what CRT members can expect in the postdisaster environment, including pragmatic aspects, psychological reactions to large-scale events, and suggestions for how to best shift normal operating strategies to meet these special challenges.

Large-scale crises put stress on every aspect of the local social environment—students, staff, and school functioning. The CRT may be asked to respond to the crisis and may be expected to work miracles quickly under impossible conditions. At the same time, those requesting the CRT services may themselves be impaired by the crisis.

Predicting Psychological Reactions to Disaster

While it seems intuitively true that victims would be psychologically impaired following exposure to disaster, and while the media and Hollywood reinforce that perspective, research literature is less convincing.

Currently, formal research into disaster

and recovery-period behavior provides as much confusion as it does illumination for disaster planners. Results of studies—sometimes of the same incident—are often discrepant or even contradictory. This is due in part to the relative infancy of the discipline, as well as to the varying assumptions and methodologies used. In fact, studies of victims' reactions to natural disaster seem split between those that report a high level of psychological impairment and those that report little or no impairment. The split generally falls along lines of method and discipline (see Appendix VI).

Disaster researchers in the psychiatric tradition tend to utilize a clinical approach, relying heavily on anecdotal reports, case studies, and interviews of victim populations. They look for clinical symptomology among affected populations, and they tend to find it. Calvin Fredricks, M.D., currently with the Department of Psychiatry, University of California, Los Angeles, is the leading proponent of the clinical tradition. Other clinical researchers include Charles Figley of Florida State University and Bonnie Green at Georgetown University. The major institutional proponent of this position is the National Institute of Mental Health.

Researchers in this group have consistently found serious and widespread psychological impact from natural disasters. They note functional impairment at the time of the disaster and delayed psychopathological reactions later. According to this school of thought, disaster planners should organize widespread psychological intervention for victims, including outreach activities, on-scene intervention, and treatment follow-through.

Sociologists, on the other hand, using more widespread surveys and less clinically sensitive instrumentation, have arrived at different estimates of the nature and extent of psychological reactions to disaster. Key researchers following this tradition include E. L. Quarantelli and Kathleen Tierney of the Disaster Research Center, University of Delaware.

Researchers in this group have found that on-scene reactions tend to be far less chaotic than one might expect and that very little posttraumatic symptomology can be attributed to the event itself.

Research on the psychological effects of non-natural, or "man-made" disaster is less ambivalent, however, citing more clearly the negative effects on individuals and the community.

Two perspectives prove useful to remember at this point. First, much of the psychological distress that proves difficult for schools to deal with is at the subclinical level. This means that a child does not need to be in full-blown Acute Stress Response to negatively affect his or her own learning or the tenor of the entire class. Following disaster, the majority of students' needs are likely to be at this subclinical level. Second, intervention has two aims: the needs of the individual and the organizational needs of the entire school. Crisis Response Teams need to deal with subclinical students and staff for their own well-being and that of the school.

Certainly, the clinical aftermath of mass shooting incidents is clear. Fear, anger, and confusion permeate the community, and aftermath issues will arise for a long period of time following the incident (see sidebar "Columbine High School at Year's End" in Chapter 1).

One of the troubling issues related to such shootings is the seeming assault on the predominant values of the school or community implied in the incident. As in cases of suicide, the group must confront questions concerning whether or not the life of the community, its culture, mores, and lifestyles are meaningful and life affirming. These questions will be raised repeatedly—often implied in behavior—in the months following a shooting.

Factors Complicating CRT Response

Crisis Response Teams prepare for and normally handle smaller incidents. Large-scale events differ in several ways that affect CRT response. The following factors may complicate CRT operations following disaster (see Figure 8-6):

Numbers and intensity. Following large-scale crises, the CRT may be stunned by the scope of need. The sheer numbers of adversely impacted students, the volume of work to be done, and the intensity of victims' reactions may overwhelm them.

Limited CRT resources. While student and staff reactions may be less severe following a disaster than following other types of incidents, they will be more widespread. Even if most needs are subclinical in nature, they demand time and resources. Three factors combine to reduce team effectiveness during the period of peak demand. First, due to the widespread impact of the incident, many CRT members may be unable to respond because of more pressing obligations in their primary assignment or their physical inability to get through to the location of CRT operations. Second, once on scene they may be negatively impacted themselves and perform in a substandard or unacceptable manner. Finally, the school organization—in leadership, decision making, or communications—may be impaired and unable to utilize and support CRT assistance.

Deployment problems. Effectively deploying limited CRT resources to maximize effectiveness may be hampered by the changing nature of the situation. As information emerges about the true extent of the crisis, team managers are faced with a planning dilemma. With too little planning flexibility, emerging and more pressing needs go unmet while the team plods on completing tasks that were begun before the more important needs were identified. With too much flexibility, the team wastes its time and energy rushing to each new brushfire. Constantly reassigning members to new tasks squanders the team's efforts.

Site staff impairment. Site staff members often live in the impacted community. They are emotionally invested in the welfare of their peers and their students, and they are likely to be suffering themselves during disaster. At best, they will probably be tired and strained by increased student need, organizational problems, and concern for their own families. They may respond by seeking CRT assistance or by denying its need both for themselves and their students. Administrators may experience a crisis in leadership. Teachers may be underfunctioning or exhausted. They may experience irritability, territorial disputes, interpersonal problems, and personal dysfunction, which may make CRT operations more difficult.

CRT member impairment. Due to their own involvement in the crisis and the demands and expectations placed on them by those in crisis, CRT members are likely to overinvest themselves in their crisis work. They may become self-sacrificial, pushing too hard and too long and ignoring their own needs. As a result, they might become exhausted long before completing the job. This places them at risk of Acute Stress Response in the short run and demoralization and burnout in the long run. Their work on scene may suffer or even be counterproductive, and they may leave more crisis work to be dealt with later.

Administrative panic. Administrators have much to lose during crisis; they are at high risk for psychological distress. As a result, they are also at risk for dysfunctioning in their role as leader during the crisis. They can negatively impact the Crisis Response Team through their mixed messages, withdrawal of support, obstructions, and unrealistic demands.

Media intrusion. Media interest in crisis is legendary. Pain sells. During a large-scale emergency, the media can be expected to arrive and conduct itself irresponsibly through confrontational interviews, circumvention of limitations set by law and by the administration, violations of confidentiality, and intrusion into the psychological space of victims who are least able to resist. On the bright side, a large-scale disaster is usually so widespread that there are not enough reporters to be everywhere at once.

The extent to which complicating factors are present depends on the nature of the incident, the extent of impact, and background factors in individuals, the organization, and the community.

Operational Suggestions

Crisis Response Teams must anticipate widespread need and limited resources following a

disaster. Because of the uncertainty of the extent of psychological reactions, the limitations of the team itself, and the various factors that complicate CRT operations, normal routines and procedures need to be modified after large-scale incidents. The following guidelines are presented for adapting normal CRT operations to the postdisaster setting (see Figure 8-7):

1. **Make the care of CRT members first priority.** Follow the principles of self-care set forth in Chapter 9. Rotate members as frequently as necessary, make sure the team takes adequate breaks, and monitor each member's functioning. Only attempt tasks that are reasonable in scope. Make certain that team leadership stays sufficiently removed from operations to ensure perspective in supervising members.

2. **Provide a center.** Establish a team center for planning and coordinating CRT functions districtwide. The team emergency operations center (EOC) should be close enough to the district EOC to maintain ongoing coordination at the highest levels. This allows for situational updates and clear communication.

3. **Assess the situation adequately.** Spend adequate time assessing the configuration of needs as they emerge over time. As new information surfaces, reprioritize needs and balance flexibility in order to confront emergent needs while completing earlier tasks.

4. **Locate resources.** Find out about surrounding communities where other CRTs operate. Contact them to determine their level of commitment and degree of availability to assist if necessary. Expedite any necessary procedural and logistical arrangements in advance of calling them on site.

5. **Adopt an educational model.** Maximize the team's impact by reverting to an indirect educational model if resources for direct services are unavailable or overextended. Adapt prepared materials for the current situation. These materials can include take-home fliers, resource and presentation mate-

rial for staff, bulletin board material, media presentations, press releases, and public presentations.

6. **Prioritize CRT services.** When demands for service exceed your resources, screen and utilize consultation and educational strategies rather than direct intervention in order to maximize care. Place those strategies within a context whereby the CRT can assist in strengthening the organization itself to meet the new set of needs created by the disaster. Focus team efforts on

   - administrative consultation

   - educational outreach

   - staff support

   - coordination of outside volunteer mental health resources

   - screening and referral of serious cases

   - planning for recovery services

7. **Adapt to command structure.** During large incidents, command of the incident may shift to fire or law enforcement agencies or even a multiagency "Incident Command." CRT services may shift accordingly. This may result in confusion, unless the school district has worked out a school safety plan that outlines such an eventuality (see sidebar "Five Functions of the Incident Command System for School Systems" in Chapter 4). If no such plan is in existence, or if the team is receiving directions from more than one source, follow the site administrator's direction unless he or she indicates otherwise.

8. **Utilize community resources and volunteers.** Large incidents will draw volunteer mental health or community Crisis Response Team workers. They can be utilized for crisis intervention and defusing, as well as support. It is imperative that they be screened, given adequate orientation and direction, and then supervised. Crisis can attract people with personal agendas, and

children's well-being is at stake. Do not allow volunteers to provide direct services to children or staff unless you are sure that they do not themselves represent an intentional or unintentional threat.

Many CRTs nationwide find that networking among local teams provides a buffer against the overwhelming demands of disaster or other large-scale incidents. Leadership, experience, and the availability of trained human resources make such networking valuable in unusual crisis situations. Combined trainings, shared resources, and continued updating are excellent ways to build working relationships with other teams.

The next section discusses self-care principles and strategies with special relevance to postdisaster intervention.

Suggestions for Community Mental Health and Crisis Response Teams

When Crisis Response Teams respond to incidents, they must also deal with staff members who are involved in the crisis as much as or more than their students. The school environment itself sets up educators for vulnerability to crisis. As our society strains under the combined social pressures of increasing crime and social ills and decreasing reliance on the family as the primary socializing institution, the schools become more than dispensers of knowledge. Society expects staff members to fix whatever is wrong with its students. Educators today must contend with the following:

- **Too many students/too many students acting out.** In addition to unmanageably large class sizes, the numbers of students who are acting out is increasing. The proportion of latency and early-adolescent suicidal children is on the increase, as is substance abuse among older elementary-age children.

- **Too much work.** In addition to creating a

balanced curriculum of basic skills and enrichment, teachers must meet a continual round of politically inspired programs. Each year's new curricular push means new materials, new preparation, new corrections...and more work.

- **Too little time.** While most educators entered the field to help individuals, they do most of their work with groups. Every moment spent with an individual is purchased at the group's expense. Most teachers and administrators put in late hours or do school work at home.

- **Role strain.** Educators exist within a matrix of competing demands; everything they do is a compromise between competing needs. The fishbowl nature of schoolwork subjects educators to the scrutiny and criticism of whimsical and fickle parents, community groups, legislators, and the media.

- **Little social reward.** Many other cultures esteem education as a profession. The attitudes of their students reflect the general public respect. In the United States, however, this is not the case. Violence toward teachers is on a dramatic increase, creating a climate of fear, particularly in inner-city schools.

All of these conditions place educators at risk of trauma during crisis events, particularly if they are responsible for students or staff members.

Educators' Traits

Many occupational groups can be characterized by shared personal characteristics. Educators tend to possess certain common traits that set them up for being traumatized by critical incidents. Many of these traits motivated them to pursue and be selected for school work in the first place; many of these traits contribute to their success. Educators tend to be the following:

"People People." Most administrators start out as teachers; most teachers become teachers to help children. They care; they want their students' lives to be happy and rewarding. They find significance, purpose, and meaning in what they do. As such, educators are vulnerable to overcommitment. They frequently identify with their students; as a result, they suffer when their students suffer.

Perfectionists. Educators tend to be perfectionists. They seem compelled to adopt an $n+1$ criterion of acceptability for each of their endeavors, especially their performance during crisis. If they did well, they "really should have done better." If they did very well, "it's too bad they let the incident occur in the first place." As such, they are vulnerable to unlimited self-blame and feelings of incompetence.

Idealists. Along with their feelings of mission and perfectionism, many educators expect themselves to be "on" every day. They do not have the cynicism many older, more shopworn colleagues give in to. This sets them up for disillusionment if they recoil from critical incidents and "turn off" to protect themselves. They may interpret this temporary regrouping as cynicism, which can undermine their self-confidence and morale.

Controllers. Like police and fire fighters, educators tend to have a high need for control. They want to be the ones deciding how the classroom, school, or program runs. Given the unpredictable nature of crisis incidents, educators are vulnerable to frustration, feelings of inadequacy, and resentment.

By their very nature, critical incidents are those in which people are hurt and things are not going well. "Perfect" responses are not only unlikely but also sometimes impossible, and control is marginal. Thus, in times of crisis, the very traits that often inspire educators create vulnerability to the stress of crisis events.

Educator-Specific Symptoms

Informal and clinical observations indicate that staff members who have undergone critical incidents experience the following symptoms. Apart from the symptoms of Acute Stress Response, more general subclinical reactions include:

Feeling overwhelmed by responsibilities. Educators are quick to lose their perspective and the ability to cope with role conflicts, environmental pressures, and the necessity of prioritizing their actions in order to deal with the crisis at hand. They become increasingly less effective and often isolate themselves rather than call upon resources available to them.

Overinvolvement. While educators may have entered the profession to involve themselves with students, a loss of boundaries between themselves and their students or other staff members is both the result of and cause for increasing stress. Overinvolvement ties the professional's self-image to the outcome of student intervention.

Impaired performance. As crisis-related stress accumulates beyond the educator's tolerance level, interest and motivation lapse and performance declines. This affects the level of professionalism and self-image. Because schools are social institutions, interpersonal relationships and general school climate suffer as a result of this impaired performance.

Withdrawal. Educators may distance themselves from the crisis situation by depersonalizing their relationships. Just as nurses may refer to patients as "the coronary in 316," educators may find themselves identifying and perceiving students and other staff as just so many obstacles in their day.

Decreased satisfaction. Educators enter schoolwork to reap the satisfaction of successful teaching and administration. Following crisis, they can "bum out." The effects of critical incident and cumulative stress deplete one's energy and sap creativity. What once served as a reward no longer outweighs the effort.

These are subclinical responses, which may or may not register on a diagnostic scale. They tend to arise in the weeks and months following a school crisis and are generally related to the educator's background vulnerability, the extent of involvement in the crisis, and the extent of support the individual receives. Educators' delayed symptoms have a profound effect on school morale and climate and warrant intervention.

Guidelines for Intervention

Intervention with staff members typically occurs in two contexts. The first is during the crisis itself. Sometimes staff members voluntarily come forward and identify themselves to team members as having difficulty with the incident. Sometimes other team members notice signs of distress in particular staff members and inquire about it. Sometimes team members are alerted to needful staff members by administrators, colleagues, or even students.

The second context for intervention occurs after the crisis, when the staff member contacts a team member and complains of difficulties or when a supervisor asks a team member for follow-up consultation regarding a troubled employee.

Following are six guidelines for conducting intervention with staff members (see Figure 8-8):

1. **Follow basic crisis intervention procedures.** Utilize the same basic intervention strategies used with students but geared to an adult level. Work toward validating the severity of the situation and the normalcy of their reactions. Define their current problems and elicit a plan for managing their personal lives. Connect them with personal support systems and/or community resources. Be aware of employee assistance or other district benefits. Include their spouses if possible and a supervisor if appropriate.

2. **Remember your place.** Keep your role in mind. Educators are your peers, and you are not their doctor, even though they might treat you as such. You are working in an advisory capacity only. Even if you are an outside, licensed mental health professional, your function as a crisis team member places restrictions on the scope of your practice.

3. **Maintain professionalism.** Follow basic crisis intervention protocol; show respect and follow team procedure. While effective intervention requires good contact, modeling professionalism elicits a similar professional response in the educator. This provides a source of strength.

4. **Respect confidentiality.** Any information shared by staff members with team members should be kept private. If delicate information is indiscriminately shared with supervisors, family, or colleagues, the victim is further victimized, and the team loses credibility. Do not even discuss the incident in such a way that participants could be identified, even if not named.

5. **Enlist a supervisor.** If you have doubts about an individual's fitness for duty:

   - work to maintain professional self-esteem

   - work to engage voluntary compliance in limiting duties; facilitate this with an administrator

   - present your observations and concerns to an administrator if efforts to gain voluntary self-limitation fail and if you feel that the individual, the students, or supervisees are at risk because of the staff member's dysfunction; work with the administrator to curtail the affected individual's actions, limit his or her duties, and gain outside assistance

6. **Keep aware of transference issues.** Crisis Response Team members may encounter staff who have unrealistic expectations of what CRT members can do. It is helpful to clarify the team members' abilities, knowledge, and function. In addition, it is easy to overidentify with the educator's position or to develop an unhealthy relationship with the employee.

   Recently CRT members have been encountering a unique set of postcrisis symptoms in school staff members and in themselves. The reaction to multiple critical incidents is addressed in the next two chapters.

CHAPTER 9

Taking Care of Yourself

Intervening with staff and students in crisis is a risky business. If you doubt that, look around in the staff room next time you think of it. How many in your staff who work with students in crisis are looking a little frayed around the edges, a little burned out?

CRT members wear two hats. They serve two masters—their normal position and their crisis duty. This position puts very special demands upon them. While it provides a changing pace in their professional life, it also makes them vulnerable to professional stress. To survive such stress, it helps to have some insight into the nature of these demands, along with access to useful steps to manage them.

It is quite normal to feel off balance in a crisis intervention session, particularly when the situation involves professional vulnerability, victims with a great deal of suffering, or personal issues. Everyone has some history of unmet basic needs, often as a result of prior trauma or loss. That unfinished business creates a vulnerability to the corresponding life issue, which can result in personal distress and professional malfunctioning (see Figure 9-1).

During or following an intense debriefing session, CRT members may experience the following essentially normal reactions (see Figure 9-2): They may fear professional and legal liabilities stemming from their involvement in the crisis. They may feel helpless, guilty about perceived "inadequacies." Anger at the situation is fairly normal, as is the urge to rescue those who are victimized by it. Distrusting the school system, law enforcement, and social agencies is

quite common. CRT members frequently feel turmoil, needfulness, and self-doubt later on.

CRT members in a difficult intervention can experience acute stress reactions similar to those of the victims. In order to monitor team members' responses, CRT leaders must keep themselves sufficiently removed from hands-on intervention. They must also designate at least one other person to monitor their (the leaders') stress levels. If leaders feel "stressed out," or if the designated monitor or other team members report "stressed out" behavior by the leader, then it is time for serious reflection and reconsideration. Rotating leadership is preferable to dysfunctional leadership.

CRT members may also experience delayed stress reactions similar to those experienced by posttrauma victims. Typically, delayed stress reactions develop when prior trauma is reawakened or when, because of unforeseen events, an intervention becomes unusually and unexpectedly intense.

Burnout is also a very big issue in CRT circles. Crisis team members come to their work looking for a setting where they can make a difference in people's lives, and this personal involvement sets them up for stress. Stress is old news for educators, but it has a unique twist in the crisis response setting. Rescuer stress occurs when the unique stressors of helping become too great, and interveners experience psychological trauma caused by working closely with people who have themselves been traumatized. This is called vicarious trauma.

Vicarious Trauma

Because people who work with traumatized people tend to become traumatized themselves, psychological debriefings are now being done with emergency workers following disasters and with school personnel following on-campus shootings and other crises.

Listening to the victims is painful, and it can leave lasting symptoms. Most symptoms of vicarious trauma are subclinical, although DSR may result (see Figure 9-3). "Subclinical" means that the symptoms are not dramatic enough to warrant clinical diagnosis, but they are enough to make life miserable. One of the risks of entering into relationships with traumatized, grief-stricken, depressed, or suicidal people is that you can end up becoming

- burned out
- anxious
- cynical
- depressed
- distrustful
- suicidal
- suspicious
- irritable
- pessimistic
- cold and unfeeling
- alienated
- despairing
- fearful
- ineffective

...not to mention difficult to live and work with.

Traumatized people take special energy, elicit compassion, trigger unfinished business, and their experiences and suffering disturb CRT members. It is impossible for anyone to do this work and remain unmoved. The delayed stress reactions CRT members experience tend to be less the cognitive, emotional, physical, and behavioral signs of DSR than the more elusive symptoms of "sickness of the spirit."

CRT members hear this a lot: "I just could not do the work that you do. How do you keep from taking it home with you?" There are two answers to this question. First, CRT members keep from taking it home by distancing themselves psychologically. Second, sometimes they get too involved and they do take it home. The main defense against vicarious trauma—psychological distancing—is mainly a factor of the receptivity CRT members display toward the students and staff members with whom they work.

Receptivity

In order to work their magic, CRT members enter into a closer relationship with students and staff than is normally possible. CRT success depends on a number of things, but openness and receptivity to student and staff experiences and needs is essential.

Receptivity is not a black-or-white proposition. It admits a wide range of responses (see Figure 9-4). The continuum of receptivity extends from complete psychological absence at the low end, to fusion at the high extreme. The extremes are where people get hurt.

1. **Absent.** The team member is in no way affected by the victim. The member is absorbed in his or her own world, and the victim might as well not exist.

2. **Distant.** The member is present, but has reduced the victims to just so many obstacles and categories in the way. If the member was in a hospital setting, patients would be reduced to "the cardiac in 103" or "the bleeder in 502."

3. **Objective.** The CRT member remains enough apart from the victim to keep perspective on the overall situation and is analytical regarding the victim's needs.

4. **Empathetic.** The member is in a state of

balanced openness to whatever the victim presents. While not becoming personally involved in or identifying with the issues, the member fully recognizes the issues as he or she has experienced them and is sensitive to the effect upon the victim.

5. **Sympathetic.** The member has shifted from balanced openness to clearly being "on the victim's side." The situation is interpreted from the victim's point of view; the intervener perceives himself or herself as the student or staff member's ally in relation to the issues involved.

6. **Identified.** The CRT member sees himself or herself and his or her own issues in the victim's situation. Whether aware of it or not, the member responds emotionally to the victim and the victim's situation as if it were the member's situation. Sometimes this is the result of parallel life situations or concerns, similar prior trauma, or unresolved developmental issues in the member's life.

7. **Fused.** The member becomes so identified with the victim that it is impossible to separate whose issue, whose problem, or even whose crisis it is. The net result is that the intervener is unable to maintain the role of leader, guide, or adult in the situation.

The first and last positions are clearly destructive. Faced with psychological absence, the victim learns (perhaps once again) that he or she is not worth the energy it would take to listen. On the other end of the scale, fusion with the intervener disorients and confuses the victim, just as it destroys the CRT member through vicarious trauma.

While not necessarily destructive, the positions of distance and identification are clearly at risk. When the intervener is distanced, it is unlikely that he or she will provide the victim with the necessary psychological validation and support. With identification, on the other hand, it is unlikely that the victim will receive balance and perspective from the intervener and likely that the intervener will suffer vicarious trauma.

The three middle positions—objectivity, empathy, and sympathy—form the effective working zone where victims' needs are most likely to be met and CRT members are least subject to psychological wear and tear. A savvy intervener will move back and forth between these three positions as the situation dictates.

Developing an inner working sense of your own receptivity level is one critical survival skill for interveners. Monitoring personal receptivity and changing posture to fit the demands of the situation not only provide better intervention but also protect against vicarious trauma.

Hot Spots

Every person has sensitive personal issues. These may result from unfinished business, painful past experiences, or felt inadequacies. If external situations parallel past events or recall prior injury, they remind us of our own weaknesses or confront us with issues we have been trying to avoid. In this situation, we are likely to overreact. We probably will not have our normal resilience to stress, and we are more likely to make misjudgements, bad decisions, or come across poorly.

Hot spots cause us to focus on one issue to the exclusion of others. Alternately, they may cause us to ignore pressing issues and focus upon inconsequential ones. They cause us to feel inadequate and unable to help when in fact we might be a great deal of help. Thus, situations involving issues that are hot spots to us will increase our stress and vulnerability.

Sometimes we are aware of our hot spots, sometimes not. When we are, we have a better chance of managing ourselves or removing ourselves from the situation. When we are not consciously aware of these issues, we can become aware of our vulnerability to hot spots by observing our emotional and physical reactions.

Our body and nervous system might be compared to a large radar antenna. We are able to take in large volumes of data simultaneously, but our consciousness can only apprehend one focus at a time. The rest of the data remain on a subconscious level often deemed irrelevant or nonsensical. Sometimes denial can relegate threatening data to the subconscious level. Thus, our perception often screens out information that is considered "hot."

While we may not be aware of information that we have received but screened out, our body and emotions may reflect its presence. Many interveners discover physical and emotional signs that indicate the presence of elusive information. They learn to read their own reactions for data about themselves and the victims with whom they are working (see Figure 9-5).

Some have discovered that when they are feeling anxious and agitated or cold and distracted, they may be too tired to continue. Alternatively, they may be avoiding something in the situation that they are not comfortable confronting.

Some have found that aches, pains, and other physical discomfort means that they are picking up on subtle verbal or nonverbal messages. Others have learned that their feelings of being overwhelmed, underpowered, or helpless/hopeless are specific signs of overidentifying with students or employees. These reactions often indicate that the crisis taps major personal issues.

Finally, many have become aware that when they are feeling parental toward, sexually attracted to, or "the rescuer" of the victim, it means one of several things: (1) The intervener is being manipulated by a dependent victim, (2) the intervener has allowed personal issues to become paramount, or (3) the intervener has lost objectivity and is overidentifying with the victim.

Taking Care of Ourselves

In our normal duty mode, we pace ourselves emotionally and manage to protect ourselves. When crisis duties arise, we shift gears. We feel the gravity of the situation and expect more of ourselves. There is hurt in the world, and we can help. The more we do, the less others suffer. When we can provide assistance to others, it is difficult to slow ourselves down.

In the unusual and dramatic context of crisis, we become vulnerable to stress, vicarious trauma, and burnout. In the interests of our performance at the incident, our own health and well-being, our long-term employability, our friendships, and our family, it is critical that we take care of ourselves.

Preventing such detrimental effects of CRT work requires proactive self-care measures. We must take action in our own behalf prior to any incidents, during interventions and crises, and after the crises are "over" (see Figure 9-6).

Precrisis

Much can be done to minimize vulnerability to the negative effects of involvement before school crises. The objective of precrisis crisis prevention is to increase personal resilience during crisis.

- Build your own interpersonal skills, including awareness of and control over your level of receptivity. This involves actively seeking out opportunities to interact in real and simulated conditions where feedback and reflection are possible. Counselors in clinical training often spend many hours in simulated or supervised settings developing these skills. It is only through this method that we can develop sensitivity to our own internal states and changes, and only by receiving good feedback that we can accurately gauge our effects on others.

- Know your own personal hot spots. Become aware of your personal needfulness and vulnerable areas. Take what the twelve-step-program adherents call a "searching and fearless moral inventory" and discover what parts of you are likely to get bruised doing crisis work.

- Be aware of your current needs and stress level. Needfulness and overwhelming stress leave little room for gracious giving. Pick up your favorite personal stress inventory and go over it occasionally. If you are facing particular types of stressors, remember your vulnerability. Keep them in mind when you accept assignments. It is better to sit out a few calls than to do a bad job in one.

- Keep informed about school and community background situations and the district and community resources that are available to you and your team. Crises never occur in a vacuum. Political, social, and historical events shape the response to events. Resources evolve and devolve. Know what is currently available for assistance and referral.

During crisis

Once you are called upon to respond to a crisis, honestly assess whether or not you are ready to go. Determine your level of vulnerability, the nature and extent of the situation, and the personal resources you have available. Recommit yourself to taking care of yourself first. The objective of self-care during crisis is to avoid exhaustion, vicarious trauma, and excess stress.

- Stay in touch with your own feelings and needs. Maintain an ongoing inventory of personal reactions, energy levels, and your capacity to continue. Be honest about your needs, and find ways in the situation to meet them.

- Set limits for your own involvement. Stay aware of your receptivity level, and attempt to assess your degree of objectivity. Keep a healthy perspective, and take a break if you feel you are "losing it" or if someone on your team suggests that you might be losing it. Consider filling a different role or going home if you cannot bring it under control.

- Listen to your hunches. Explore possibilities that are suggested by your gut-level reactions. Don't act upon unsubstantiated intuition, but do look for substantiation. Assume that your own physical reactions may be in response to knowledge that your overworked consciousness might be unable to focus on. Ask, "What might be going on in this situation to make me feel like that?"

- Monitor your receptivity level. Review the above discussion on receptivity. Distance yourself appropriately. If you are feeling overwhelmed, hopeless/helpless, or undergunned, back off. If you are feeling unaffected, rational, and under firm control, consider seeing things more from the victim's perspective.

- Pull in help any time you need it. It is essential that CRT members approach their work with humility. "I can tough it out!" has no place in work where others' well-being is at stake.

Postcrisis

Self-care following an incident begins by taking the incident seriously. It also means prioritizing your own well-being over your performance. Performance reviews are necessary and essential to team operations, but your own thoughts and feelings generated by the incident are more important. Talking it over with people involved in the incident, those not involved, and those who are on your side takes precedence.

- Review the incident with yourself, staff members, outsiders, and/or another consultant. Get some perspective about how the incident was experienced by others and how they perceived you. Avoid faultfinding, and celebrate your successes.

- Obtain a psychological debriefing when it might help. Use a mental health professional who specializes in emergency care and who is familiar with the school context. You may feel more comfortable with an alternative form of therapy such as therapeutic massage, but make sure that you are not simply deceiving yourself and dodging confrontation.

- Eat well, exercise well, and rest well. Avoid excesses and avoid alcohol or other maladaptive coping devices. Find normalizing experiences and ways to lighten up.

- Talk about it at home. Don't worry about hurting your husband, wife, or significant other by your stories. If you don't tell your loved one what you are going through, you are sowing seeds of isolation. The issue is not so much what happened, but rather what it meant to you and how you felt about it. Children, however, do not need to hear about how uncertain and brutal the world can be. Learn how to communicate your need for additional space following intervention.

The Dilemma

CRT members face a dilemma: If you stay too far removed from the students and staff with whom you intervene, they suffer. If you stay too close, you and the students and staff suffer. You must work out a balance. If you feel bored, disinterested, and judgemental, you probably need to become more involved—"walk a mile in their shoes." If you feel overwhelmed and paralyzed by their problems, you probably need to back off and get some distance.

If you suffer from some of the symptoms listed in the first section above, consider the possibility that you are experiencing vicarious trauma. You would do well to think about your receptivity level and how you are handling yourself with the students. You might consider seeing a counselor to explore just what within you—what memories, old hurts, personal issues—identifies with your students' struggles. Building appropriate distance does not mean shutting down. Remember your proper role, your limitations, and your need to endure.

Suggestions for Community Mental Health and Crisis Response Teams

School personnel are heavily invested in their students and tend to take crises personally. When working with school personnel, remember that staff members are likely to be as impacted as their students, but lack the luxury of giving in to their reactions. Assume that they hurt, but will go on anyway. This is as true in the short run as the long run, yet harder to see. It amounts to a "symptom contagion" effect.

Recent work has been done to describe this "symptom contagion." Charles Figley (1995) points to a set of symptoms paralleling those of PTSD that he terms Secondary Traumatic Stress Disorder—emphasizing the reexperiencing of images and feelings relayed by clients and subsequent persistent arousal—and names the resulting dysfunction "Compassion Fatigue." McCann and Pearlman (1990) use the term "vicarious traumatization" to describe the phenomenon of symptom contagion, and Pearlman and Saakvitne (1995) extend the term to describe the subtle and not-so-subtle characterological changes that result from long-term exposure to clients' suffering. Familiarize yourself with this growing body of literature, as it will provide direction for your work with staff members.

To the extent staff will allow you, help them to work at a deliberate program of personal stress management, including obtaining psychological assistance as preventive care. Help them to examine the way the incident has challenged their spiritual and core beliefs and forced a reconstruction of their "givens," values, and world view.

Remember, as well, that all of this applies to you. Repeated exposure to indirect accounts of trauma can be traumatic. Carefully monitor your own reactions to crisis work in schools. Many countertransference issues are raised when working with children in pain and confusion, and others are raised when working with staff.

Most importantly, take care to follow your own best advice.

CHAPTER 10

Taking Care of Our Teams

The closing of this decade added civil disorder and mass murder to the litany of difficulties facing schools. The budgetary woes lessened, but social pressures increased, bringing increased litigation, the continuing unending flow of federal and state mandates, political tidal waves, and increasingly brutal violence in the streets, homes, and communities served by the schools. The educational process continues to be tumultuous, and impact of these difficulties is felt in Crisis Response Team conference rooms throughout the world.

Critical incidents affecting schools appear to be increasing in frequency, complexity, and intensity. As a result, a whole new category of crises that no longer fits the model presented thus far is emerging in many schools. This category includes critical incidents that occur within a context of chronic traumas experienced by the individual or group. Explanations, projections, and interventions based upon single-incident crises seem to miss the mark in many school settings. A new way of describing and responding to crisis is needed; that new model may be termed Cumulative Traumatic Stress (CTS).

Crisis Response Teams must begin systematically to address the needs of their responders. In order to meet staff and student needs in this setting and in an increasing number of settings like it, the model of classroom and staff debriefings for Critical Incident Stress must be modified. The modifications need to address more than individual symptoms and team cohesion and must confront larger, deeper social issues. Accordingly, this chapter will outline Operational Debriefings and Cumulative Trauma Debriefings.

Operational Debriefings

Crisis Response Teams do not last forever. Normal attrition, changes of assignment, and funding account for loss of personnel. And, some teams fall apart because their members cannot sustain the personal drain the work can exact. Cumulative Traumatic Stress builds up in team members who, as was discussed in the last section, time and again vicariously experience their clients' pain. This stress can undermine team dynamics and pull teams apart.

Three strategies can help offset these demands and should be incorporated into the normal operating procedures of every Crisis Response Team. First, have mandatory team member participation in planning stress management for, during, and after operations. Second, provide special debriefings for Cumulative Stress whenever possible, as discussed later in this chapter. Third, conduct an operational debriefing after every intervention; make it mandatory for all members, whether they participated in intervention or not.

Operational Debriefings are similar in format to other debriefings (see Figure 10-1). After an introductory phase, the fact phase allows participants to gain consensus on what happened, what order it happened in, and what role each team member played. As distinct from other debriefings, an Operational Debriefing includes an assessment phase that reviews the team's performance. If the incident was diffi-

---

Case: Inner-city elementary school district in the Midwest

Situation: Following the report of an off-campus shooting death of a first-grader, the CRT responded to the school and classroom of the victim. After a routine post-violent-death intervention, the team saw an unexpected drop in morale. This reaction came as a surprise for all involved because the team had dealt with a number of incidents more critical than this.

Complications: Precedents for the incident were disclosed. The police were investigating the shooting, which was considered to have occurred under suspicious circumstances. The child's 13-year-old brother, who had pulled the trigger of the shotgun, had previously been investigated for killing a third sibling with a shotgun two years earlier. In addition, the staff indicated that this incident was not an exception to the chronic high levels of traumatic incidents that they responded to several times a week. The staff attributed the incidents to the social and economic depression triggered in the past several years by the closing and relocating of several giant manufacturing plants that had employed a large percentage of the population. Neighborhoods that used to be nice were now decimated, populated by those too disadvantaged to move. Homes were deteriorating, burned down, or inhabited by transients. Drugs, violence, and crime were increasing. With the homefront a battlefield, the schools played an increasingly pivotal role in stabilizing the lives of their students.

Reactions: Individual team members universally complained of overwhelming personal stress symptoms. In relation to their work, they showed signs of spiritual depletion, manifested in depression, isolation, pessimism, numbness, and concern that their work no longer had meaning or purpose. On the team level, there was evidence of contagious job burnout, organizational distrust, and collective despair.

---

cult, take care to ensure that members do not criticize on a personal level, but rather keep it to a "what worked and what didn't" level. Once this phase is completed, give individuals the opportunity to discuss their personal reactions during the incident as well as current reactions. The interpretation phase gives professionals a chance to make sense of the event professionally, fulfilling their need to understand the situation with regard to lessons learned for future interventions. Finally, the team needs to establish any plans to implement the lessons learned. Then, the debriefing may close.

Cumulative Traumatic Stress

While a critical incident is an event so intense as to overwhelm the individual's capacity to cope, Cumulative Trauma consists of a number of such incidents experienced with greater frequency and intensity than can be satisfactorily adapted to either the individual or the group.

Human service professionals, by virtue of their close contact with clients in crisis, can be indirectly traumatized. Professionals in close contact with clients who experience a variety of ongoing crises and traumas may develop posttraumatic symptoms; their exposure to a number of such experiences has a cumulative effect. Teachers and mental health and health professionals can be similarly affected. Indirect trauma can be debilitating to both individuals and the teams they serve.

Cumulative Trauma refers to a set of critical incidents affecting a clientele with sufficient intensity and frequency so as to result in

1. Chronic individual delayed stress symptoms among individual service providers

2. Disintegrating effects on service teams

Work-related effects of Cumulative Trauma in individuals include chronic work-related symptoms commonly associated with Delayed Stress Response. Individuals suffering from Cumulative Traumatic Stress exhibit a host of signs of physical, emotional, attitudinal, and spiritual exhaustion. The composite signs of depression—including apathy, lack of caring, sense of powerlessness, and chronic fatigue— plague those who have experienced too much trauma. The individual may initially become isolated and tend to overidentify with the team to the extent that relationships with family and friends suffer. The stressed worker's attitude will eventually reflect unhappiness and dissatisfaction with work, which can result in detachment from or even hostility toward clientele.

Perhaps even more characteristic, too much direct or indirect traumatic stress leads to a decline in optimism, personal sense of purpose, and faith that an individual's work is meaningful and useful. In extreme cases, this spiritual depletion can extend to the individual's view of his or her entire life or all of life itself (see Figure 10-2). The individual impact of indirect trauma was discussed in Chapter 9.

Cumulative Traumatic Stress affects more than the individual. When it is a work-related phenomenon, CTS is likely to affect all members of the team. This is because CTS stems from incidents affecting the entire team and because it is contagious. CTS initially manifests itself on the team level through morale problems and relational difficulties within the team. It develops into distrust of leadership

Staff Reactions to the Colombine High School Shooting

Jo Anne Doherty

Following the Colombine High School shootings, staff members from the entire school district as well as from CHS were highly impacted. Prior to April 20, Columbine High School had not had any serious problems affecting the safety or welfare of its students. CHS was known essentially as a college prep school—with a high percentage of kids who go on to college—and for having an excellent athletic program. Many staff members, as well as parents, were shocked that something like this could happen at CHS. The shootings rocked their basic sense of safety and of the future.

In spite of the significant emotional toll, CHS staff needed to return to teaching 10 days after the shootings. Staff in other schools continued teaching. It was critical that staff have the opportunity to deal with their feelings as well as address any concerns regarding their own safety or that of their students. School administration had many meetings with CHS staff to answer their questions about what happened and to address their concerns. Information was shared with staff regarding how they could easily access individual counseling, and 24-hour crisis lines were also made available. Drop-in debriefings were provided by mental health staff and victims' assistance staff at four different locations in different parts of the county, three times a day (totaling 12 per week). Drop-in debriefing groups and staff support groups were ongoing through the summer.

It is well documented that mental health staff who work with persons who are impacted by mass trauma may be secondarily traumatized themselves. Staff who responded to the initial and ongoing effort of responding to the shootings on April 20 were no exception. Staff reported many symptoms, including sleep disturbance, difficulty concentrating, and emotional reactivity. Mental health for the caregiver was essential. The Jefferson Center for Mental Health (JCMH) already had a policy of mandatory debriefing for any staff involved in a traumatic event. In this situation, there were so many staff who were deployed and therefore impacted that the center had to rely on numerous professional resources, including other community mental health centers, to provide the debriefings and decompressions for our staff. Though staff would often be reluctant to take time away from the pressing demands of their work, once they did, they most often were grateful that they had the opportunity, finding relief in the debriefings. Debriefings and decompressions were also provided for victims' assistance and other agency staff who assisted in the efforts.

Jo Anne Doherty, MS, RN, CNS, is Vice President of Clinical Services and Chief Operating Officer of the Jefferson Center for Mental Health.

and the supporting organization and takes the form of defensiveness at various levels. As a whole, the team suffers from contagious job burnout. This can eventually lead to a collapse of team mission and purpose and collective despair (see Figure 10-3).

Cumulative Traumatic Stress leads to both personal distress and team disintegration.

CTS Debriefings

Like Critical Incident Stress, Cumulative Traumatic Stress responds well to early intervention. When you define the traumatic nature of the set of incidents, outline complicating factors, acknowledge individual reactions, adopt coping strategies, and address team dysfunction, you can turn around the disintegrative process of CTS.

Cumulative Traumatic Stress Debriefing (CTSD) is a group intervention similar to Critical Incident Stress Debriefing (Everly and Mitchell 1999) or a classroom debriefing (Johnson 1999; Johnson et al. 1999). The goals are basically the same: to address and moderate traumatic stress symptoms and to build group cohesiveness among participants. CTSD differs in that it is designed to specifically address issues that are eroding individual and team functioning. Because of the complexity of the incidents leading up to a debriefing, the chronic and diverse reactions, and the team factors addressed, CTSD tends to utilize more props such as flipcharts, blackboards, and checklists, although use of these techniques may vary with the style of the leader.

Like classroom or adult debriefings, the CTSD protocol follows a specific, predetermined set of phases. These phases include incidents, complications, reactions, and planning (see Figure 10-4).

The process is explained below. It assumes a group and, more specifically, a working team of adults. Different applications of this basic process (such as use with individuals, older children, or with groups not traumatized together or not belonging to the same team) will be discussed in the section "Suggestions for Community Mental Health and Crisis Response Teams."

The introduction phase consists of the same basic format as in other debriefings: explain the purpose of the meeting, introduce the leader, outline the format of the meeting, and lay ground rules.

Incidents Phase

The incidents phase of CTSD serves two purposes. First, it allows the group to narrow the focus of discussion to the three or four most difficult incidents experienced in the recent past. This involves the group reaching consensus on which incidents were, in fact, the most difficult. This process leads to the second purpose, which is for individuals to express and acknowledge their experiences.

This phase follows a generally orderly flow, from determining the events and the temporal relationships, to the individuals' roles in each of these, to their basic reactions at the time (see Figure 10-5).

At this point the leader should consider several aspects of the situation. The leader should observe each participant's reactions to this phase and his or her functioning level. If participants seem to be showing signs of Acute Stress Response, the group process should be interrupted to arrange for an immediate mental health consultation on an individual level.

If the group is unable to reach consensus on key incidents, a rift between members may be apparent. When this is the case, conflict resolution becomes a primary agenda.

Finally, any legal action or investigations conducted concurrently to the debriefing will affect the comfort level, intensity of reactions, and the degree of disclosure possible for the individuals in the debriefing.

A good approach to facilitate the incidents phase begins by having participants write down three or four key incidents that they feel affected the team during the past six months. The leader can have participants call out the incidents they have written down. Using a blackboard or flipchart, the leader lists them, placing checks after repeat mentions of specific events. After the list is complete, the leader can suggest that the group decide together which were the three or four most important incidents.

The leader can consolidate the list chronologically, with at least one inch of space between incidents. Alternately, a horizontal time line can be drawn, indicating the key incidents and leaving a space under each one. Individual roles and responses can be recorded under each incident. Discuss each incident, noting each participant's role to the left and reactions to the right. The virtue of using flipcharts is that sheets can be torn off and taped to the wall as they are filled, thus creating a visual record for reference during the course of the debriefing.

Sometimes during another type of debriefing, the leader becomes aware of the intrusion of other incidents and determines that the original incident under discussion cannot be dealt with unless the others are discussed as well. Transition to the CTSD format can occur by using the method of writing down reactions to each incident.

Complications Phase

Events do not take place in a social vacuum; their meaning and effects need to be understood within their context. The purpose of this phase is to identify and acknowledge the various factors that complicate the key incidents and the ongoing postincident environment.

Complications can include the following:

- the nature of the client community
- background factors and precedents
- key themes
- organizational issues
- practical and logistical problems
- the interpersonal context

A good approach for assessing these factors begins by having participants fill in a checklist of possible complications. The checklist should provide prompts as well as include space for individual comments and additions; the latter can be incorporated into the overall list. The leader asks participants to call out factors they have listed, while he or she writes them on a flipchart or large paper. Then each factor is discussed, allowing the group to express reactions and reach consensus on each. The group does not have to reach agreement on each entry, but it does need to acknowledge that each is at issue and is a point of difference. The final list is saved for use at a later phase (see Figure 10-6).

A major consideration during this phase is the presence of supervisory personnel, a presence that may inhibit or exacerbate the group process. Because of the nature of team operations and the complexity of team needs, there is no easy formula to determine the ideal composition of the debriefing group. Supervisory or

EXAMPLE
INCIDENT #1: SHOOTING 3/29

TEAM MEMBER	ROLE	REACTION
Sandra	Team leader Consult with administration Liaison with district office	Confused Pressured Angry Saddened
Tom	Classroom debrief Individual consult	Overwhelmed by student acceptance Headache
Martha	Classroom debrief Individual consult	Overwhelmed by student acceptance Uncertainty

managerial personnel are likely to dampen team discussion of organizational issues or may cause the group to polarize and get enmeshed in a political struggle over peripheral issues. On the other hand, supervisors are an integral part of team functioning and operations and can provide valuable perspective and assistance in dealing with future difficulties.

The decision to include or not include supervisors, or the determination of who is or is not functioning in a supervisorial capacity, should take into consideration all the factors discussed here. One way of resolving the issue is to bring together those members of the team who clearly are not supervisors. This should be in the introductory phase, after explaining the purpose and format of the meeting. At this time, raise the issue of inclusion of supervisors for group decision. If even one participant objects, consider any supervisor's inclusion risky.

Reactions Phase

This phase explores, acknowledges, and validates current individual and team reactions to cumulative stressors. The process begins with personal assessment and continues by sharing these individual reactions (see Figure 10-7). Once the composite personal reactions are brought into the open, a pattern emerges showing cumulative stressor effects upon team members as individuals. At this point the discussion shifts to exploring ways in which overall team functioning has been affected.

Due to the wide range of possible symptoms and team members' tendency to minimize their own symptoms or dysfunction, a printed checklist is useful to help members identify their own distress. Figure 10-2 presents such a list and can be used as the basis for the checklist. Responses to this list can be handled in one of at least two ways. The leader must decide how comfortable the group is with disclosure. The group members can share their reactions verbally, with the leader listing responses on the board as they are called out, or members can submit their reactions on paper for the leader to then list on the board anonymously. Discussion of the reactions aims to acknowledge the

extent and universality of chronic stress reactions within the group.

Be aware of individuals who indicate a need for referral. Assess the extent of personal dysfunction, especially with regard to an individual's ability to carry out job or team duties. Assess the advisability of the individual continuing his or her job or team assignment; do this separately, following the debriefing if necessary. During the discussion, incorporate members' observations of one another's signs of CTS. Exercise caution, however, to keep this on a constructive level. For example, include double-blind observations where neither the observer nor the person observed is identified. Or, create an informal system where each member solicits feedback from others regarding his or her functioning.

Figure 10-3 provides a list of possible ways team-level functioning has been affected. This is a sensitive area of discussion; remember that this is simply an opening of discourse, not an exhaustive treatment. Be aware that the discussion must be managed carefully to avoid individuals being singled out, management unfairly dumped on, or group divisions polarized. Helpful strategies include keeping the discussion general, constructive, and focussed upon the list.

The leader should be capable of guiding the group in the ways just described. It is important to consider these types of skills when choosing a leader.

Planning Phase

This final phase has two major purposes: to explore the effect of Cumulative Traumatic Stress on team functioning and to develop a plan for incorporating team-level stress management into team preparedness and operations (see Figure 10-8).

The planning phase begins with reviewing both the types of incidents the group encountered and the complications listed during the complications phase. Discuss individual plans for cumulative stress management. Explore individuals' current use of stress management strategies, and identify key additional means of coping that members can incorporate into their individual stress plans.

Then, the team explores the following areas for possible change: client community; broader organization; team preparation, training, and conditioning; team policies, operations, and communications; and interpersonal relationships. In addition, each member is asked what he or she needs from other team members. This exploration may be best conducted with individual checklists brought up for group consideration. The checklist simply lists the areas of change, leaving space under each for a response sentence or two. A flipchart or blackboard may be helpful to list the various suggestions. After prioritizing the list, consider the next steps to institutionalize changes.

Close the planning phase with a general review of incidents, complications, individual reactions, and group reactions. Reinforce plans for individual and group changes, and note referral resources. To complete the debriefing, offer a final opportunity for each participant to express anything left unsaid and to address personal hopes for the future.

When deciding whether to use props such as checklists, the leader should consider the extent to which group members are open and able to learn from and share with one another. Healthy group functioning and the degree of mutual support determine whether the leader should be didactic or facilitative. The stronger the group, the more facilitative the leader should be. For example, to modify this process appropriately for a large but supportive group, the leader might have participants divide into triads and mutually reinforce new coping strategies.

Suggestions for Community Mental Health and Crisis Response Teams

Community professionals and teams are vulnerable to vicarious traumatic stress as discussed in Chapter 9. Accordingly, they are equally at risk for the cumulative effects of trauma. Thus

the considerations discussed in this chapter are relevant beyond the school grounds. Consider taking advantage of CTS debriefings as a part of individual and team care.

When working with school personnel, outside professionals are sometimes startled to discover the cumulative nature of staff symptomatology. The CTS protocols are often useful in consultation contexts and can be used with almost seamless transition.

There are several contexts, however, where the CTS approach can be useful for outside consultants other than with staff. Sometimes the basic crisis intervention protocol is inadequate when working with individual adults, ad hoc groups without a shared incident, or with groups of older children.

Individual Applications

In crisis intervention contexts, individuals sometimes disclose that they are in crisis because of the combination of a number of past incidents and current complications. They struggle with daily decisions about life choices and practical strategies for the future. This situation presents a puzzling glut of information for team leaders to work through, unless some system of organization is used to keep the session from being sidetracked and bogged down.

If the situation is a crisis intervention, complete the chart during the session, assessing appropriately the individual's risk factors and need for structured support. If the situation marks the beginning of an ongoing counseling relationship, use several sessions to gather more comprehensive data. When working with an individual, use the complications stage to explore the complications considered in team debriefings, along with personal factors such as family issues, individual background, and prior trauma. The planning phase can investigate practical issues, but it can also be used to define direction for future clinical work (see Figure 10-9).

Ad Hoc Groups without a Shared Incident

The CTSD model presented so far is intended

for adult work teams who experienced a set of stressors together, whose work together is compromised by the experiences, and who will function together as a team in the future. There are, however, some other group settings that do not meet these criteria but where the CTSD approach can be useful as well. Group CTSD can be very successful on occasions where the background factors, individuals, and traumatic stressors are similar enough that the benefits of group interaction outweigh the fact that the individuals are not otherwise related. For example, individuals working in the same type of setting, their spouses, or those who have been traumatized in a similar fashion are good candidates for group debriefing. In such an application, the planning phase focuses on ways in which each individual can work more productively with his or her own family or work setting.

To make this application successful, use the following minimal criteria to consider group composition (see Figure 10-10):

- similar precipitating incident (such as gunshot, assault) or condition (such as disability, relationship with victim)

- similar living environment

- similar stage of adjustment to situation

- similar developmental issues

Children

While the CTSD model is designed primarily for adult populations, it can be used with children if the basic process is modified. The major limiting factor for using CTSD with children has to do with children's relatively immature cognitive development. People cannot understand such concepts as *cumulative stress* and *complicating factors* until they have at least reached adolescence. This is true even if the terms are used operationally. Bringing up more than one painful incident at a time can also be overwhelming for children. Even if the leader does not bring up other incidents or issues, other children in the group may do so, or they may discuss the incidents insensitively. Finally,

younger children are sometimes unable to distinguish others' hurts from their own; they are likely to experience another's talk about a past incident as a current incident directly affecting them. For these reasons, CTSD should not be used with younger children at all, and used with older children only according to the following considerations (see Figure 10-11).

When discussing traumatic incidents with older elementary children, use activities and discussions that follow the standard CTS model. Because of children's conceptual difficulties, eliminate the complications section unless the children initiate discussion; then, pursue the discussion only if it makes sense to all the participants and is not likely to cause further distress. Generalize during the planning stage. Emphasize stress management techniques and focus the group energy into a meaningful closure project, as in standard classroom debriefings.

With middle school students, the CTSD format can be followed using an opening activity and structured discussion. Be alert to contagious feelings among students of this age. Open the complications phase only with general and leading comments. Respect the students' conceptual limitations and their need to win approval from others. Do not allow children to overdisclose in ways they might regret later; confidentiality is virtually impossible.

CTSD in high school can follow the adult model, with the exception of using an introductory activity. The activity will format the discussion in a familiar manner for students.

At each level, CTSD should not be the group intervention of choice, but rather should be regarded as an approach to be taken when a normal classroom debriefing uncovers a number of prior traumas that must be considered during the discussion. CTSD's usefulness lies in addressing the children's need to discuss and make meaning out of discrepant, overwhelming, and troubling crisis experiences.

Note that the CTSD model itself, as well as the various adaptations, can be used in both school and clinical settings. Cumulative stress debriefings, whether in a school or clinic, emphasize different aspects of the basic approach, reflecting their different missions and respective scopes of practice. In school settings, the intervention furthers educational goals by stabilizing individual students, groups of students, and staff. In clinical settings, the intervention furthers the therapeutic goals of psychologically processing the incidents.

Red flag signs that indicate the inappropriateness of CTS activities in school settings help give direction and focus to clinical intervention. While each type of intervention may use all of the following strategies, some generalizations may provide an appropriate focus for each (see Figure 10-12). School applications stress a form of questioning that uses cognitive prompts, while clinical applications freely utilize affective prompts. Administrators in school contexts use global impressions and memories, while clinicians often use specific sensory impressions. Schools focus on problem solving and analysis, while clinics explore the impact of crisis and encourage individual catharsis. Using discussion and talking about feelings are appropriate for school applications, while enactment and other means to help work through feelings may be more beneficial to clinics.

CHAPTER 11

Issues:
Legal and Otherwise

While strategies are developing for dealing with suicides, shootings, and the host of other calamities befalling students, some particularly difficult issues begin to emerge. Should schools provide psychotherapy services? Should teachers and counselors explore children's feelings and family relationships? Are schools "deviating" from their primary mission of education when they assist their children in adjusting to catastrophe?

Providing crisis response services, particularly assessments of threat and crisis intervention, raises several issues of legal, moral, and practical importance. Most of these issues concern the role of the school and school personnel.

This book cannot, and makes no attempt to, provide an adequate analysis of the legal liabilities incurred by districts that provide crisis services. Laws vary from state to state, and are revised and updated regularly. Legal counsel must determine the liability of the district and of the individual CRT members. Prior to operations, guidelines for minimizing risk should be formalized and then followed.

Under no circumstances should CRT personnel circumvent legal counsel, district policy and procedures, or their own professional judgement in their urgency to meet human need during crisis. The resulting legal and organizational liability makes such "freelancing" not only unwise, but also harmful to the overall mission of the CRT. A team slow to organize and respond is infinitely better for students and staff than no team at all.

Some Concerns

The following comments about legal issues have been made by workshop participants and administrators from many districts. They are intended only as an impetus for further discussion and exploration by team administrators and district counsel.

Certain case precedents have been held to apply to crisis service providers and deserve investigation by district counsel:

1. Some cases support liability of CRT work: *Mullins v. Pine Manor College* (1983) and *Miller v. State of New York* (1984) are examples of such cases

2. *Tarasoff v. Regents of the University of California* (1976) established that CRTs should warn threatened individuals or their guardians

3. Most states have some mandated reporting laws covering cases of suspected child abuse and neglect

To protect the team and its individual members, establish a record-keeping system to document observations, concerns, and actions taken, although remind members of confidentiality issues.

Develop clear policies and procedures regarding legal issues after consultation with knowledgeable legal counsel. Furthermore, have district administration and the governing board formalize and approve CRT operational procedures.

Individual crisis responders, whether school personnel or outside mental health professionals, should explore issues of personal liability with their supervisors, their professional organization, and their malpractice insurance carrier.

As claims against schools and other public agencies continue to rise in number, cases against Crisis Response Teams are also expected to grow. Knowledgeable team leaders and administrators will explore liability issues and take them into account when formulating team policies, procedures, and training.

The political dimensions of the community and district relate to and interact with legal issues. Crisis events create fodder for political cannons. Newspapers and other media are attracted to incidents, thus raising the visibility of these incidents to the public. The critical incident itself may pale in comparison to the organizational crises that follow.

Some Suggestions

Particularly with the passage of current school safety legislation, the most effective way to prevent misunderstanding and resistance is to create in advance a clear crisis policy and plan, with governing board approval. This plan must clearly protect the rights of individuals, as well as carry out the obligation of the school to provide for the well-being of its students. Such a plan must ensure that CRT personnel function within their scope of practice. The plan should articulate the district and CRT's position on several key issues, such as participation, affective education versus therapy, levels of involvement and training, and parent permission.

Participation

Participation in school intervention must always be optional. By its very nature, the intervention process is conducted at a time when students are vulnerable to their own feelings and the effects of others. Emotions can run high, and students may feel barely able to maintain themselves without further reawak-

ening of feelings. They may feel violated when well-meaning professionals attempt to poke and prod into their private lives. Although conferencing or debriefings may be exactly what the student needs in order to feel better and work better in class, he or she may resist participating out of fear.

School personnel have the responsibility to provide the opportunity to talk about a critical incident; yet it is important to realize that most people will be reluctant to begin the process. A good way to make the opportunity available without coercing participation is to strictly enforce the right-to-pass rule. Encourage students to remain in the class, but reassure them that participation is not necessary. A student does not have to speak, share anything, or do anything other than give others the chance to share and respect their confidence. This is usually enough, although an occasional student may protest attendance. In case of such protest, arrange another activity for that child. While each student should have the right to pass, or even to not attend, missing a debriefing will be an isolating factor from the group.

Therapeutic Learning Versus Doing Therapy

School personnel are often afraid of "doing therapy" in the classroom, and well they should be—it is beyond their training and beyond their scope of practice. It is also a political issue. Parent groups abound who believe that the school already intrudes in the lives of children and families. For staff to attempt psychotherapy with children would be to tempt fate. Nevertheless, that does not excuse school personnel from not dealing with the effects of critical incidents, both for the sake of the students' well-being and for the sake of the learning environment in the classroom. For this reason, it is important to clarify the difference between emotionally supportive learning experiences and therapy.

Bloom's Educational Taxonomy distinguishes between cognitive and affective domains. Many well-accepted educational programs, such as Magic Circle and Stages 1 and 2, use group learning experiences to further affective development in children. These experiences may have therapeutic benefits for students in the areas of increased self-understanding and interpersonal communication, but they are not therapy.

While there are different kinds of therapies (some that are little more than straight classroom behavior modification and cognitive relearning), most therapies involve attempts at transforming emotional disposition and primary relationships. More than learning about feelings, therapy involves the treatment of emotional, behavioral, and relational dysfunction.

Affective education, on the other hand, limits itself to teaching, sharing, and communicating about feelings, behavior, and relationships. Individual differences are explicitly respected and accepted. Education emphasizes encouraging mutual understanding rather than changing people's emotional disposition. Interventions following a crisis are normally affective educational experiences designed to encourage learning about one's own and others' perceptions and feelings following critical incidents.

Levels of Involvement and Training

As indicated above, the classroom intervention model presented here can be used as an educational process or as a therapeutic strategy, depending on how it is carried out. When school personnel utilize the intervention to rebuild group cohesiveness and teach about postcrisis reactions, intervention is primarily an educational process. When utilized by mental health professionals to effect emotional or behavioral change within group members, intervention is primarily a therapeutic process. The therapeutic process implies a deeper level of involvement and must be lead by someone with specialized training in therapeutic intervention. Such specialists include psychiatrists, clinical or counseling psychologists, clinical social workers, family therapists, or other clinicians trained and experienced in group work. If an intervention or part of an intervention is done

on such a basis, Crisis Response Teams should employ a clinically trained leader and apprise the parents of the nature of the intervention. Further, they must clarify the legal status of the activity.

Parent Permission

When the intervention is intended to be counseling following an incident, parent permission is normally required, although this varies from state to state. Check out local regulations. When the intervention is led by school personnel, is intended to be an educational experience, and will be limited to the parameters of affective education outlined above, there should be no need for parent permission. Again, review local policies.

Politically, however, such educational activities may be controversial in certain areas. If so, the potential danger of moving ahead without parental permission outweighs the risk of unenlightened parents' prohibiting their children from participating. This is a judgement call; if the situation permits, it is probably prudent to be conservative. Phrasing the permission in a general way (such as, "I hereby give permission for my son/daughter _____ to participate in a group discussion regarding the _____ incident that occurred on May 15 at school. I understand that the discussion will be lead by _____ ") presents a less threatening image to parents than a specific description in more technical language that would be liable to misinterpretation. Some districts have found that a "negative" permission slip (such as, "Sign below if you wish your child NOT to be included in a group discussion regarding _____ ") results in fewer children being deprived of the opportunity. Again, however, this depends on the political climate.

Other Issues

In the decade since the publication of the first edition of this book, school Crisis Response Teams have become an accepted management strategy, and team development has become widespread. Most schools and districts have some sort of team, although the size, training, and organization of these teams vary widely. With this development, a number of important issues have come to be recognized, among them the changing functions of CRTs, the increased emphasis upon interdisciplinary and even interagency cooperation, emerging school-community partnerships, changing training needs, and the development of national professional standards.

Breaking the Community-School Barrier

While some partnerships have been formed between school districts and community agencies and teams, we must acknowledge a general failure of outside crisis responders to gain entry to schools and of schools to effectively access those resources.

All across the United States and Canada—and indeed in many countries throughout the world—schools feel isolated in dealing with the overwhelming demands upon them, including crisis management. Paradoxically, they are typically surrounded by enormous human and material resources. Many of these outsiders want to help, yet feel blocked by the bureaucratic morass they face when approaching schools.

This is particularly true in the area of crisis management. Significant cultural, procedural, legal, and practical differences exist between schools and other community organizations and institutions. Most people working outside the schools cannot appreciate the demand characteristics of even the small neighborhood elementary school, much less a large secondary school or entire district. When crisis strikes, school personnel, already stretched far too thin, attempt to don their emergency hats and therapy coats and do what they have never been trained to do.

At the same time, most communities have some sort of crisis response organization trained to do crisis management. Linking up these resources with the schools who need them has traditionally been difficult. The problem seems to be training crisis providers to understand the unique context and limitations of the school and getting them to modify their normal procedures and protocols to fit the needs of children and staff within the school setting.

With the goal of meeting this need, several organizations provide training in school response to crisis. The National Organization of Victims Assistance has provided training for school personnel for years. Various governmental agencies have sponsored research and practice guidelines, and several educational organizations have provided material development. A relatively small number of private clinicians and school people have also prepared materials and given presentations to school and community audiences. Fortuitously, a current banner in educational circles is the School-Community Partnership movement, which has made schools more open to community-based assistance.

One organization that holds great promise is the International Critical Incident Stress Foundation. Founded by Jeffrey Mitchell and George Everly, the ICISF has established crisis teams in most major communities throughout the United States and in many countries abroad. Not long before the shooting at Columbine High School in Littleton, Colorado, the Foundation began the development of a specialized training for both its community crisis management teams and educators in school crisis response. The purpose of the training is to establish a common set of goals, shared concepts and language, and a set of standard intervention approaches that allow the ICISF community teams to function comfortably within the school context and allow school personnel to understand how to use them. As the ICISF training develops, it is becoming increasingly process-oriented, focusing upon issues of integrating services and making those services more accessible to the schools.

Another organization that is making gains on a different front is the American Academy of Experts in Traumatic Stress. Under the leadership of Mark Lerner, the AAETS has developed a board-certification program in School Crisis Response. While the concept of professional standardization is new to the area of school crisis management, it is certainly a worthy project. Learner's well-organized and concise handbook *Crisis Response in Our Schools* is available from the AAETS (www.aaets.org).

The U.S. Department of Education recently funded a resource document entitled "Early Warning, Timely Response: A Guide to Safe Schools" (Washington, D.C.: U.S. Department of Education). This project was conducted by Kevin Dwyer, Principal Investigator, National Association of School Psychologists; and David Osher, Project Director, American Institutes for Research. Of particular interest in this resource is the excellent research bibliography. The report is a public document available on the project's Web site (www.airdc.org/cecp/guide).

Legislative Trends

The promise of emerging legislation such as mandated crisis planning in California, South Carolina, Nevada, and other states is that it forces schools to write crisis intervention plans in event of emergency. This is certainly good news for students and staff who are likely to be impacted by violence and other crises. These acts specify planning for large-scale incidents. Indeed, some states require trained Crisis Response Teams. Unfortunately, such laws—and such planning—can be fleeting. In the aftermath of the string of natural disasters in the early 1990s, public laws mandating disaster planning were enacted. Now, extensive disaster plans, and even Crisis Response Team Handbooks, line the shelves in many of those districts and schools, gathering a great deal of dust. The Third Law of Thermodynamics—entropy—applies to team development as readily as it applies to molecular systems. Those who do the initial planning, and those who form the initial teams, eventually move away. Team maintenance and readiness present greater challenges than team design and implementation. Many districts find themselves in the position of recreating teams that existed years ago.

The good news is that much of the initial groundwork has already been done, and the needs of those districts have been considered. Review of such plans provides a starting point. More importantly, new plans should address the area of team institutionalization and development to prevent the same gradual eroding of current efforts and readiness.

Windows of Opportunity: Intervention to Planning

Given the increasingly visible role played by school crisis responders following recent high-profile incidents, one might wonder why districts are resistant to developing school Crisis Response Teams. Or why they tend to develop elaborate crisis plans only following the sieges of natural disaster, civil disorder, and terrorism. Part of the answer lies in the politically responsive nature of schools and part in good old-fashioned denial.

Schools are complex, political beasts. Schools are committee-driven, and many decisions governing operations are made as a result of group decision making. As such, they are subject to the changing tides of political controversy. Educational buzzwords are usually formed within political discourse. Politics, in turn, directs educational research, budgets, programs, and planning. Various banners pass by with a life span of three to five years, and experienced educators know that if they are unhappy with a particular set of priorities, they need but wait. Things move in cycles.

It is the same with such vital issues as safety and student well-being. If no one seems to be interested in the development of crisis prevention curriculum or intervention resources this season, be patient. The next catastrophe will renew interest in crisis preparedness.

Crisis responders, however poorly prepared and organized, will be sought after following a suicide, accidental death, or act of random violence. It is important for responders to take advantage of the situation to force long-range planning in the face of a short-range incident.

Districts and sites often give indications that school CRTs would be welcome, and then go about setting up roadblocks to team development. Part of the resistance is a homeostatic desire to avoid change. Part is territorial; it is unclear how the team will affect decision making during emergencies. To assuage this worry, offer reassurance that the role of the team is solely as a supplemental resource.

Other strategies include the following:

- Gain the preliminary blessing of the superintendent as well as the school psychology department. This will hinge upon political and territorial considerations.

- Give awareness training to selected site guidance and/or principal management teams. Demonstrate how the team's function will supplement existing power and decision-making relationships.

- Create a demand. Provide informational fliers following emergencies (on site and elsewhere); make presentations to the school board, parent faculty association, and staff.

- Work several incidents, taking an increasingly central role. Act in a conservative, helpful manner within the school structure. Build credibility.

- Blend with the administration; enlist administrators on the team in liaison and planning roles.

- Create a liaison group on site, articulating the developing role of the team within the existing scope and practice of the school. Troubleshoot resistance and obstacles together.

- Where helpful and appropriate, incorporate liaison and resource persons in incidents at other sites and districts.

- Emphasize administrative consultation; assist with decision making during incidents.

Afterword

School crisis management has developed qualitatively as well as quantitatively since the publication of the first edition of this book. Teams have formed and grown throughout the world. This development has been exciting and productive, and thousands of children have been helped to reclaim their lives partly as a result of the efforts of school crisis managers. With the growth of the field has come diversity. School crisis management has been challenged to move past its exclusive focus upon aftermath issues and address a growing role in the management of unfolding critical incidents.

Crisis Response Teams provide a proactive approach to managing the various tragedies that increasingly beset schools today. School interventions assist staff, students, and parents in adjusting to critical incidents that could otherwise threaten their psychological well-being, school climate, and classroom performance. With sufficient planning and training, Crisis Response Teams can accomplish these objectives while respecting the rights of individuals and families, operating within the scope and practice of the professionals involved, and carrying out the primary educational mission of the school.

As the discipline has matured, new techniques and strategies have evolved. Within each district, team policies, procedures, training, acceptance, and utilization will continue to mature and evolve. As in any endeavor, team success depends on its institutionalization. Unless the team is trusted and utilized within the district, it will cease to exist and cease to provide the services for which it was created.

The key to institutionalization lies in the team's usefulness to others. Be prepared, respect political boundaries, build support, network resources, and most of all, deliver when the time comes. Do not work at odds with the organization you seek to serve. More important than any of the work the CRT seeks to do is the stabilizing factor of the school itself in the lives of children in crisis. Finally, in the face of resistance, ignorance, and setback, keep the faith that the work done by the CRT is good work.

Appendix I:
What Therapists Can Offer Educators and What Educators Can Offer Therapists

There is often a long distance between the school and the clinic; this distance is measured by more than miles. Educators and therapists may view each other alternately as obstacles and saviors. Further, they often view each other's work as a black box, as something they do not understand. Yet each occasionally relies on the other, and certainly each has much to offer the other to assist in meeting the needs of students in crisis.

The following represents the culmination of an interactional process with 120 educators and private therapists involved in a training program at HCA Hospital, North Richland Hills, Texas, in August 1990. Therapists and educators were evenly matched in structured discussion groups of eight participants; each group addressed the questions separately. The participants documented suggestions and eliminated duplicated answers.

What Therapists Can Provide Educators

By virtue of their training and scope of practice, therapists possess in-depth knowledge of individual reactions to trauma. They can provide educators information that is useful in structuring classroom activities and providing for expectations. Ultimately, this interchange can result in classroom experiences that reinforce therapeutic goals.

Release of information. Where possible, obtain permission from parents for open communication with school personnel. Then, provide educators with a signed release-of-information form. Be clear about the limits of confidentiality affecting school employees.

Intervention recommendations. Give strategies for intervening with students or their classes, including rationales, contingencies, and considerations for dealing with the crisis. Help educators explore and implement strategies.

Range of likely reactions. Inform educators of possible reactive behavior that they may anticipate in students. This can include what to look out for and what is and is not likely to be serious.

Level of pressure students can tolerate; how much support they need. Provide educators with an estimate of the students' capability of tolerating challenging tasks and their need for support. Work and interaction can be balanced accordingly.

Ways to work with the family. Suggest options and strategies for working productively with the family in the interests of the student. Administrators and teachers frequently have considerable contact with families and can have considerable effect.

Perspective. Help educators put the student's experiences and reactions into a meaningful context. Let them know how serious the response is or isn't and how resilient the children are.

Support. Provide personal support for teachers. Take time to listen, and give feedback about expressed reactions. Avoid making assumptions based on limited observations.

Recommendations to reinforce therapy. Suggest various classroom activities and learning experiences that further the goals of therapy. Activities can cross disciplinary lines (e.g., English, social studies, health) and utilize various means (e.g., writing, artwork, enactment, discussion).

Alternative explanations of behavior. Provide different ways of explaining, interpreting, and understanding the student's behavioral responses to crisis, including distractibility, lack of focus, hyperactivity, and preoccupation.

Professional services to the educator. Let the educator know that having intense reactions is normal, that crisis events can bring up personal unfinished business and stress current family functioning. Offer your professional services, or let the educator know where such services are available.

Realistic expectations. Provide a realistic appraisal of what the educator can expect of the child in terms of academic, behavioral, and social functioning, both immediately and in the long run. Emphasize that such projections are strictly tentative and depend on background, personal, and support variables.

Specific skills the child may need. Pass on observations of the child's need for coping and adaptive skills. Present a variety of techniques appropriate to the classroom setting that might help the child develop those skills.

Signs of child abuse or family dysfunction. Communicate observations and concerns about any signs of abuse or dysfunction. Request collaborative observations from teachers and assist in reporting and/or intervention.

Changes in the child. If the therapist has had greater precrisis contact with the child than the school has, the therapist should provide observations of cognitive, physical, and emotional changes since the crisis, including the length of time the problem behavior has existed.

Family information. To the extent it would be helpful and confidentiality allows, share background information regarding the student's history, his or her family, and the precipitating events.

Family as a resource. Let educators know the assessment of the extent the family supports the child and the school and whether the family can be utilized as a resource.

Assessing stage of recovery. Update educators about the student's stage of recovery. Provide periodic progress reports to teacher; treat teacher or support personnel as part of the recovery team.

Structure and discipline recommendations. Give recommendations regarding the child's disciplinary and social structure needs. These can include performance expectations, ways in which the class can be supportive, and disciplinary systems that take the child's vulnerability into account.

Visibility and availability. Be accessible; make availability apparent. Avoid intrusiveness, but be present enough that professionals can contact you spontaneously.

Parental involvement. Help parents become involved in their child's recovery and adjustment at school. Coach teachers in orchestrating an outreach to affected families, either directly or indirectly through take-home material.

Empowerment techniques. Let teachers know various ways they can give the child an increased sense of control and mastery over the situation. Focus on exploring situational management strategies and building awareness of personal power.

Medication information. If the child takes medications, explain the purpose of the medications as well as any side effects. In addition, let educators know about the process of establishing the correct dosage and the need for both patience and feedback regarding the process.

Mediation and facilitation between parent, child, and teacher. Become an "outside party" to assist parents, teachers, and other adults in resolving conflicts or increasing communication. Work toward establishing alternative means of addressing personal needs or working out relational issues.

Guidelines for handling certain children. While classroom management is the educator's domain of expertise, therapists can provide guidelines for handling certain children or certain groups of children.

Resource information. Direct educators to community resources that might be useful for the teacher, the parents, or the family. These may include specialized or low-cost counseling, facilities, or programs.

What Educators Can Provide Therapists

While educators do not normally possess the training therapists receive to understand and deal with human pain, they have much to contribute. First, they spend far more time with students than do therapists. Second, they orchestrate students' social milieu. Third, they observe students in a far more natural setting. Consequently, they can provide therapists with key information and assistance. In return, the therapist's information, assistance, and attainment of therapeutic goals furthers the educator's own mission.

Release of information from parents. Proper releases let professionals discuss otherwise confidential information and allow transmission of the information. This flow encourages each professional to coordinate his or her efforts with the other.

Key incident preceding the behavior. Provide a detailed description of the incident. This incident should be described in terms of events leading up to it, the incident itself, the student's role in the incident, the student's immediate reactions, and any interventions already done.

Behavior of the child at school, home, and in different environments. Educators spend more time with children than therapists and see them in varied contexts. Thus, they can provide detailed and realistic assessments of the child's behavior.

Context and circumstances in which problem behavior occurs. Similarly, descriptions and assessments of functioning can include detailed information regarding the context and circumstances in which particular behavior occurs, as well as any current behavior management strategies used with the child.

Family dynamics. Within the limits of confidentiality, provide therapists with observations of family functioning, particularly regarding issues that you believe affect the child's emotional well-being, performance, functioning, and recovery from crisis. In particular, attend to issues of psychological support.

Peer dynamics. Assess and let the therapist know about the child's social relationships. Determine the extent to which those relationships support and are conducive to recovery.

School and health records, medical history. Within the bounds of confidentiality and with parental permission, pass on school and health records that may be germane to understanding the child's reaction or that may bear on the progress of recovery.

Apparent discrepancies between emotions and behavior in school. Discrepancies between emotions and behavior can indicate serious reactions. Pass on information about such suspected discrepancies, which can be valuable to therapists.

Behavioral changes. Cite behavioral changes the child exhibits in class or that are reported by others. Indicate when observations are secondhand. Emphasize changes that have occurred since the incident; update as observations indicate new patterns.

Socialization skills. Let therapists know about the child's level of socialization. They may find useful information in the child's patterns of interaction with peers and adults, particularly any changes in behavior following the crisis.

Information on special stresses. Special stressors can impact both recovery and recovery-related school behavior. Educators are often privy to ongoing changes in home and social situations; such information can then be forwarded to the therapist.

Estimate of child's self-esteem. Give the therapist an indication of the child's self-esteem. Provide anecdotal descriptions that support the assessment when possible. Focus on the child's self-image and self-esteem as a personal resource during recovery.

Frequency of problem behavior. Chart or otherwise document the frequency of problem behaviors that affect classroom functioning. Let the therapist know of these behaviors, with reference to precrisis baseline levels.

Behavioral observations and descriptions in very specific terms. Explain all observations in specific terms. Distinguish between observations and impressions or interpretations. Reference behaviors to their context, with attention to particular situations that seem to precede behaviors.

Differences from other classmates. Because therapists deal primarily with individuals, they sometimes need to be oriented to peer and cohort norms. Contrast the referred student's behavior and functioning with that of his or her classmates.

Positive reinforcers and discipline systems that work. Any information that orients therapists to successful management strategies with the student can be very helpful. In particular, tell them of discipline methods and reinforcers that have worked in the past.

Which recommendations work. Information regarding therapists' recommendations that have proved helpful is very valuable in the process of fine-tuning both therapeutic and school interventions. This information should be fed back to the therapists from the educators who experience the results day after day.

Communication patterns. School staff, particularly classroom teachers, usually have extensive experience dealing with individual students. They are in the best position to relate communication patterns and techniques that work with the child.

Referring teacher's home number. Teachers are very difficult to reach for case conferencing, and therapists' high-traffic hours—late afternoon—usually coincide with teacher preparation time. This makes conferencing very difficult. Although evening calls are draining for everyone, they may be the only possible times to share information.

Baseline behavior prior to trauma. It is critical for therapists to know what the student's behavior was prior to the crisis. If the behavior was as extreme before the crisis as after, assume the crisis had less effect.

Testing results. The usefulness of any student testing results done at school is hard to foresee. But such results may provide useful data for determining the effectiveness of different therapeutic approaches or the appropriateness of therapeutic goals.

Staff reactions. Feelings and reactions in staff evoked by the child's behavior can be useful information to the therapist, whether or not the therapist works with the staff. The staff's reactions can mirror more subtle conditions in the student often missed by normal observational reports.

The school's expectations of the therapist. Schools refer students to therapists for particular reasons and usually they have expectations for the outcome of the therapy. Communicating such expectations at the outset helps therapists define their task more quickly.

Attendance and parent contacts. Attendance and parent contact records provide therapists with insight into the family's support for the child's school efforts. In addition, they may give clues about family issues and functioning.

Special education records. Special education testing and records of service may give therapists valuable insight into student needs. The therapeutic approach can be varied to take these needs into account.

Perceptions of testing needs. Schools generally cannot administer psychological tests that are not directly related to academic learning, but school personnel are often aware of specific testing needs that they cannot provide. Informing therapists about these needs facilitates their gathering of helpful data.

Learning modality. Information regarding learning modality assists therapists in designing clinical intervention. Pass on basic modality information (auditory, visual, kinesthetic), as well as information about particular activities or instructional vehicles that have been successful with the student.

Resources available through school. Let therapists know what services (such as resource teachers, language specialists, special education, health services, home tutorial, technical support, groups, and counselors) are available through the school.

Appendix II:
Crisis Consultant's Checklist

PROVIDE ADEQUATE CAMPUS SECURITY	COMMENTS
☐ Take measures to ensure physical security ☐ Gain input from police and emergency services ☐ Gain administrative approval for actions ☐ Inform staff of measures taken ☐ Provide brief inservice to staff on status ☐ Monitor staff reactions and leadership needs ☐ Provide buffer against unnecessary crisis-related stimuli ☐ Inform students, parents, community	
REESTABLISH ROUTINE	
☐ Resume normal class schedule ☐ Instruct staff regarding information ☐ Instruct teachers regarding class discussion ☐ Orchestrate crisis response with minimal disruption ☐ Isolate crisis response areas ☐ Provide catchment areas for distressed children	
CONTROL FLOW OF INFORMATION	
☐ Develop official narrative ☐ Manage incoming information ☐ Develop sources of information ☐ Liaison with central administration and linking agencies ☐ Designate spokesperson ☐ Manage reporters ☐ Manage rumors ☐ Respond to inquiries	

MONITOR & SUPPORT STAFF	COMMENTS
☐ Train in advance	
☐ Identify and monitor at-risk staff	
☐ Provide information	
☐ Maintain close supervisory contact	
☐ Provide relief as necessary	
☐ Arrange support services	
☐ Adapt management strategies	
☐ Provide informal training	
☐ Network	
IDENTIFY & MONITOR AT-RISK STUDENTS	
☐ Letters and fact sheets home	
☐ Coordinate schedule for periodic checking in	
☐ Personal contacts with parents	
☐ Attend to student talk	
☐ Train all staff to identify signs of distress and refer	
☐ Develop a referral system	
☐ Alert staff to monitor changes	
☐ Identify a case manager for monitoring	
☐ Create resource file for referring out	
☐ Centralize documentation	
PROVIDE CRISIS & GRIEF COUNSELING	
☐ Prepare staff	
☐ Have disaster response plans	
☐ Utilize CRT or other resources	
☐ Facilitate return to school	
☐ Provide individual support	
☐ Provide grief support groups	
☐ Organize memorials	
☐ Plan commemorative anniversaries	

TEACH STRESS MANAGEMENT	**COMMENTS**
☐ Teach teachers	
☐ Turn off TV in classroom	
☐ Protect students from information overload	
☐ Monitor classroom themes	
☐ Modify diet	
☐ Provide rest periods	
☐ Check out student perceptions	
☐ Incorporate stress management into curriculum	
PROVIDE OUTREACH TO HOMES	
☐ Provide crisis-related material	
☐ Encourage parent- or PTA-led meetings	
☐ Increase staff-parent conferencing	
☐ Sponsor parent emergency baby-sitting pool	
☐ Encourage visits to home by staff	
☐ Sponsor a parent newsletter	
☐ Increase conferencing for at-risk students	
☐ Send positive notes to home	
☐ Encourage parent volunteering	
☐ Invite parent participation in task force projects	
☐ Encourage updates on family	
PROVIDE SUPPORTIVE CLIMATE IN ALL CLASSROOMS	
☐ Provide support groups to at-risk students	
☐ Provide supportive in-class discussions	
☐ Ensure safe dialogue	
☐ Create opportunities for undirected expression	
☐ Use class projects that identify student with class	
☐ Utilize crisis-related art, writing, and enactment activities	
☐ Make crisis-related activities OPTIONAL	

BUILD COMMUNITY AT SCHOOL	COMMENTS
☐ Implement group-building activities in classes	
☐ Utilize school climate improvement activities on campus	
☐ Teach facilitation skills to all students	
☐ Provide extra training in crisis intervention skills to peer counselors	
☐ Introduce special section in student newspaper	
☐ Take on whole-school projects	
☐ Bring in outside speakers	
PROVIDE EMPOWERING ACTIVITIES	
☐ Infuse curricular activities that encourage expression	
☐ Take on community service projects	
☐ Provide clear information	
☐ Encourage letter writing	
☐ Sponsor fund-raising	
☐ Profile student contributions	
PROVIDE ONGOING SUPPORT	
☐ Provide ongoing psychological first aid	
☐ Increase conferencing	
☐ Develop school counseling program	
☐ Develop peer coaching/counseling program	
☐ Encourage community volunteers	
☐ Provide recognition	
☐ Encourage selective participation in special projects	
☐ Encourage physical activity	
☐ Provide after-school activities	
☐ Monitor home	

Appendix III:
Assessing Depressive Reactions

	"NORMAL" *Counseling helpful*	SUBACUTE *Needs referral for counseling; therapy necessary*	ACUTE *Emergency: needs immediate psychiatric evaluation for possible medication or hospitalization*
THINKING	Loss of meaning Lowering of interest in people, things Lack of concentration on routine tasks Dwelling on events of the past	Slowing Lack of interest in people, things Lack of focus Self-blame	Some disorientation as to time, place, person Some delusions regarding sin, guilt, disease Hyperresponsibility for events Interrupted thought process / speech
EMOTIONS	Numbness Discouragement Despair Frustration Anger Guilt	Dejection Hopelessness Low self-worth Feelings of failure Mood swings	Profound feelings of worthlessness Lack of feeling
PHYSICAL	Appetite loss Increased illness Psychosomatic illness	Weight loss, weakness Digestive disorders Menstrual irregularity Impotence / rigidity Unexplained pain	Slowing of physical functions
BEHAVIOR	Uncontrollable emotions in the work-place or in private Sleep loss or excessive sleeping Irritability Crying Helplessness	Slow motor skills Aimlessness Speaking in monotone Suicidal preoccupation; attempts possible Episodes of manic / hyperactive behavior Disheveled appearance Withdrawal	Increasingly slower motor skills Isolation Agitation; hand-wringing Mild hallucinations Manic episodes become irrational / ritualistic; unresponsive

Appendix IV:
Risk of Suicide Assessment

ISSUE	LOW RISK	MODERATE RISK	HIGH RISK
Anger / hostility	Mild	Moderate	Severe
Anxiety	Mild	Moderate	Severe / panic
Coping strategies	Constructive	Marginal	Destructive
Depression	Mild	Moderate	Severe
Disorientation / disorganization	None	Mild / moderate	Moderate / severe
Family / friends	Several available	One available	None available
Functioning	Good	Moderate	Poor
Ideation	Some vague	Frequent	Continual, specific
Lifestyle	Stable	Marginal	Unstable
Plan	Ideation /no plan	Vague plan	Specifice, lethal
Prior attempts	None	None or one with low lethality	Multiple or one with high lethality
Prior counseling	No history, or positive results	Yes, some reservations	Yes, views as negative
Resources	Adequate	Marginal	Inadequate
Substance use, abuse	Infrequent	Frequent, to excess	Continual abuse
Withdrawal	Mild withdrawal	Moderate withdrawal	Isolation

FAMILY MAPPING

Here are two family maps

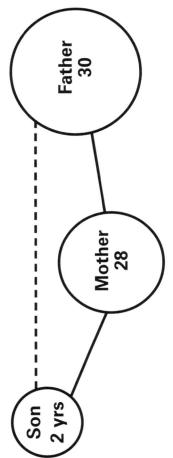

This family consists of three, mother being central, father close and more powerful, son closer to mother with broken communication with father.

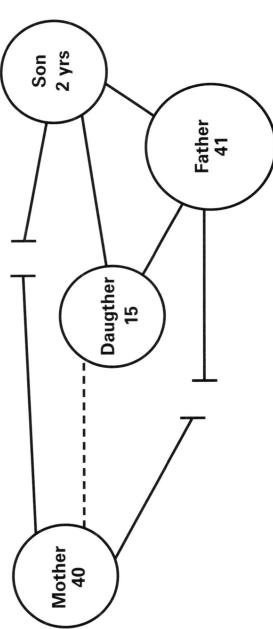

In this family, father is more powerful and central, and mother is estranged with only broken communication with daughter. Father, son, and daughter have a close relationship with solid communication

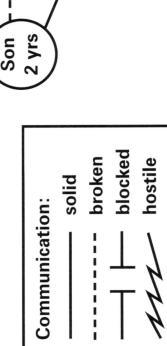

Communication:

——	solid
- - - -	broken
⊢⊣	blocked
/\/\/	hostile

1. Map your family before the crisis occurred.

2. Map your family a day or so after the crisis.

3. Map your family a week to a month after the crisis.

4. Map your family after it restabilized or as it is now (indicate which).

PSYCHOLOGICAL EFFECTS OF NATURAL DISASTER

	Clinical	Sociological
Orientation	Clinical	Sociological
Leading Researchers	Fredericks Figley Tichner	Quarentelli Drabek Tierney
Leading Institutions	NIMH	DRC
Types of Effects	Extensive clinical effects: ASR / DSR / PTSD	Some limited subclinical effects largely due to inefficient relief efforts
Duration	Long lasting	Transient
Scope	25% or more ASR 10% or more debilitating DSR	Little or no dysfunction ASR or DSR related to traumatic effects of the event

School Crisis Management © *2000 Kendall Johnson, Ph.D.*

References

American Psychiatric Association. 1980. *Diagnostic and Statistical Manual of Mental Disorders*. 3rd ed. Washington D.C.: APA.

American Psychiatric Association. 1987. *Diagnostic and Statistical Manual of Mental Disorders*. 3rd ed., rev. Washington D.C.: APA.

American Psychiatric Association. 1994. *Diagnostic and Statistical Manual of Mental Disorders*. 4th ed. Washington, D.C.: APA.

Ayalon, O. 1979. "Community Oriented Preparation for Emergency: COPE." *Death Education* 3 (4):222–244.

Ayalon, O. 1992. *Rescue: Community Oriented Prevention Education for Coping with Stress*. Ellicott City, MD: Chevron Publishing Corporation.

Ayalon, O. 1993. "Post Traumatic Stress Recovery." In *International Handbook of Traumatic Stress Syndromes*, ed. J. Wilson and B. Raphael, 855–66. New York: Plenum Press.

Ayalon, O. 1997. "Creative Methods Offered to Caregivers to Prevent or Deal with Secondary Traumatization." In *Trauma Recovery and Training*, ed. D. Ajdukovic. Zagreb, Croatia: Society for Psychological Assistance.

Ayalon, O. 1998. "Community Healing for Children Traumatized by War." *International Review of Psychiatry* 10:248–257.

Ayalon, O., M. Lahad, and A. Cohen, eds. 1998. *Community Stress Prevention* 3.

Ayalon, O., M. Lahad, and A. Cohen, eds. 1999. *Community Stress Prevention* 4.

Donaldson, M. A., and R. Gardner. 1985. "Diagnosis and Treatment of Traumatic Stress among Women after Childhood Incest." In *Trauma and Its Wake,* ed. C. Figley. New York: Brunner/Mazel.

Erikson, E. 1968. *Identity, Youth and Crisis*. New York: Norton.

Eth, S., and R. Pynoos. 1985. "Developmental Perspective on Psychic Trauma in Childhood." In *Trauma and Its Wake,* ed. C. Figley. New York: Brunner/Mazel.

Everly, G. 1989. *A Clinical Guide to the Treatment of the Human Stress Disorder.* New York: Plenum Press.

Everly, G. S., and J. Lating, eds. 1995. *Psychotraumatology: Key Papers and Core Concepts in Psychological Trauma*. New York: Plenum.

Everly, G., and J. Mitchell. 1999. *Critical Incident Stress Management*. Ellicott City, MD: Chevron Publishing Company.

Figley, C. 1995. *Compassion Fatigue: Coping With Secondary Traumatic Stress Disorder In Those Who Treat The Traumatized*. New York: Brunner/Mazel.

Freud, S. 1920. "Beyond the Pleasure Principle." In *Standard Edition* 18, ed. J. Strachey. London: Hogarth Press.

Freud, S. 1926/1959. "Inhibitions, Symptoms and Anxiety." In *Standard Edition* 20, ed. J. Strachey. London: Hogarth Press.

Horowitz, M. 1975. "A Prediction of Delayed Stress Response Syndromes in Vietnam Veterans." *Journal of Social Issues* 31:67–80.

Horowitz, M. 1976. *Stress Response Syndromes.* New York: Jason Aronson.

Johnson, K. 1999. *Trauma in the Lives of Children.* Alameda, CA: Hunter House.

Johnson, K., D. Casey, B. Ertl, G. Everly, and J. Mitchell. 1999. *School Crisis Response: A CISM Perspective.* Ellicott City, MD: Chevron Publishing Company.

Kübler-Ross, E. 1969. *On Death and Dying.* New York: Macmillan.

Lahad, M. 1997. "BASIC Ph: The Story of Coping Resources." In *Community Stress Prevention* O. Ayalon, M. Lahad, and A. Cohen (eds.) 1 2:117–145.

McCann, L., and L. A. Pearlman. 1990. "Vicarious Traumatization: A Framework for Understanding the Psychological Effects of Working with Victims." *Journal of Traumatic Stress* 3 (1):131–149.

Mitchell, J. 1983. "When Disaster Strikes: The Critical Incident Stress Debriefing Process." *Journal of Emergency Services* 8:36–39.

Mohandie, K., and G. Boles. 1999. "School Violence Prevention for Educators, Mental Health, and Law Enforcement." Los Angeles: Los Angeles County Office of Education

Pearlman, L. A., and K. Saakvitne. 1995. *Trauma and the Therapist: Countertransference and Vicarious Traumatization in Psychotherapy with Incest Survivors.* New York: W.W. Norton.

Pynoos, R., and K. Nader. 1988. "Psychological First Aid and Treatment Approaches to Children Exposed to Community Violence: Research and Implications." *Journal of Traumatic Stress* I (4):445-473.

Quarantelli, E., and R. Dynes. 1976. "Community Conflict: Its Absence and Its Presence in Natural Disasters." *Mass Emergencies* 1:139–52.

Scurfield, R. 1985. "Post-trauma Stress Assessment and Treatment: Overview and Formulations." In *Trauma and Its Wake,* ed. C. Figley. New York: Brunner/Mazel.

Trimble, M. 1985. "Post-Traumatic Stress Disorder: History of a Concept." In *Trauma and Its Wake,* ed. C. Figley. New York: Brunner/Mazel.

Van der Kolk, B., A. McFarlane, and L. Weisaeth. 1996. *Traumatic Stress: The Effects of Overwhelming Experience on Mind, Body, and Society.* New York: Guilford Press.

Wilson, J. 1978. *Identity, Ideology and Crisis: The Vietnam Veteran in Transition.* 2 vols. Washington, D.C.: Disabled American Veterans.

ELEMENTS OF CRISIS

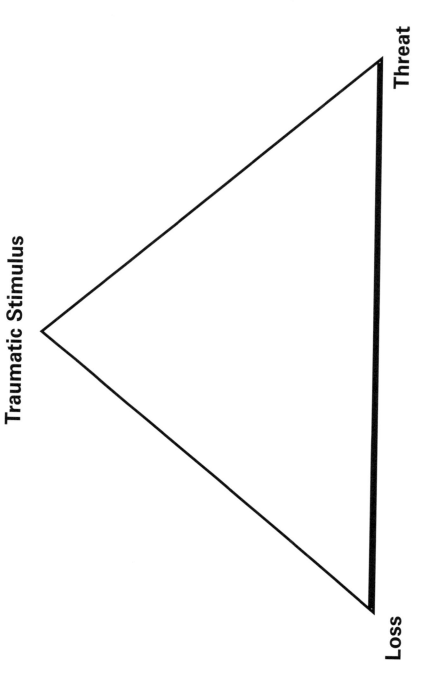

Traumatic Stimulus

Threat

Loss

School Crisis Management © 2000 Kendall Johnson, Ph.D.

Figure 1-1

REACTIONS TO CRITICAL INCIDENTS

The more extensive the impact of an event upon our lives (in terms of both threat to our basic needs and intensity of the experience) the greater our response at the time and later.

School Crisis Management © 2000 Kendall Johnson, Ph.D.

Figure 1-2

REACTIONS TO CRITICAL INCIDENTS

INITIAL REACTION

- Capacity to cope overwhelmed
- Heightened suggestibility and negative learning
- Fear and inadequacy

SECONDARY REACTION

- Cognitive
  - negative expectations
  - negative judgments
  - negative sets
  - impairments
- Emotional
  - under- or overreactivity
  - lowered self-esteem
- Physical
  - psychosomatic illness
- Behavioral
  - maladaptive coping efforts

School Crisis Management © 2000 Kendall Johnson, Ph.D.

Figure 1-3

REACTIONS TO CRITICAL INCIDENTS

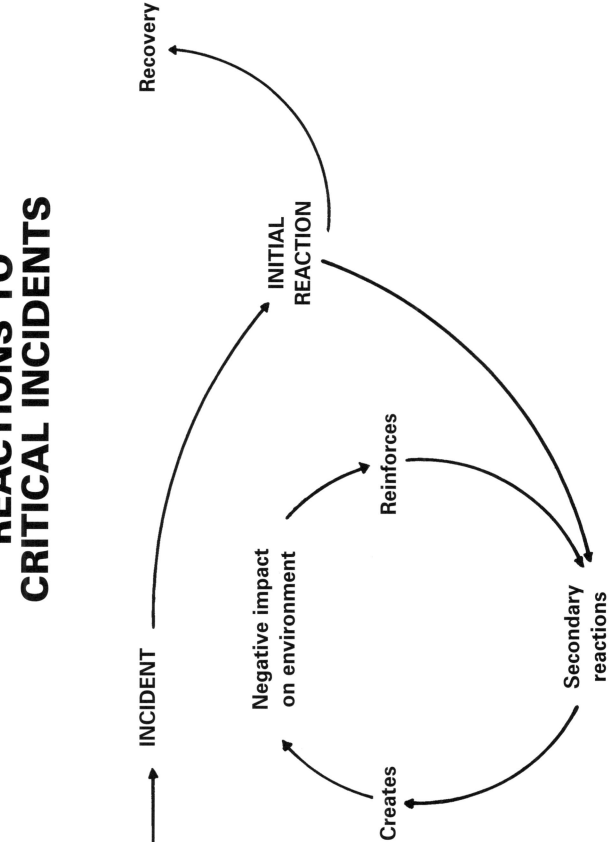

INCIDENT → INITIAL REACTION

Recovery

Negative impact on environment

Reinforces

Secondary reactions

Creates

School Crisis Management © 2000 Kendall Johnson, Ph.D.

Figure 1-4

ASR, DSR, AND PTSD

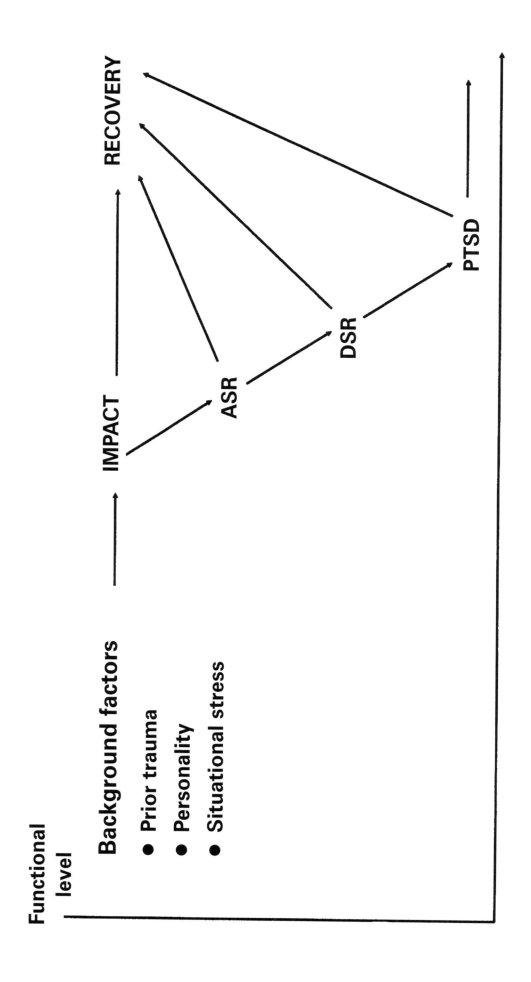

School Crisis Management © 2000 Kendall Johnson, Ph.D.

Figure 1-5

DURING THE INCIDENT

COGNITIVE SIGNS

- Confusion
- Difficulty solving problems
- Trouble prioritizing
- Time distortions
- Memory loss
- Anomia
- Dissociation

PHYSICAL SIGNS

- Headache
- Heart palpitations
- Nausea
- Cramps
- Profuse sweating
- Rapid breathing
- Faintness
- Other signs of shock

Figure 1-6

DURING THE INCIDENT

EMOTIONAL

- Fear
- Anxiety
- Anger
- Irritability
- Frustration

BEHAVIORAL

- Slowing
- Aimless wandering
- Dejection
- Hysteria
- Memory problems
- Hyperactivity
- Muffled hearing

School Crisis Management © *2000 Kendall Johnson, Ph.D.*

Figure 1-7

AFTER THE INCIDENT

COGNITIVE

- Fear of going crazy
- Preoccupation with incident
- Orientation toward past
- Denial of incident's importance
- Problems concentrating

PHYSICAL

- Fatigue
- Psychosomatic symptoms
- Increased illness
- Physical concerns

Figure 1-8

AFTER THE INCIDENT

EMOTIONAL

- Depression
- Grief
- Numbing
- Resentment / rage
- Guilt
- Fear of recurrence
- Phobic reactions

BEHAVIORAL

- Substance abuse
- Self-destructive behavior
- Sudden lifestyle change
- Social withdrawal
- Sleep disorders
- Compulsive talking
- Avoidant behavior
- Problems at work
- Family problems
- Flashbacks, nightmares, or other intrusive imagery

School Crisis Management © 2000 Kendall Johnson, Ph.D.

Figure 1-9

VULNERABILITY FACTORS

- Prior trauma

- Background stress

- Family disruption

- Feelings of inadequacy

- Psychological need

- Physical fatigue

- Recent changes, losses

- Overly optimistic or pessimistic attitude

- Certain beliefs

Figure 1-10

POSTTRAUMATIC STRESS DISORDER
(APA, DSM-IV)

A. Exposure to traumatic event

B. Reexperience of event

C. Avoidance and numbing

D. Inappropriate arousal

E. Distress or impairment of functioning

Acute: duration <3 months

Chronic: duration >3 months

Delayed: onset >6 months

School Crisis Management © *2000 Kendall Johnson, Ph.D.*

Figure 1-11

CRITERION B:
EVENT REEXPERIENCED

One of:

1. Recollections, repetitive play

2. Dreams

3. Feelings of recurrence, reenactment

4. Psychological distress to internal / external cues

5. Physiological reactivity to internal / external cues

School Crisis Management © 2000 Kendall Johnson, Ph.D.

Figure 1-12

CRITERION C:
AVOIDANCE AND NUMBING

Three of:

AVOIDANCE OF:

1. Associated thoughts and feelings
2. Similar situations

NUMBING:

3. Amnesia
4. Diminished interest in significant activities; regressive behavior
5. Detachment
6. Constricted affect
7. Foreshortened future

Figure 1-13

CRITERION D:
INAPPROPRIATE AROUSAL

Two of:

PROBLEMS WITH:

1. Sleeping
2. Irritability
3. Concentration
4. Hypervigilance
5. Startle response

Figure 1-14

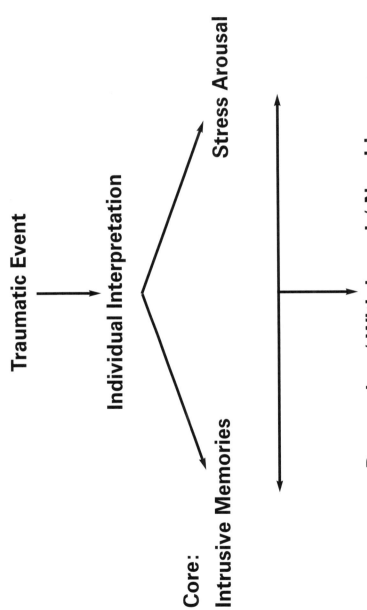

PTSD:
NEUROPHYSIOLOGICAL MODEL

(Everly and Lating 1995)

Premise: lowered activation threshold
of limbic (arousal) system

Traumatic Event

Individual Interpretation

Stress Arousal

Core:
Intrusive Memories

Depression / Withdrawal / Numbing

School Crisis Management © *2000 Kendall Johnson, Ph.D.*

Figure 1-15

CRISIS AND DEVELOPMENT

(Erickson 1968; Wilson 1978)

STAGE	CRISIS	REGRESSIVE ATTRIBUTE
Infancy	Trust	Mistrust: anxiety, dependency, withdrawal
Play age	Autonomy	Shame / doubt: overcontrol, impulsiveness, helplessness
Younger school age	Initiative	Guilt: loss of purpose and rootedness, need for protectors
Older school age	Industry	Inferiority: futility, work paralysis, incompetence
Adolescence	Identity	Identity diffusion: lack of commitment, self-consciousness, prolonged moratorium

Figure 1-16

CHILDREN'S IMMEDIATE REACTIONS TO TRAUMA

(adapted from Eth and Pynoos 1985)

- Disorganization
- Primitivization
- Deverbalization
- Somatization

Figure 1-17

CHILDREN'S
ACUTE STRESS REACTIONS TO TRAUMA

(adapted from Eth and Pynoos 1985)

HYPOACTIVE

- Appearance
  — pale
  — submissive
  — shocklike

- Affect
  — blunted
  — numb

- Behavior
  — slowed
  — automatic
  — paralyzed
  — immobilized

HYPERACTIVE

- Appearance
  — flushed
  — sweating
  — agitated

- Affect
  — panicked
  — enraged
  — "hysterical"

- Behavior
  — rapid / frenzied
  — ineffectual
  — uncontrolled

Figure 1-18

School Crisis Management © 2000 Kendall Johnson, Ph.D.

CHILDREN'S POSTTRAUMA SIGNS PRESCHOOL / KINDERGARTEN

COGNITIVE SIGNS

- Shorter attention span
- Confusion regarding
  - event
  - locations
  - sequencing
  - death

PHYSICAL SIGNS

- Loss of appetite
- Overeating
- Bowel / bladder problems
- Sleeping disturbances

Figure 1-19

CHILDREN'S POSTTRAUMA SIGNS PRESCHOOL / KINDERGARTEN

(continued)

EMOTIONAL

- Generalized fears
- Nervousness, anxiety
- Irritability
- Fearful of reminders

BEHAVIORAL

- Bedwetting
- Thumbsucking
- Nightmares
- Repetitive play, reenacting trauma
- Anxious attachment, clinging
- Aggression, disobedience

Figure 1-20

CHILDREN'S POSTTRAUMA SIGNS
ELEMENTARY

COGNITIVE SIGNS

- Confusion regarding

  — event

  — sequencing

- Inability to concentrate

PHYSICAL SIGNS

- Complaints (vision, stomach)

- Headaches

- Nausea

- Itching

- Sleeping disturbances

Figure 1-21

CHILDREN'S POSTTRAUMA SIGNS ELEMENTARY

(continued)

EMOTIONAL

- Fear of recurrence, related stimuli
- Wanting to be fed, dressed
- School phobia, avoidance of large groups
- Responsibility, guilt over performance
- Aggression
- Overconcern for family safety

BEHAVIORAL

- Clinging
- Resumption of outgrown habits
- Competition with siblings
- Repetitive talking, reenacting incident
- Disobedience
- Drop in school performance
- Nightmares

School Crisis Management © 2000 Kendall Johnson, Ph.D.

Figure 1-22

CHILDREN'S POSTTRAUMA SIGNS
MIDDLE SCHOOL / SENIOR HIGH SCHOOL

COGNITIVE SIGNS

- Problems concentrating
- Overconcern regarding health

PHYSICAL SIGNS

- Headaches
- Vague complaints, pains
- Skin rashes
- Loss of appetite, overeating

Figure 1-23

CHILDREN'S POSTTRAUMA SIGNS
MIDDLE SCHOOL / SENIOR HIGH SCHOOL
(continued)

EMOTIONAL

- Depression
- Anxiety

BEHAVIORAL

- Can't meet responsibilities
- Resumes earlier coping styles
- Emancipation setback
- Social withdrawal
- Antisocial behavior
- Survival guilt
- Drug, alcohol abuse
- Drop in school performance
- Sudden changes in
  - attitudes
  - lifestyles
  - relationships
- "Too old too soon"
- Precipitous life decisions (dropping out, pregnancy, marriage)

Figure 1-24

School Crisis Management © 2000 Kendall Johnson, Ph.D.

SOME EFFECTS OF TRAUMA ON LEARNING

1. ADHD students have disproportionate rates of prior trauma; posttrauma behavior mimics ADHD

2. Heightened physiological arousal disturbs concentration

3. Heightened startle reflex disrupts attention

4. Regression and reenactments interfere with socialization

5. Memory difficulties frustrate retention and retrieval

6. Dissociative reactions affect attention

7. Behavior caused by dissociation and attention and concentration difficulties is interpreted as a conduct and discipline issue

8. Preoccupation with traumatic experience disengages child from schooling process

School Crisis Management © *2000 Kendall Johnson, Ph.D.*

Figure 1-25

STAFF / CLASSROOM RESPONSE

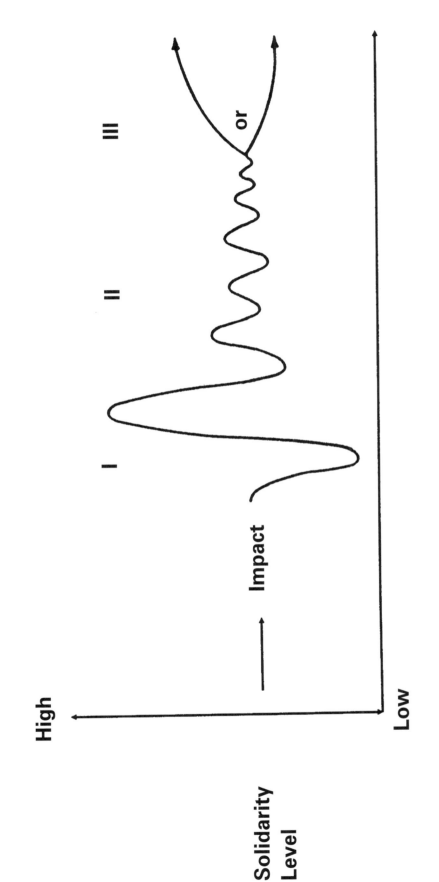

I = Recoil

II = Reorganization

III = Restabilization

Figure 1-26   *School Crisis Management © 2000 Kendall Johnson, Ph.D.*

ORGANIZATIONAL INDICATORS OF CRISIS

PROCESS DYNAMICS

- Contractual disputes
- Role rigidity
- Homeostatic resistance
- Distance polarity

CONTENT DYNAMICS

Changes in patterns of

- Attachment
- Affiliation
- Values
- Goals
- Beliefs

School Crisis Management © *2000 Kendall Johnson, Ph.D.*

Figure 1-27

SCHOOL CRISIS MANAGEMENT: GOALS AND OBJECTIVES

1. Provide adequate campus security

2. Reestablish routine

3. Control flow of information

4. Monitor and support staff

5. Identify and monitor at-risk students

6. Provide crisis and grief counseling

7. Teach stress management

8. Provide outreach to homes

9. Provide supportive classroom climate

10. Build community at school

11. Provide empowering activities

12. Provide ongoing support

Figure 2-1   *School Crisis Management © 2000 Kendall Johnson, Ph.D.*   153

PROVIDE ADEQUATE CAMPUS SECURITY

- Take measures to ensure physical safety

- Gain input from police and emergency services

- Gain administrative approval for actions

- Inform staff of measures taken

- Provide brief inservice to staff on status

- Monitor staff reactions and leadership needs

- Provide buffer against unnecessary crisis-related stimuli

- Inform students, parents, and community of security measures

Figure 2-2   *School Crisis Management © 2000 Kendall Johnson, Ph.D.*   154

REESTABLISH ROUTINE

- Resume normal class schedule

- Instruct staff regarding procedures to be followed

- Instruct teachers regarding class discussion

- Orchestrate crisis response with minimal disruption

- Isolate crisis response areas

- Provide catchment areas for distressed children

Figure 2-3   *School Crisis Management © 2000 Kendall Johnson, Ph.D.*   155

CONTROL FLOW OF INFORMATION

- Develop official narrative

- Manage incoming information

- Develop sources of information

- Liaison with central administration and linking agencies

- Designate spokesperson

- Manage reporters

- Manage rumors

- Respond to inquiries

Figure 2-4   *School Crisis Management © 2000 Kendall Johnson, Ph.D.*   156

MONITOR AND SUPPORT STAFF

- Train in advance

- Identify and monitor at-risk staff

- Provide information

- Maintain close supervisory contact

- Provide relief as necessary

- Arrange support services

- Adapt management strategies

- Provide informal training

- Network among staff, other schools, and community resources

Figure 2-5   *School Crisis Management © 2000 Kendall Johnson, Ph.D.*   157

IDENTIFY AND MONITOR AT–RISK STUDENTS

- Send letters and fact sheets home

- Coordinate schedule for periodic checking in

- Personal contacts with parents

- Attend to student talk

- Train all staff to identify signs of distress and refer

- Develop a referral system

- Alert staff to monitor changes

- Identify a "case manager" for monitoring

- Create resource file for referring out

- Centralize documentation

Figure 2-6   *School Crisis Management © 2000 Kendall Johnson, Ph.D.*   158

PROVIDE CRISIS AND GRIEF COUNSELING

- Prepare staff

- Have disaster response plans

- Utilize CRT or other resources

- Facilitate return to school

- Provide individual support

- Provide grief support groups

- Organize memorials

- Commemorate anniversaries

Figure 2-7   *School Crisis Management © 2000 Kendall Johnson, Ph.D.*   159

TEACH
STRESS MANAGEMENT

- **Teach teachers**

- **Turn off TV in classroom**

- **Protect students from information overload**

- **Monitor classroom themes**

- **Modify diet**

- **Provide rest periods**

- **Check out student perceptions**

- **Incorporate stress management into curriculum**

Figure 2-8   *School Crisis Management © 2000 Kendall Johnson, Ph.D.*   160

PROVIDE OUTREACH
TO HOMES

- Provide crisis-related material

- Encourage parent- or PTA-led meetings

- Increase staff-parent conferencing

- Sponsor parent emergency baby-sitting pool

- Visits to home by staff

- Sponsor a parent newsletter

- Increased conferencing for at-risk students

- Send positive notes to home

- Encourage parent volunteering

- Invite parent participation in task force projects

- Encourage updates on family

Figure 2-9   *School Crisis Management © 2000 Kendall Johnson, Ph.D.*   161

PROVIDE SUPPORTIVE CLIMATE IN ALL CLASSROOMS

- Provide support groups to at-risk students

- Provide supportive in-class discussions

- Ensure safe dialogue

- Create opportunities for undirected expression

- Use class projects that identify student with class

- Utilize crisis-related art, writing, and enactment activities

- Make crisis-related activities OPTIONAL

BUILD COMMUNITY AT SCHOOL

- Implement group-building activities in classes

- Utilize school climate improvement activities on campus

- Teach facilitation skills to all students

- Provide extra training in crisis intervention skills to peer counselors

- Introduce special section in student newspaper

- Take on whole–school projects

- Bring in outside speakers

PROVIDE
EMPOWERING ACTIVITIES

- Infuse curricular activities that encourage expression

- Take on community service projects

- Provide clear information

- Encourage letter writing

- Sponsor fund-raising

- Profile student contributions

- Provide support during recovery period

PROVIDE ONGOING SUPPORT

- Provide ongoing psychological first aid

- Increase conferencing

- Develop school counseling program

- Develop peer coaching / counseling program

- Encourage community volunteers

- Provide recognition

- Encourage selective participation in special projects

- Encourage physical activity

- Provide after-school activities

- Monitor home

CENTRALIZED CRISIS RESPONSE TEAM

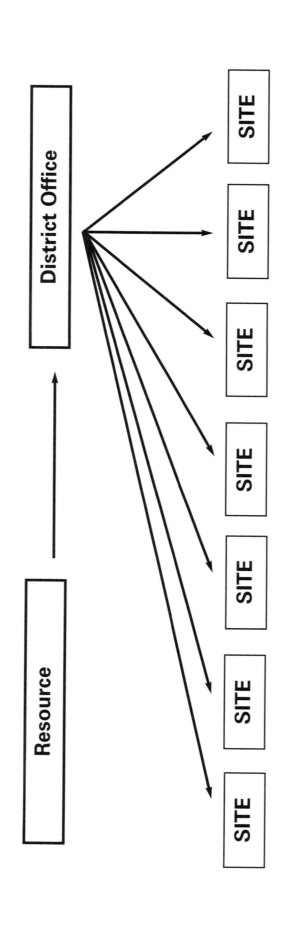

Resource → **District Office**

SITE | SITE | SITE | SITE | SITE | SITE | SITE

ADVANTAGES

Administrative control

Quality control

Efficiency (in small incidents)

DISADVANTAGES

Easily overwhelmed

Site dependency

Underutilizes outside resources
and expertise

Figure 3-1

School Crisis Management © 2000 Kendall Johnson, Ph.D.

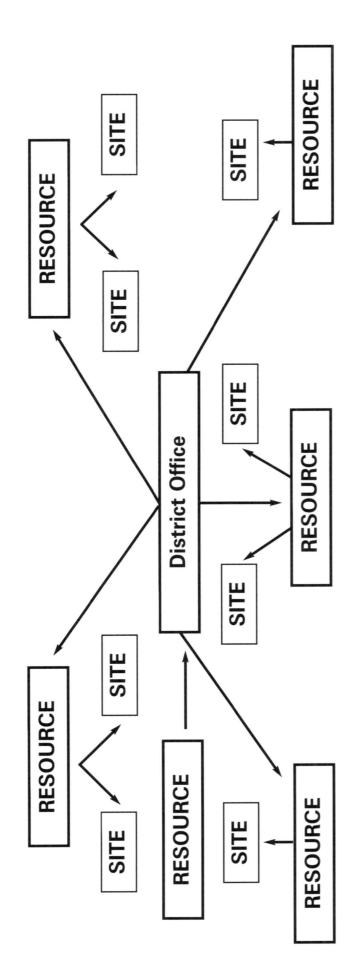

DECENTRALIZED CRISIS RESPONSE TEAM

RESOURCE

SITE

SITE

SITE

RESOURCE

SITE

District Office

SITE

RESOURCE

SITE

RESOURCE

SITE

SITE

RESOURCE

SITE

RESOURCE

DISADVANTAGES

Increased training cost

Lowered quality control

Lowered administrative control

Lowered efficiency (in small incidents)

ADVANTAGES

Resource availability

Site empowerment

Utilization of outside expertise

Figure 3-2

School Crisis Management © *2000 Kendall Johnson, Ph.D.*

CRISIS RESPONSE TEAM STRATEGIES

1. Administrative consultation

2. Staff consultation

3. Informational briefing and fact sheets for home

4. Parent meetings

5. Identification of community, school resources

6. Liaison

7. Individual consultation and assessment

8. Parent consultation

9. Classroom discussion, defusing, debriefing

10. Classroom follow-up activities

Figure 3-3

School Crisis Management © 2000 Kendall Johnson, Ph.D.

CRT STRATEGY 1: ADMINISTRATIVE CONSULTATION

TARGET

District and site administrators

PURPOSE

1. Assess functioning

2. Input situational assessment

3. Facilitate planning

4. Empower leadership

METHOD

One-one-one, small group

CONSIDERATIONS

1. Recognize administrator's vulnerability and stress

2. Do not undermine authority

3. Observe for ASR, dysfunction

4. Assist with self-assessment, self-management

5. Consider recommendations regarding unfitness only as last resort

---

Figure 3-4 *School Crisis Management © 2000 Kendall Johnson, Ph.D.* 169

CRT STRATEGY 2:
STAFF CONSULTATION

TARGET

Staff

PURPOSE

1. Assess functioning, feedback to administrator
2. Input information regarding situation, reactions, role
3. Provide resources, assistance, support
4. Refer to administrator or resources, if appropriate

METHOD

One-on-one; small, informal groups; didactic sessions; formal debriefings

CONSIDERATIONS

1. Staff must be empowered and supported to stabilize campus
2. Observe for ASR, dysfunction relative to duties
3. Offer assistance and information
4. Determine ability to provide necessary leadership and support to students
5. Determine openness to assistance

Figure 3-5   *School Crisis Management © 2000 Kendall Johnson, Ph.D.*   170

CRT STRATEGY 3: INFORMATIONAL BRIEFING AND FACT SHEETS

TARGET

All

PURPOSE

Provide information regarding:

1. Situation, explanation
2. Most recent actions taken by school
3. Possible reactions by students and steps to relieve them
4. Specific strategies to reinforce family support and stability
5. Resources through school or community

METHOD

Didactic presentation, fact sheets for distribution, media releases

CONSIDERATIONS

1. Keep information simple, direct, and current
2. Anticipate needs and questions
3. If didactic, leave time for questions, clarification
4. Gather information from variety of sources
5. Learn about rumors, provide clarification
6. Anticipate effect of information

Figure 3-6   *School Crisis Management © 2000 Kendall Johnson, Ph.D.*   171

CRT STRATEGY 4: PARENT MEETINGS

TARGET

Parents, guardians, interested community members

PURPOSE

Provide information regarding:

1. Situation, explanation
2. Update actions taken by school
3. Possible reactions by students and steps to relieve them
4. Specific recommendations to reinforce family support and stability
5. Resources through school or community

METHOD

Large group meeting, preferably on site

CONSIDERATIONS

1. Prepare for wide range of response and reaction
2. Be honest, be detailed
3. Have one spokesperson for school
4. Have high-level administrator (principal or above)
5. Have resource representatives available
6. (but don't turn meeting over to them)
7. Have plans set for managing media

Figure 3-7   *School Crisis Management © 2000 Kendall Johnson, Ph.D.*   172

CRT STRATEGY 5: IDENTIFICATION OF COMMUNITY, SCHOOL RESOURCES

TARGET

All

PURPOSE

1. Determine resources available through school and community for impacted staff, students, and families

2. Make information available to all who would benefit

METHOD

Inventory through district administration, community agencies

CONSIDERATIONS

1. Consider wide range of needs

2. Consider cost and availability

3. Determine how to access services

4. Determine contact persons, locations, and phones

5. Centralize and organize information

6. Disperse information to all who might benefit

Figure 3-8   *School Crisis Management © 2000 Kendall Johnson, Ph.D.*   173

CRT STRATEGY 6: LIAISON

TARGET

District administrators and community resources

PURPOSE

1. Facilitate flow of information between site, district, and outside
2. Facilitate access to resources as needed
3. Limit need for extraneous personnel at site

METHOD

Telephone and meeting between one designated district-level and one site-level administrator and appropriate outside resource spokespersons

CONSIDERATIONS

1. Do not interfere with normal chains of command
2. Do not undercut site-level authority
3. Insulate decision makers from unnecessary distraction
4. Facilitate important communication
5. Take into account issues of professional "face"

Figure 3-9   *School Crisis Management © 2000 Kendall Johnson, Ph.D.*   174

WHAT YOU MAY OBSERVE IN EMPLOYEES AND ADULT VICTIMS DURING AND IMMEDIATELY FOLLOWING A CRITICAL INCIDENT

Behavioral Signs

AGITATED

Frantic

Doing too much

Lack of follow-through

Lack of control

Rapid, broken speech

Emotionally overreactive

Panic

DEPRESSED

Slowed

Aimless wandering

Disconnected / detached

Overly controlled

Slow speech, mumbling

Emotionally underreactive

Dejection

Physical Signs

AGITATED

Flushed appearance

Sweating

Hyperventilation

Glassy stare

Vomiting

DEPRESSED

Pale appearance

Other signs of shock

Figure 3-10

School Crisis Management © 2000 Kendall Johnson, Ph.D.

WHAT YOU MAY OBSERVE IN EMPLOYEES AND ADULT VICTIMS IN THE WEEKS AND MONTHS FOLLOWING TRAUMA

- Seem disconnected / preoccupied

- Not as neat: dress and habits

- Late, absences, fatigued

- Low morale, change of attitude toward work

- Avoid certain situations / places

- Talk compulsively, or not at all about incident

- Irritable, conflicts with others, and possibly with you

- Drinking, drug use

- Sudden change in lifestyle

- Aches, pains, illnesses

- Unhappiness, dissatisfaction

School Crisis Management © *2000 Kendall Johnson, Ph.D.*

Figure 3-11

ASSESSING THREATS TO OTHERS: GENERAL FACTORS

- History of violence
- History of threats
- History of conflict and anger
- History of impulse control problems
- History of emotional instability
- Precipitating incident

This list is general and not to be construed as exhaustive; it is only a starting point for further inquiry. Significantly dangerous cases may not fit the profile.

School Crisis Management © *2000 Kendall Johnson, Ph.D.*

Figure 4-1

ASSESSING THREATS TO OTHERS: GENERAL SIGNS

- Credible witnesses of threat
- Inappropriately expressed anger
- Expressed or implied intent
- Bizarre thoughts or behavior
- Plans and preparation
- Threat / plans realistic
- Records, notes, records of conversation where threats are made

This list is general and not to be construed as exhaustive; it is only a starting point for further inquiry. Significantly dangerous cases may not fit the profile.

Figure 4-2

ASSESSING THREATS TO OTHERS: PROTOCOL

- Gain input from others who know and observe individual

- Look for corroborating evidence

- Establish contact, rapport

- Express concern

- Ask directly

DETERMINE

1. Was there a precipitating incident?

2. Are any significant predictive factors present?

3. Can the direct or indirect signs be collaborated?

4. Are there signs of distorted thinking?

5. Does the student have a plan?
   — Is it specific as to how?
   — Is it specific as to when?
   — Are the means available?
   — How lethal are the means?

This list is general and not to be construed as exhaustive; it is only a starting point for further inquiry. Significantly dangerous cases may not fit the profile.

Figure 4-3

School Crisis Management © 2000 Kendall Johnson, Ph.D.

CRT STRATEGY 7: INDIVIDUAL CONSULTATION AND ASSESSMENT

TARGET

All

PURPOSE

Assist Individuals in

1. Situational assessment and understanding
2. Determining responsibilities and roles
3. Assessing personal reactions and level of functioning
4. Planning for decision making

METHOD

Private conversation and crisis intervention

CONSIDERATIONS

1. Determine what decisions the individual must make
2. Keep consultation oriented to problem assessment and solution
3. Assess level of functioning relative to responsibilities and needs
4. Utilize basic crisis intervention format unless unnecessary
5. Assess need for direct vs. indirect suggestions and planning
6. Assess need for structured intervention and support

Figure 5-1   *School Crisis Management © 2000 Kendall Johnson, Ph.D.*   180

CRISIS INTERVENTION FORMAT

1. Build rapport, trust

2. Assess functioning

3. Define problem

4. Ventilate reaction

5. Explore resources

6. Teach stress management

7. Plan action

Figure 5-2

SAFER Model Protocol

(adapted for schools from Everly and Mitchell 1999)

STABILIZE THE SITUATION

1. Provide distance from the situation
2. Build alliance and encourage trust

ACKNOWLEDGE CRISIS

1. Facilitate talk about what happened
2. Establish cognitive set
3. Assist individual in articulating reaction
4. If safe, allow ventilation of reaction

FACILITATE UNDERSTANDING

1. Identify nature and implications of crisis
2. Reinforce cognitive processing
3. Frame reactions as "normal"

ENCOURAGE ADAPTIVE COPING

1. Assess ability to function (ongoing process)
2. Explore and identify coping skills
3. Explore personal, school, community resources

RESTORE AUTONOMOUS FUNCTIONING OR REFER

1. Identify and access further resources
2. Provide structure and make referrals if necessary

Figure 5-3   *School Crisis Management © 2000 Kendall Johnson, Ph.D.*

PSYCHOLOGICAL FIRST AID
Preschool / Kindergarten

AIM:

- Reestablish trust and security

- Reestablish self-control and autonomy

APPROACHES:

- Provide physical comforts (e.g., warm milk, holding, food, rest)

- Reestablish routines

- Assure and provide adult protection

- Let sleep in parents' room

- Help child draw, act out, and discuss incident

- Clarify event, misconceptions, and misunderstandings

- Be calm

School Crisis Management © *2000 Kendall Johnson, Ph.D.*

Figure 5-4

PSYCHOLOGICAL FIRST AID
Elementary

AIM:

- Bolster self-esteem
- Relieve guilt
- Reestablish productivity
- Provide reassurances of safety

APPROACHES:

- Encourage expression of thoughts and feelings
- Validate normalcy of reaction
- Lessen requirements for optimal performance
- Reinforce age-appropriate behavior
- Provide structure as behavior indicates
- Allow expression of feelings of responsibility; clarify misconceptions
- Talk directly about dreams
- Provide opportunities for success

School Crisis Management © *2000 Kendall Johnson, Ph.D.*

Figure 5-5

PSYCHOLOGICAL FIRST AID
Middle School / Senior High School

AIM:

- Reassure of normalcy
- Inoculate against secondary reactions
- Emphasize stress management
- Facilitate identity development
- Reaffirm life direction

APPROACHES:

- Encourage discussion / expression
- Validate normalcy of reaction
- Lessen requirements for optimal performance
- Teach healthy stress management
- (Individualize)
  - Provide opportunity for positive action
  - Provide monitoring, guidance
  - Provide conceptualization of incident, reactions, situations

School Crisis Management © 2000 Kendall Johnson, Ph.D.

Figure 5-6

CONFERENCING STUDENTS "STUCK" IN DELAYED REACTION

1. Provide clear description of problem

2. Inform student of your concern that reaction may be incident-related

3. Work out set of mutually agreed upon bottom-line expectations

4. Focus on problem, issue, or behavior—not on the person

5. Work to maintain student's self-confidence and self-esteem and your professional image

School Crisis Management © 2000 Kendall Johnson, Ph.D.

Figure 5-7

CRT STRATEGY 8: PARENT CONSULTATION

TARGET

Parents

PURPOSE

Assist parents in

1. Situational assessment and understanding
2. Determining proper parental role
3. Assessing student and personal reactions and level of functioning
4. Planning for decision making

METHOD

Private conversation and Crisis Intervention

CONSIDERATIONS

1. Convey support
2. Recognize displaced anxiety or anger; keep balance
3. Listen to specific concerns, determine problem definition
4. Keep consultation oriented to problem assessment and solution
5. Assess level of functioning relative to responsibilities and needs
6. Assist parent in assessing child's needs
7. Utilize basic Crisis Intervention format unless unnecessary
8. Assess need for direct vs. indirect suggestions and planning
9. Assess need for structured intervention / respite / support

---

Figure 5-8   *School Crisis Management © 2000 Kendall Johnson, Ph.D.*   187

CRISIS RESPONSE TEAM ASSESSMENT MUST BE

- Informal

- Approximate

- Conservative

- Unobtrusive

- Tentative and ongoing

School Crisis Management © 2000 Kendall Johnson, Ph.D.

Figure 6.1

INDICATORS:
DIRECT VS. INDIRECT SUGGESTION

DIRECT   **INDIRECT**

–	Internal controls	+
–	Empowerment	+
–	Resource availability	+
–	Cognitive function	+
–	Absence of ASR	+
–	Toleration of ambiguity	+

School Crisis Management © *2000 Kendall Johnson, Ph.D.*

Figure 6-2

IMMEDIATE REFERRAL SIGNS
COGNITIVE

When		Has become
Slight disorientation	$\longrightarrow$	Can't tell name, date, event
Problems prioritizing	$\longrightarrow$	Exclusive preoccupation
Denial of severity	$\longrightarrow$	Denial of incident
Flashbacks	$\longrightarrow$	Hallucinations
Self-doubt	$\longrightarrow$	Paralysis
Numbing	$\longrightarrow$	Disconnection
Problems planning	$\longrightarrow$	Life skills dysfunction
Confusion, misperceptions	$\longrightarrow$	Acting on bizarre beliefs

Figure 6-3

IMMEDIATE REFERRAL SIGNS
EMOTIONAL

When

Has become

Upset, crying $\longrightarrow$ Hysteria

Anger, self-blame $\longrightarrow$ Threat to others, self

Dulled response $\longrightarrow$ No response, rigidity, fetal position

Anxiety $\longrightarrow$ Panic

Fatigue, slowness $\longrightarrow$ Physical shock

School Crisis Management © *2000 Kendall Johnson, Ph.D.*

Figure 6-4

IMMEDIATE REFERRAL SIGNS

BEHAVIORAL

When | | **Has become**

Excessive talk, laughter $\longrightarrow$ Uncontrolled

Restlessness, excitement $\longrightarrow$ Unfocused agitation

Frequent retelling $\longrightarrow$ Ritualistic, continual enactment

Pacing, hand-wringing $\longrightarrow$ Ritualistic, continual and repetitive

Withdrawal $\longrightarrow$ Immobility, rigidity

Disheveled appearance $\longrightarrow$ Inability to care for self

Figure 6-5

School Crisis Management © *2000 Kendall Johnson, Ph.D.*

ASSESSING RISK:
Threats to Self

FACTORS

Recent attempts

Recent losses

Critical incidents

Prior traumas

Isolation / withdrawal

Substance abuse

Destructive coping styles

Disorientation

Inadequate support

Precipitating incident

This list is general and not to be construed as exhaustive; it is only a starting point for further inquiry. Significantly dangerous cases may not fit the profile.

School Crisis Management © *2000 Kendall Johnson, Ph.D.*

Figure 6-6

ASSESSING RISK:
Threats to Self

SIGNS

Threats

Final arrangements

Risk taking

Preoccupation with death, suicide, and death-oriented youth culture

Changes in

— personality

— attitude

— appearance

— performance

— substance use

This list is general and not to be construed as exhaustive; it is only a starting point for further inquiry. Significantly dangerous cases may not fit the profile.

School Crisis Management © *2000 Kendall Johnson, Ph.D.*

Figure 6-7

ASSESSING RISK:
Threats to Self

- Gain input from others who know and observe individual

- Look for corroborating evidence

- Establish contact, rapport

- Express concern

- Ask directly

DETERMINE

1. Was there a precipitating incident?

2. Are any significant predictive factors present?

3. Can the direct or indirect signs be collaborated?

4. Are there signs of distorted thinking?

5. Does the student have a plan?

   — Is it specific as to how?

   — Is it specific as to when?

   — Are the means available?

   — How lethal are the means?

This list is general and not to be construed as exhaustive; it is only a starting point for further inquiry. Significantly dangerous cases may not fit the profile.

Figure 6-8

School Crisis Management © *2000 Kendall Johnson, Ph.D.*

SOCIAL SUPPORT

	Family	Friends	Neighbors	Coworkers	Professionals	Agencies
Emotional						
Material support						
Task assistance						
Guidance						
Information						
Resource linkage						

School Crisis Management © 2000 Kendall Johnson, Ph.D.*

Figure 6-9

CRT STRATEGY 9: CLASSROOM DISCUSSION, DEFUSING, DEBRIEFING

TARGET

Classrooms or groups

PURPOSE

Assist group in

1. Situational assessment and understanding
2. Approximating goals of crisis intervention
3. Raising incident as topic of discussion
4. Providing clarification and information
5. Integrating experience into life of the group

METHOD

Group discussion, defusing, or debriefing

CONSIDERATIONS

1. Observe for individual and group red flags
2. Assess for referral needs
3. Maintain control of discussion
4. Utilize discussion, defusing, or debriefing formats as appropriate
5. Gain prior necessary administrative and parental permission
6. Observe developmental differences
7. Have one-on-one follow-up and support available

Figure 7-1   *School Crisis Management © 2000 Kendall Johnson, Ph.D.*   197

CLASSROOM DISCUSSION AND DEFUSING: GENERAL CONSIDERATIONS

- Find a comfortable place
- Maintain calm
- Be honest with yourself
- Read between the lines
- Validate feelings
- Listen well
- Show belief
- Dispel fault
- Explore fears
- Provide information
- Walk through the process
- Explore resources
- Find friends
- Stress your availability

Figure 7.2

CLASSROOM DEFUSING

(adapted from Everly and Mitchell 1999; Johnson et. al. 1999)

1. INTRODUCTION

— State purpose

— Set rules for discussion

— Describe process

2. EXPLORATION

— Ask students to describe what happened

— Work toward consistency of group experience

— Share initial reactions

3. INFORMATION

— Summarize perceptions

— Clarify misconceptions

— Normalize experiences and reactions

— Provide appropriate information

— Outline expectations

— Suggest stress management strategies

School Crisis Management © 2000 Kendall Johnson, Ph.D.

Figure 7-3

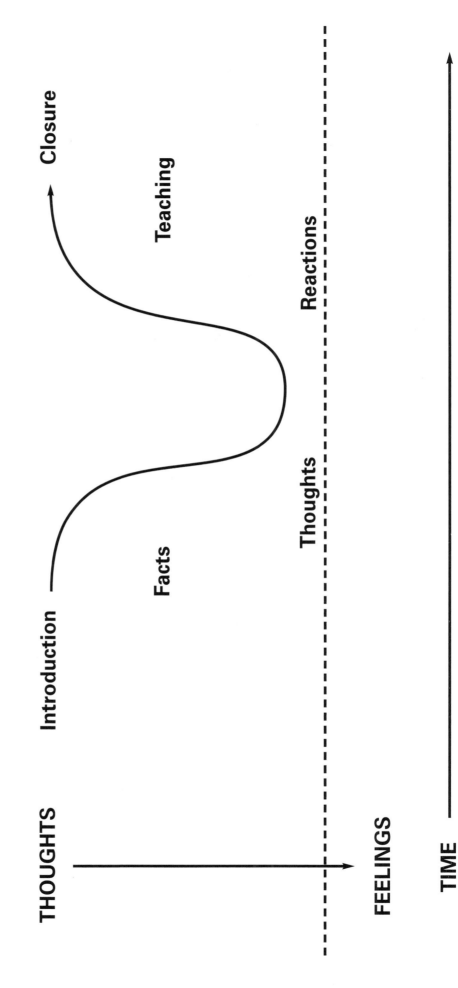

CLASSROOM DEBRIEFING

(adapted from Everly and Mitchell 1999; Johnson et. al. 1999)

THOUGHTS

Introduction

Closure

Facts

Teaching

Thoughts

Reactions

FEELINGS

TIME

RED FLAGS

INDIVIDUAL

- Acute Stress Response signs

GROUP

- Nonsupportive class
- Polarized needs
- Politicized classroom
- Highly impacted families

School Crisis Management © 2000 Kendall Johnson, Ph.D.

Figure 7-5

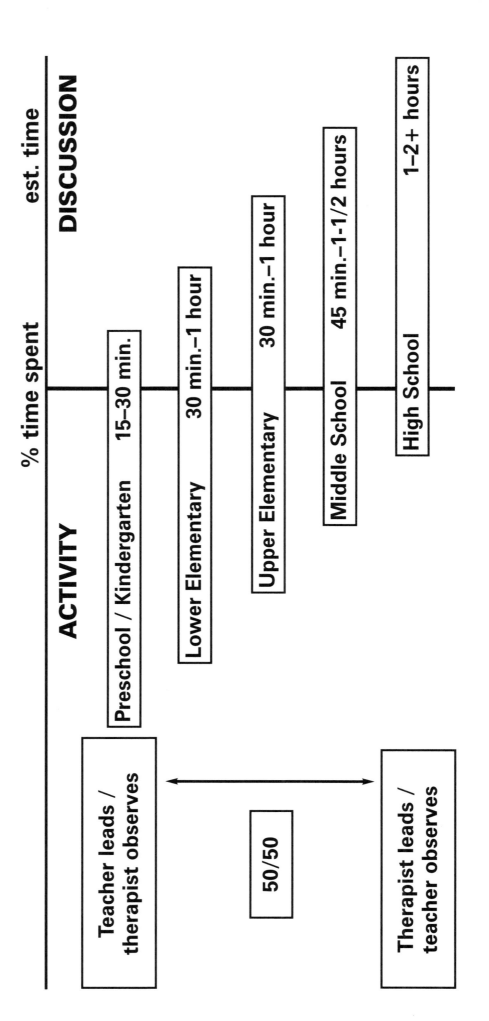

Figure 7-6

CRT STRATEGY 10: CLASSROOM FOLLOW-UP ACTIVITIES

TARGET

Students

PURPOSE

Individual and group integration of experience

Monitor long-term reactions and functioning

Counteract isolation

Assess need for further intervention

METHOD

Writing, art, or enactment activities led by teacher or
CRT personnel

CONSIDERATIONS

1. Assess for posttrauma symptoms
2. Lessen impact of activities to meet needs and vulnerabilities
3 Observe for group and individual red flags
4. Utilize basic Crisis Intervention format unless unnecessary
5. Share observations with staff and parents
6. Assess need for structured intervention and support

Figure 7-7   *School Crisis Management* © 2000 Kendall Johnson, Ph.D.   203

CLASSROOM ACTIVITIES FOLLOWING CRISIS

USEFUL WHEN

- the group or class would benefit from structure

- students are feeling isolated and need assistance in sharing about the incident

- discussion would benefit from impetus, direction, and context

- they are used with consideration toward student sensitivities

AVOID WHEN

- the group or class has a history of being nonsupportive, hurtful, or divisive

- the group's needs relative to the crisis are polarized

- some class members are highly traumatized or have suffered serious loss

Figure 7-8

School Crisis Management © 2000 Kendall Johnson, Ph.D.

THE IMPACT OF ACTIVITIES CAN BE SOFTENED WHEN THE PROMPTS REQUIRE

- individual rather than group activity

- cognitive rather than affective responses

- general rather than specific responses

- universal rather than personal responses

- principles rather than consequences

- problem solving rather then dwelling on the impact

- global impressions rather than sensory images

- writing rather than art activities

- art rather than enactment activities

Figure 7-9

SUICIDE INTERVENTION

RULE OF THUMB #1

The more detailed, workable, lethal, and imminent the plan and the greater the psychological and physiological disturbance, the higher the risk of completion

RULE OF THUMB #2

TAKE ALL THREATS SERIOUSLY

School Crisis Management © 2000 Kendall Johnson, Ph.D.

Figure 8-1

LOW-RISK
SUICIDE INTERVENTION

- Alert staff

- Notify outside agency (e.g., crisis center)

- Contact parents

- Counsel student

  — determine precipitating event

  — diffuse despair, empower cognitive controls

  — identify triggers

  — explore new perspectives, problem solving

  — refer to outside help

School Crisis Management © *2000 Kendall Johnson, Ph.D.*

Figure 8-2

HIGH-RISK
SUICIDE INTERVENTION

- **Do not allow to leave, assign staff member, maintain visual contact at all times**

- **Notify police and appropriate agency for professional evaluation**

- **Notify parents**

- **Inform student what has been done**

- **Facilitate transition to police, hospital**

- **Follow up later**
  - **consider a "no-suicide pact"**
  - **build peer support network**
  - **coordinate with therapy**

School Crisis Management © 2000 Kendall Johnson, Ph.D.

Figure 8-3

POSTSUICIDE / MURDER INTERVENTIONS

- **One person in charge**
- **Get help from outside**
- **Designate spokesperson**
- **Staff briefing**
  - Facts
  - Planning for school response
  - Planning for student meetings
  - Assess staff members for role in meetings
  - Introduce outside resources
- **Classroom debriefings to affected classes**
- **Materials / notifications home**
- **Staff debriefing**
- **Follow-up student services; actions as appropriate**
- **Memorial**

School Crisis Management © 2000 Kendall Johnson, Ph.D.

Figure 8-4

DISCUSSING LOSS WITH CHILDREN

- Remember ages and stage

- Start by asking

- Keep it simple

- Minimize theorizing

- Give hope

School Crisis Management © 2000 Kendall Johnson, Ph.D.

Figure 8-5

CRISIS RESPONSE TEAM
LARGE-INCIDENT COMPLICATIONS

- Numbers and intensity
- Limited CRT resources
- Deployment problems
- Site staff impairment
- CRT member impairment
- Administrative panic
- Media intrusion

School Crisis Management © 2000 Kendall Johnson, Ph.D.

Figure 8-6

CRISIS RESPONSE TEAM
LARGE-INCIDENT OPERATIONS

- Prioritize CRT members

- Establish a center

- Assess adequately

- Locate resources

- Adapt educational model

- Prioritize services

- Adapt to command structure

- Screen and utilize community resources and volunteers

School Crisis Management © *2000 Kendall Johnson, Ph.D.*

Figure 8-7

STAFF INTERVENTION

- Follow crisis intervention procedure

- Remember your place

- Maintain professionalism

- Respect confidentiality

- Enlist supervisor

- Stay aware of transference issues

School Crisis Management © 2000 Kendall Johnson, Ph.D.

Figure 8-8

HELPER VULNERABILITY

People (including professionals) can have histories of unmet basic needs, often as a result of prior trauma or loss. This unfinished business creates a vulnerability to the corresponding life issue.

School Crisis Management © *2000 Kendall Johnson, Ph.D.*

Figure 9-1

PERSONAL REACTIONS

DURING OR FOLLOWING AN INTENSE SESSION, YOU MAY FEEL

- Fear over professional responsibilities and legal liabilities
- Guilt over "inadequacies"
- Feelings of helplessness
- Anger at the situation
- Urge to rescue
- Distrustful of department or helping system
- Personal unfinished business reemerging
- Turmoil, needfulness, doubt later on

School Crisis Management © 2000 Kendall Johnson, Ph.D.

Figure 9-2

SUBCLINICAL SIGNS OF VICARIOUS TRAUMA

Burned out

Cynical

Distrustful

Suspicious

Pessimistic

Alienated

Fearful

Anxious

Depressed

Suicidal

Irritable

Cold and unfeeling

Despairing

Ineffective

...not to mention difficult to live with

Figure 9-3

School Crisis Management © 2000 Kendall Johnson, Ph.D.

LISTENER RESPONSE

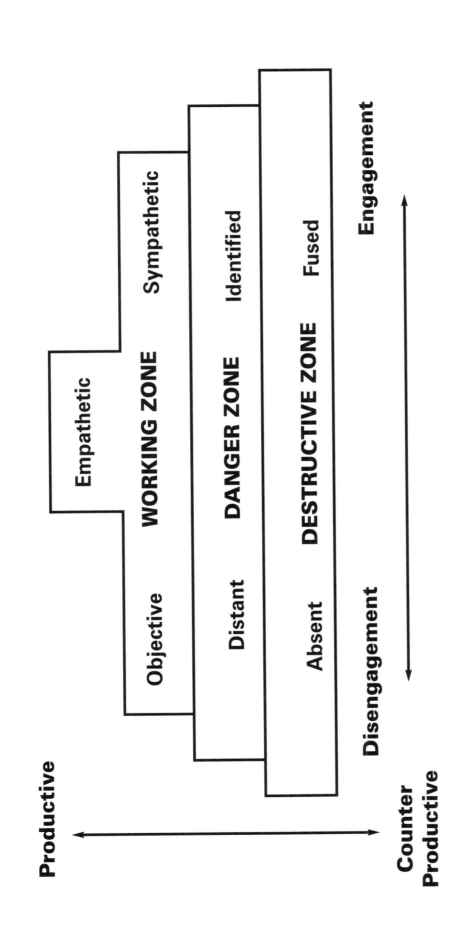

School Crisis Management © 2000 Kendall Johnson, Ph.D.

Figure 9-4

HOT SPOTS

IF YOU'RE FEELING	YOU MAY BE
Anxious and agitated or cold and distracted	Too tired, or avoiding something you are not comfortable with
Physically uncomfortable, pains, aches, etc.	Picking up on a subtle, nonverbal message
Overwhelmed	Overidentifying with student or employee, or with issues
Parental, sexually attracted, or "the rescuer"	Being manipulated by dependent student, employee, have personal, unfinished business of your own, or have lost objectivity

Figure 9-5

TAKING CARE

BEFORE INCIDENT

1. Build your skills

2. Know your "hot spots"

3. Be aware of your needs and current stress level

4. Get background information

DURING INCIDENT

1. Stay in touch with your feelings and needs

2. Set limits

3. Listen to your feelings and hunches

4. Stay aware of your receptivity level

5. Distance yourself

6. Get help when you need it

AFTER INCIDENT

1. Review incident with yourself, outsider

2. Debrief when necessary

3. Talk about it at home

Figure 9-6   *School Crisis Management © 2000 Kendall Johnson, Ph.D.*   219

OPERATIONAL DEBRIEFINGS

1. Introduction

2. Facts

3. Assessment

4. Reactions

5. Interpretations

6. Plans, closing

School Crisis Management © 2000 Kendall Johnson, Ph.D.

Figure 10-1

INDIVIDUAL SIGNS OF CUMULATIVE TRAUMATIC STRESS

- Spiritual depletion

- Depression

- Chronic fatigue

- Sense of powerlessness

- Apathy

- Hostility toward clientele

- Unhappiness / dissatisfaction

- Isolation / overidentification with team

School Crisis Management © 2000 Kendall Johnson, Ph.D.

Figure 10-2

TEAM LEVEL SIGNS OF CUMULATIVE TRAUMATIC STRESS

- Morale problems

- Collapse of sense of team mission and purpose

- Organizational distrust

- Distrust of leadership

- Contagious job burnout

- Collective despair

- Defensive posture at multiple levels of the organization

- Pervasive diminution of team self-esteem

- Relational difficulties within team

Figure 10-3

School Crisis Management © 2000 Kendall Johnson, Ph.D.

CUMULATIVE TRAUMATIC STRESS DEBRIEFING PHASES

Incidents	**Reactions**
Complications	**Planning**

School Crisis Management © *2000 Kendall Johnson, Ph.D.*

Figure 10-4

CTSD:
INCIDENTS PHASE

PURPOSE

- Consensus regarding key events
- Relate individual experiences

FLOW

1. Determine time sequence
2. Determine individual role
3. Note on-scene reactions

CONSIDERATIONS

- Participant's functioning level
- Trust levels
- Inclusion of supervisors

STRATEGIES / PROCEDURES

Flipchart

Chalkboard

Reactions checklist

Figure 10-5

CTSD:
COMPLICATIONS PHASE

PURPOSE

- Identify complicating factors

FLOW

1. Factors checklist
2. Group discussion and consensus on effect of each
3. Save list on flipchart

CONSIDERATIONS

Explore

- Nature of client community
- History / background
- Themes, key events
- Organizational issues
- Practical problems
- Interpersonal context

STRATEGIES / PROCEDURES

- Checklist
- Flipchart

Figure 10-6

CTSD:
REACTIONS PHASE

PURPOSE

- Acknowledge personal reactions
- Define team needs

FLOW

1. Identify reactions with checklist
2. Share reactions
3. Validate essential normalcy of reactions

CONSIDERATIONS

- Assessment of dysfunction
- Indications of referral needs
- Advisability of continuing assignment
- Need for further team intervention
- Avoid conflict, polarization

STRATEGIES / PROCEDURES

Checklists
- DSR signs
- Subclinical signs of CTS
- Team-level signs of CTS

Figure 10.7

CTSD:
PLANNING PHASE

PURPOSE

- Determine effect of CTS on team function

- Develop team CTS management plan

FLOW

1. Review incidents and complications

2. Explore areas for possible change

3. Determine appropriate changes

4. Prioritize list, set agenda

5. Review individual and group plans, resources

6. Close

CONSIDERATIONS

- Client community, broader organization

- Team preparation / training / conditioning

- Team policies, team operations

- Communication, relationships

STRATEGIES / PROCEDURES

Checklist

Flipchart

Flipchart notes from complications phase

School Crisis Management © 2000 Kendall Johnson, Ph.D.

Figure 10-8

INDIVIDUAL APPLICATION

1. Can spread over several sessions

2. Introduction phase unnecessary

3. Complications phase can explore

   — family issues

   — development

   — personal background

   — prior trauma

4. Planning phase can

   — investigate practical issues

   — define direction for future work

School Crisis Management © 2000 Kendall Johnson, Ph.D.

Figure 10-9

AD HOC
GROUP APPLICATION

CTSD FORMAT CAN BE USED WITH UNRELATED TRAUMA VICTIMS, PROVIDING GROUP SHARES

- Similar precipitating incident or condition

- Similar environment

- Similar stage of adjustment

- Similar development issues

Figure 10-10

CTSD
WITH CHILDREN

OLDER ELEMENTARY

- Activity and general discussion
- Classroom debriefing format
- Eliminate complications and planning phases
- Teach stress management

MIDDLE SCHOOL

- Follow CTSD format
- Gloss complications section
- Respect limitations
- Observe for over disclosure, emotional contagion

HIGH SCHOOL

- Handle like adult
- Respect school limitations

School Crisis Management © 2000 Kendall Johnson, Ph.D.

Figure 10-11

APPLICATIONS

SCHOOL	VS.	CLINIC
● Screen red flags		● May include red flags
— cognitive prompts		— affective prompts
— global impressions		— specific impressions
— problem solving		— exploring impact
— analysis		— catharsis
— discussion		— enactment
— talking about it		— working through it

School Crisis Management © 2000 Kendall Johnson, Ph.D.

Figure 10-12

Index

A

acting out, student, 83
Acute Stress Response, 4, 5; in school staff, 32–33
administrators, and large scale crises, 83; consulting with, 29–31
agitation, 5
alienation, 8
American Academy of Experts in Traumatic Stress, 105
American Psychiatric Association, 8
amnesia, 8
anger, 5; channeling, 65
anxiety, 4
arousal, 7–13; inappropriate, 8; physiological, 13
art activities, 70–71
assessment, 47–48; critical situations, 38; rapid, 52–60; dependency of others, 59; families, 56–60; individuals, 47–48; medical considerations, 59; moderately impaired functioning, 53–54; safety factors, 59; seriously impaired functioning, 54–55; threat to self, 55–56
Attention Deficit Hyperactivity Disorder, trauma and, 13
avoidance, 8

B

behavioral responses, Acute Stress Response, 5, 55
Bloom's taxonomy, 104
bombings, 34–35
bonding, in traumatized groups, 14–15

brain chemistry and trauma, 12–14
burnout, 87–92; preventing, 90–92

C

catecholamines, 12, 13
centralized crisis teams, 27–28
children, and Cumulative Traumatic Stress, 100–101; depressive reactions, 11; intervention, 48–49; play, 8; posttrauma behavior, 10–12
classroom activities; debriefing, 64–68; discussion, guidelines, 61–62
codependency, 56
cognitive impairments, 5; after crisis, 54
Columbine High School, 17, 36, 63, 95
community, providing, 23
Community-Oriented Preventive Education, 65
community-school barriers, 105–106
compulsive behaviors, 56
conflict mediation classes, 23
consistency, 20–21
consultation, 47–48; administrative, 28; teachers, 29
coping skills, 22
corticosteroids, 12
counseling, individual, 21–22
crises, assessing, 38; definition of, 3; elements of, 3; large scale, 80–83; responses to, 3–7
crisis consultants' checklist, 114–117

crisis intervention, individual, 47–51
crisis management, goals and objectives, 18–24
crisis response teams, 25–35; burnout in, 87–92; composition, 1; history of, 25–26; large scale crises, 81–83; legal issues, 102–104; membership of, 26–27; models of, 26–28; responsibilities of, 31–32; roadblocks to developing, 106–107; and school cultures, 16; strategies, 28–30, 47–48, 50, 61–63, 70; training, 1–2, 26–27
Cumulative Traumatic Stress Debriefings, 96–99
Cumulative Traumatic Stress, in crisis teams, 93–99

D

debriefing, classroom, 26, 64–68
debriefings, Cumulative Traumatic Stress, 96–99
decentralized crisis teams, 28
defusing, classroom trauma, 62–63
Delayed Stress Response, 4, 5–7; in crisis teams, 87; school staff, 33
denial, 6, 8
depression, 4, 6, 8; assessing, 118; children, 11
developmental differences, group interventions, 69–70
deverbalization, 11
digestive disorders, 6
disassociation, 5

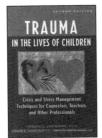

ORDER FORM

10%	DISCOUNT on orders of $50 or more —
20%	DISCOUNT on orders of $150 or more —
30%	DISCOUNT on orders of $500 or more —

On cost of books for fully prepaid orders

NAME

ADDRESS

CITY/STATE   ZIP/POSTCODE

PHONE   COUNTRY (outside of U.S.)

TITLE	QTY	PRICE	TOTAL
School Crisis Management (paperback)		@ $24.95	
School Crisis Management (spiral)		@ $29.95	

Prices subject to change without notice

Please list other titles below:

		@ $	
		@ $	
		@ $	
		@ $	
		@ $	
		@ $	
		@ $	

Check here to receive our book catalog   ☐   FREE

Shipping Costs:
*First book: $3.00 by book post ($4.50 by UPS, Priority Mail, or to ship outside the U.S.)
Each additional book: $1.00
For rush orders and bulk shipments call us at (800) 266-5592*

TOTAL	_____
Less discount @_____%	(_____)
TOTAL COST OF BOOKS	_____
Calif. residents add sales tax	_____
Shipping & handling	_____
TOTAL ENCLOSED	_____

Please pay in U.S. funds only

☐ Check ☐ Money Order ☐ Visa ☐ Mastercard ☐ Discover

Card # _____ Exp. date _____

Signature _____

Complete and mail to:
Hunter House Inc., Publishers
PO Box 2914, Alameda CA 94501-0914
Orders: (800) 266-5592   email: ordering@hunterhouse.com
Phone (510) 865-5282 Fax (510) 865-4295
☐ Check here to receive our book catalog

SCM2 6/00

LIFE Ronald Reagan

A LIFE IN PICTURES

PETE SOUZA/THE WHITE HOUSE

LIFE Ronald Reagan

A LIFE IN PICTURES

By Robert Sullivan
and the Editors of LIFE

With a Foreword by Dan Rather

LIFE Ronald Reagan
A LIFE IN PICTURES

Editor Robert Andreas

Picture Editor Barbara Baker Burrows

Art Director Ian Denning

Writer Robert Sullivan

Reporters Hildegard Anderson, Lela Nargi, Deirdre Van Dyk

Associate Picture Editor Christina Lieberman

Picture Research Lauren Steel

Copy Chief Kathleen Berger

Copy Desk Cheryl Brown, Madeleine Edmondson, Joel Griffiths, Larry Nesbitt, Pam Warren

Publisher Andrew Blau

Business Manager Craig Ettinger

Assistant Finance Manager Karen Tortora

LIFE Books
Time Inc. Home Entertainment

President Rob Gursha

Vice President, New Product Development Richard Fraiman

Executive Director, Marketing Services Carol Pittard

Director, Retail & Special Sales Tom Mifsud

Director of Finance Tricia Griffin

Assistant Marketing Director Ann Marie Doherty

Prepress Manager Emily Rabin

Book Production Manager Jonathan Polsky

Associate Product Manager Jennifer Dowell

Special thanks to Bozena Bannett, Alex Bliss, Bernadette Corbie, Robert Dente, Gina Di Meglio, Anne-Michelle Gallero, Peter Harper, Suzanne Janso, Robert Marasco, Natalie McCrea, Margarita Quiogue, Mary Jane Rigoroso, Steven Sandonato, Grace Sullivan

LIAISON AGENCY

Foreword

BY DAN RATHER

I n 1994, the world learned that Ronald Wilson Reagan was suffering from Alzheimer's disease. The news came from a brief letter, written in Reagan's own hand on stationery bearing the presidential seal and dated November 5, 1994—14 years and one day after an electoral landslide made him the 40th President of the United States. "I now begin," the letter read, "the journey that will lead me into the sunset of my life."

He has been called the Great Communicator, and his signature cadence and mellifluous rasp have ridden the American airwaves for the better part of 70 years now. In the years since Reagan embarked on that final journey, we have heard his voice only from fading bits of video, pieces of a recent past rendered so very distant by the breathtaking pace of change at century's end and century's dawn. But once that voice spoke to America directly. From the small screen and the big screen and the wireless, in the career of an actor, a corporate spokesman, a sports announcer. It spoke from the California governor's mansion and it spoke from the White House, where Reagan's eloquence in framing the American moment stands as perhaps his greatest legacy.

It is, of course, too soon for us to know how history will judge the Reagan presidency; the battle to define its legacy, and his, roils still. To the partisans of the "Reagan Revolution," his is a face that would benefit and befit Mount Rushmore; to their opposites, the Reagan White House stands at the center of a decade that memory has rendered synonymous with rapaciousness and greed. Some point first to the legislative triumphs of his first term; others to the foreign-policy malfeasance of his second. The divide is evident in how one views America's current run of economic good fortune. To some, this is the Clinton boom. To others, it is simply and self-evidently the Reagan expansion, 18 years of growth interrupted only by the brief recession of 1991.

Reagan's was the last presidency to fight the cold war from beginning to end, and there are those who credit him with winning it. Honest observers on both sides can debate over whether victory, such as it is, was the fruit of 40 years of bipartisan continuity in American foreign policy or the Reagan will to stand up to and outspend the Soviet Union wherever and whenever necessary. But however one comes down on that question, it was undeniably Ronald Reagan who had the best lines before the iron curtain came down. It was he who stood at Berlin's Brandenburg Gate in 1987, and facing East Germany and the "evil empire" beyond, intoned, "Mr. Gorbachev, tear down this Wall." Two years later, words became deed.

Whether Ronald Reagan drove the tide of history or was carried on the crest of its breaking wave is not a judgment that we can properly make. That falls to those who will come after us, long after the partisans and the detractors and the man himself have ridden into that final sunset. Posterity has so often shown us a middle view between the pressing debates of an era, and has a way of illuminating features we cannot see now with the light of a future we cannot know.

But we can recount what we know. The Reagan presidency began on the front steps of the Capitol, the inaugural ceremony facing west toward the Mall and its monuments for the first time in history. In that first inaugural address, Reagan sounded the themes he had campaigned on and would return to and repeat throughout his presidency—the need, as he saw it, to cut federal spending and the reach of big government, his hope for peace through strength and, what may be most important of all, his call to "realize that we're too great a nation to limit ourselves to small dreams."

This plea to "begin an era of national renewal" was the essence of Reagan's popular and populist appeal, as was his almost incantatory repetition of the three words that gave birth and definition to the American experiment: "We the People." We the People moved through the text of his inaugural oratory, and We were invoked in his farewell address, eight years later. He tried so often to remind us that, from We the People—not, need it be said, government—would come the solutions to our greatest problems.

He asked a nation to find within itself the greatness that he considered its birthright, and he sought to make us equal to the task by reminding us of our collective heritage. Reagan was the Great Communicator, yes, but he was also a master at communicating greatness. He understood that, as he once put it, "History is a ribbon always unfurling" and managed to convey his vision in terms both simple and poetic. From his first inaugural, as he looked west past the Mall to Arlington National Cemetery:

"Each one of those markers is a monument to the kind of hero I spoke of earlier. Their lives ended in places called Belleau Wood, the Argonne, Omaha Beach, Salerno and halfway around the world on Guadalcanal, Tarawa, Pork Chop Hill, the Chosin Reservoir, and in a hundred rice paddies and jungles of a place called Vietnam."

Then, in a trademark touch, the easy move from the grand tableau to the concrete, the personal example and exemplar:

"Under one such marker lies a young man, Martin Treptow,* who left his job in a small town barbershop in 1917 to go to France with the famed Rainbow Division. There, on the western front, he was killed trying to carry a message between battalions under heavy artillery fire.

"We're told that on his body was found a diary. On the flyleaf under the heading, 'My Pledge,' he had written these words: 'America must win this war. Therefore I will work, I will save, I will sacrifice, I will endure, I will fight cheerfully and do my utmost, as if the issue of the whole struggle depended on me alone.'"

Finally, the coup de grâce, connecting past with present: *"The crisis we are facing today does not require of us the kind of sacrifice that Martin Treptow and so many thousands of others were called upon to make. It does require, however, our best effort . . ."*

One senses that, for Reagan, the ghosts of history were entirely visible. One can imagine that when he, as was his habit, contemplated the vista from his favorite White House window, he could see the faraway smoke rising from the Battle of Bull Run, as he was told Lincoln had before him. That he addressed Con-

---

*Ed.: Treptow was actually buried in Bloomer, Wis. Reagan's speechwriters accepted the blame for the error.

gress in halls that still echoed with the voices of Webster and Clay.

Much has been made of Ronald Reagan's sentimentality, his sepia-toned vision of a Norman Rockwell past. But one is struck, looking back over what he said during eight years in the White House, with how often he used the past to illuminate the present and the future. I am not the first to call attention to this; the biographer Edmund Morris goes so far as to suggest that Reagan had little use for nostalgia in and of itself.

For Ronald Reagan, the distinctions of past, present, future, may have been irrelevant. He remained a constant in the eight years he occupied 1600 Pennsylvania Avenue, his outlook, if not always his deeds, unwavering from first word to last. And so he was able to act as a conduit to connect us to who we had been and who we could be.

His letter of November 5, 1994, poignant yet devoid of self-pity, tells us he is once again looking west. But Ronald Wilson Reagan also could not resist one more look back over his shoulder. He makes his ride confident in his knowledge that, as he wrote, "for America there will always be a bright dawn ahead."

May we all share his optimism. And may his steed hold steady as he completes his journey.

An American Boy

In the mid-1960s, Ronald Reagan, a Hollywood actor who was recasting himself as a national politician, paused to reminisce about his boyhood. He recalled gaslit streets in small Illinois towns. He talked of adventures in the woods and at treacherous swimming holes, of an existence that was "one of those rare Huck Finn–Tom Sawyer idylls." He remembered being perched on his older brother's secondhand bike, "hanging onto a hitching post in front of the house," waiting for his dad. "I was always there at noon when he came home for lunch. He would push me around in the street for a few exhilarating circles." He recalled his loving mother teaching him to read before he was five. He recounted bygone pickup football games. "The lure of sweat and action always pulled me back to the game—despite the fact that I was a scrawny, undersized, underweight nuisance," he said. "As a result, I had a collection of the largest purplish-black bruises possible. More than once, I must have been a walking coagulation. Those were the happiest times of my life."

Reagan painted lovely sepia-toned pictures of his youth. The images were charming to his audience. And were they true?

A skinny, scrappy boy who would become a strapping man, Ronald Reagan played right guard on the football team at Dixon (Ill.) High, where he also participated in basketball and track. His family was poor, and summertime meant work as well as play: caddying, laboring on a construction crew, eventually lifeguarding.

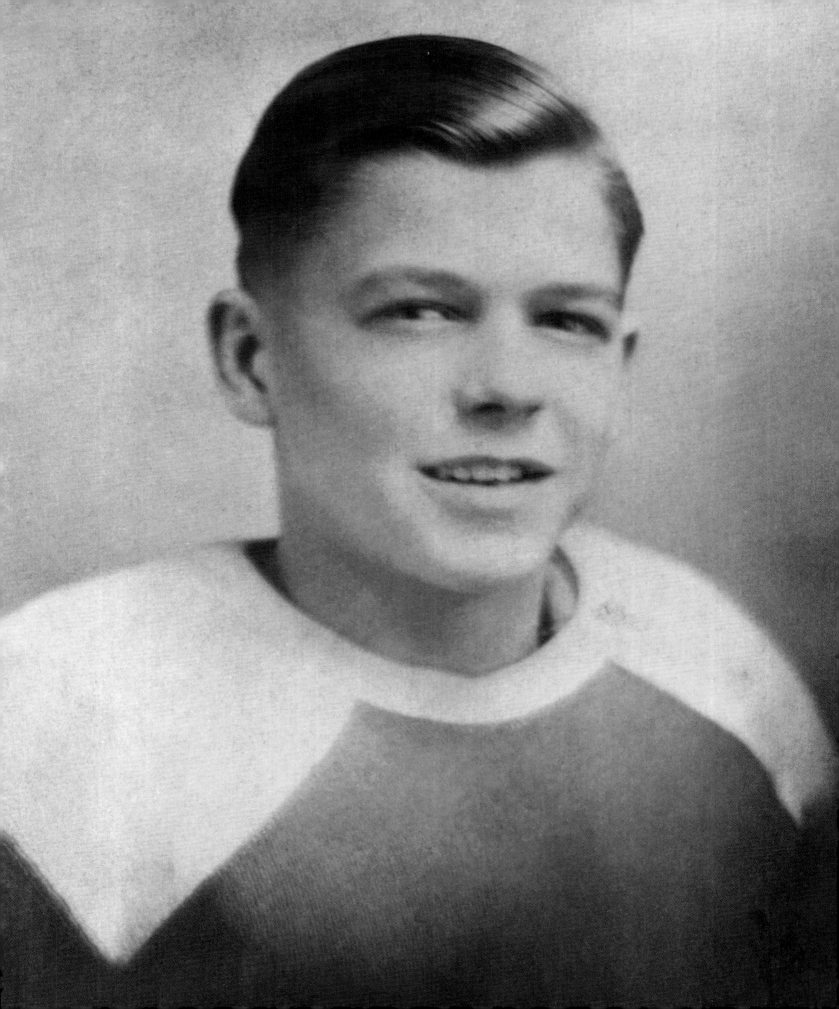

The Reagans, circa 1915: Jack, Neil, Ronald and Nelle. Years later, Ronald Reagan viewed his upbringing through rose-colored glasses. There were surely good times, but his father, an alcoholic, wouldn't shrink from "clobbering" the boys, and his mother nearly died of influenza in 1918.

On February 6, 1911, Jack Reagan heard his newborn's cry and said, "For such a little bit of a fat Dutchman, he makes a hell of a lot of noise."

"I think he's perfectly wonderful," said Jack's wife, Nelle.

The baby was not a Dutchman but the son of a first-generation Irish Catholic father and a Scotch Protestant mother—yet the nickname, Dutch, would stick his entire life. Ronald Wilson "Dutch" Reagan, the younger of two boys, was born in the country town of Tampico, Ill., to a shoe salesman and his wife. The family moved regularly from one rented home to another, and by the time Dutch was nine he had lived in several small towns and on Chicago's South Side. There were, to be sure, many fine adventures with his brother, Neil, but there was darkness as well. Jack Reagan, as tall and strong a man as Dutch would grow to be, was seriously addicted to alcohol. He went on weeklong benders and suffered from blackouts. In a 1965 memoir, *Where's the Rest of Me?*, Ronald Reagan recalled his "first moment of accepting responsibility." A boy of 11, he had returned to the family's home in Dixon to find his father on the front porch, "spread out as if he were crucified—as indeed he was—his hair soaked with melting snow, snoring as he breathed." Dutch had, theretofore, been shielded from his father's problem by Neil and Nelle—though of course he heard the shouting in the night. His instinct this time was to pretend his dad wasn't there, to walk over him and scurry to his bedroom. But no one else was there to deal with the situation, so the boy grabbed his father's overcoat, dragged him inside and got him to bed. "In a few days he was the bluff, hearty man I knew and loved and will always remember."

This postscript was characteristic. Throughout Ronald Reagan's life he

would be the optimist: He would seize upon better memories, he would seek—and find—silver linings. This aspect of his personality was immensely appealing, and while Dutch Reagan was famous as a loner with few intimate friends, he was also, from the first, charismatic and extremely popular.

Jack Reagan held strong political convictions. He was "a sentimental Democrat, who believed fervently in the rights of the workingman," Ronald recalled. A staunch Roman Catholic in an era when Catholics were second-class citizens, Jack preached tolerance in his household. Family lore maintained that he refused to let the kids see D.W. Griffith's *The Birth of a Nation* at the local movie house because it condoned racial bigotry, and that once, on a sales call, he slept a cold night in his car rather than stay at a hotel that barred Jews. Whatever the truth of these anecdotes, Dutch got from his father a passion for political thought and a belief that the Democratic party was the people's protector. The former, at least, would last a lifetime.

Despite his father's influence, Ronald

The future President spent his formative years primarily in rural towns in Illinois. At the age of eight, a pensive Dutch posed with his Tampico elementary school classmates. By the time he was entering his teens (opposite), the Reagan family had moved to Dixon, where his father became part owner of a shoe store.

DONALD REAGAN
"Dutch"

"Life is just one grand sweet song, so start the music."
Pres. N. S. Student Body 4; Pres. 2; Play 3, 4; Dram. Club 3, 4, Pres. 4; Fresh.-Soph. Drama Club 1, 2, Pres. 2; Football 3, 4; Annual Staff; Hi-Y 3, 4, Vice-Pres. 4; Art. 1, 2; Lit. Contest 2; Track 2, 3.

was very much his mother's son. Neil had been baptized a Catholic, but Ron was raised in Nelle's Disciples of Christ Church. She was an evangelist and something of a missionary, caring for the sick, visiting prisoners, giving talks, at one point even writing a play for her church in Dixon. (The Disciples of Christ supported temperance—Carry Nation was a member—and in Nelle's play a young girl says to her father, "I love you, Daddy, except when you have that old bottle.") Young Ronald worked after school at the church and acted in some of those church plays. He heard his mother's talks, and years later said that his own early speeches had been modeled on hers. Ronald Reagan inherited his mother's propensity for seeing only the good in people, as well as his mother's firm belief that God's will was at work in all things.

If mother and son were correct about this, then God did a fine job in landing Dutch at Dixon's Lowell Park. There, in 1926, he began working as a lifeguard on the Rock River for $15 a week. During the next seven summers he saved the lives of no fewer than 77 people; it is difficult to corroborate many of the tales from Reagan's early years, but by all accounts he did rescue 77 swimmers. This young man who would, in the years to come, continually float between real and illuso-

In a high school drama, Dutch played opposite his girlfriend, Margaret "Mugs" Cleaver. He followed her to college, but the relationship fizzled when, on a trip abroad, she fell in love with an attorney whom she would marry. Dixon High's yearbook says that Dutch, second from left, "took care of his tackle berth in a creditable manner, and certainly had the true 'Dixon Spirit.'"

Scrawny no longer, Dutch saved 77 lives as a lifeguard—and carved a notch into a log for each one. At Eureka College he played varsity football for three years, starred in swimming, served as president of the Boosters Club and the student senate, wrote for the school paper and was a features editor of the yearbook. And: "I copped the lead in most plays."

ry images of all-American champions was, in his late teens and early twenties, a bona fide American hero.

He graduated from Dixon High in 1928, a fair student, a fine athlete and already a leader (he was student body president). In the fall he matriculated at Eureka (Ill.) College, a religious school. He supplemented his scholarship money by washing dishes at his TKE fraternity house, meanwhile continuing his so-so academic career and his ever more vibrant public life. "I loved three things: drama, politics and sports," he later remembered. "And I'm not sure they always came in that order." He won letters in football and swimming, joined the drama club, worked on the college newspaper and became involved in school politics. When students called for the resignation of Eureka's president, they asked Reagan to speak on the issue in chapel. His rousing speech drew a roar and helped spur the students to go on strike. "That audience and I were together," Reagan said. He realized that he was a man who could connect with, and inspire, the people.

Back home, things weren't getting easier. In the midst of the Depression, Jack Reagan lost his shoe store. In the fall of 1932 he and his son Ronald voted for Franklin Delano Roosevelt for President.

REAGAN

Sporting Presidents

Ronald Reagan was a swimmer and footballer. Other Chief Executives also learned valuable lessons on the playing fields of America.

Theodore Roosevelt, Boxer
The Rough Rider was a marksman, a hunter, a tennis player and, during his days at Harvard (above), a boxer. Kinsman F.D. Roosevelt loved to swim.

William Taft, Golfer
A very big golfer, he was also a baseball fan.
In 1910 he became the first President to open the Major League season with a ceremonial toss.

George Bush, Baseball Player
As President he could play a round of golf in two hours. At Yale he hit .264 as captain of a championship team.

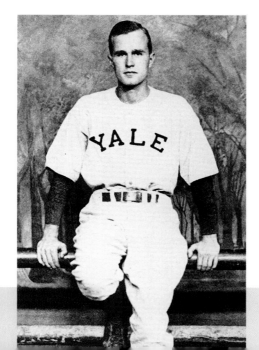

George Washington, Horseman
He not only rode in war, he also rode for recreation; on occasion he rode to hounds (above).

Gerald Ford, Football Player
Perhaps the finest athlete ever to reside at 1600 Pennsylvania Avenue, Ford received offers to play pro football after his MVP senior season at Michigan.

John F. Kennedy, Sailor
A deft hand at the tiller, he was quietly the best golfer among the Presidents; he played down his talent for this Republican game.

Dwight D. Eisenhower, Fisherman
Ike, famous as a golfer, had a putting green outside the Oval Office. The old general was also an avid fisherman.

Richard Nixon, Bowler
He bowled in the Executive Office Building (above) and had a lane installed at the White House. A foot note: Did the President's men tell him when he stepped over the line?

Hollywood Bound

The scene is a midwestern city—Des Moines—during the Great Depression. It is evening. A bus pulls in and a young woman gets off. She sets off down the street. A man follows her. Suddenly, he is on her. She feels a gun in her back, and he tells her to drop the purse and suitcase. She has only three dollars and offers that. The man grabs the purse and suitcase. Then, the hero appears in an apartment window two floors above the street. "Leave her alone," he shouts, "or I'll shoot you right between the shoulders." The mugger drops everything and flees. The hero descends the stairs and comforts the lady in distress.

The hero was played by Ronald Reagan. The woman was Melba Lohmann, playing herself. The year was 1933 and the scene was real. Reagan may or may not have had a gun; if he had one, it may or may not have been loaded. Through the years, even his accounts of the story differed. But the significant point is: Ronald Reagan could be the hero, on screen or in life. He could play it to people's satisfaction. If he embroidered, no one much cared. His audience was taken with the performance, and felt that behind it was a man they could trust.

Reagan radiated midwestern strength and exuberance in this 1942 Warner Bros. publicity still. Coming off a stellar performance in *Kings Row*, he was at the apex of his film career, but military service would limit him to just one movie from 1943 through '46.

MPTV

utch Reagan loved Eureka College, a school of 250 students founded by the Disciples of Christ, and he loved Margaret "Mugs" Cleaver, a former classmate from Dixon High who, during their final months together at Eureka, became his fiancée. In college, Dutch was distanced from—if not immune to—the country's economic misery and the struggles of the Reagans back in Dixon. He moved from glory to glory, growing stronger and more successful as an athlete, feeling the joy of a man in love, drinking the "heady wine" of being a leader.

In 1932, only 7 percent of Americans were in college, while 12 million of them—25 percent of the adult population—were out of work. That was the year Dutch graduated into the world.

He already knew he would play a large part in the survival of his family. It was he who had helped persuade his older brother, Neil, a.k.a. Moon, to join him at Eureka and improve his lot. It was he who had the best summer jobs and was able to contribute to the family pot. Now it was he who analyzed the situation and decided to be an entertainer—a Depression-proof profession. In 1932 radio was hot, so Dutch set his sights on radio.

WHO was a 50,000-watt radio station, and Dutch Reagan reached an audience beyond the Midwest with his baseball re-creations. By 1937 he had signed with Warner Bros. In those days, a studio often broke its film stars in gradually, and in Reagan's first three films, he barely had to act. He played a radio announcer, a radio announcer and (opposite, in *Swing Your Lady*) a sports reporter.

Chicago didn't want him, but Davenport, Iowa, took him. Dutch Reagan, sportscaster and announcer, went on the air at WOC (World of Chiropractic, believe it or not) in February 1933. A portion of his $100 per month—an enormous sum in that place and time—was mailed home to Dixon, where his father was unemployed.

Dutch quickly got himself fired when he failed to mention a program sponsor. WOC could not find an immediate replacement, and Reagan was still hanging around the studio, doing occasional temporary on-air work, when he was sent in the spring to work at WHO, a sister station in Des Moines. This much-larger NBC affiliate rehired Reagan as a full-time employee.

Davenport was 75 miles from Dixon, but Des Moines was 250 miles west—

In his first film, *Love Is On the Air* (1937, above), Reagan blurred fact and fiction to a delicious degree, playing a wide-eyed smalltown radio announcer. In 1939's *Dark Victory* (right) he played violently against type as a rich, bleary-eyed roué with designs on Bette Davis (who responded much as she did in real life). Reagan found his own performance wanting.

Jane Wyman and Reagan clicked in 1938 in *Brother Rat*, then accompanied Louella Parsons on her 1939 vaudeville tour. The gossip columnist, who was from Dixon, hosted a wedding reception for the couple at her home on January 26, 1940.

a world away. And Reagan's world changed. The girl he left behind, Mugs Cleaver, met a man on her European tour and broke off her engagement to Dutch. Reagan would write in his memoirs: "As our lives traveled into diverging paths . . . our lovely and wholesome relationship did not survive growing up." Also in Des Moines, Reagan got his first taste of professional success and celebrity—even a kind of stardom. His rise as a sportscaster on one of the most far-reaching radio stations in the Midwest brought him a threefold raise to $75 a week. He bought a Nash convertible, nice clothes—and still had money to send home.

It was the era of baseball re-creations, and Reagan had a distinct flair for taking black-and-white information and making it colorful. He would receive updates via telegraphy from the ballpark and would

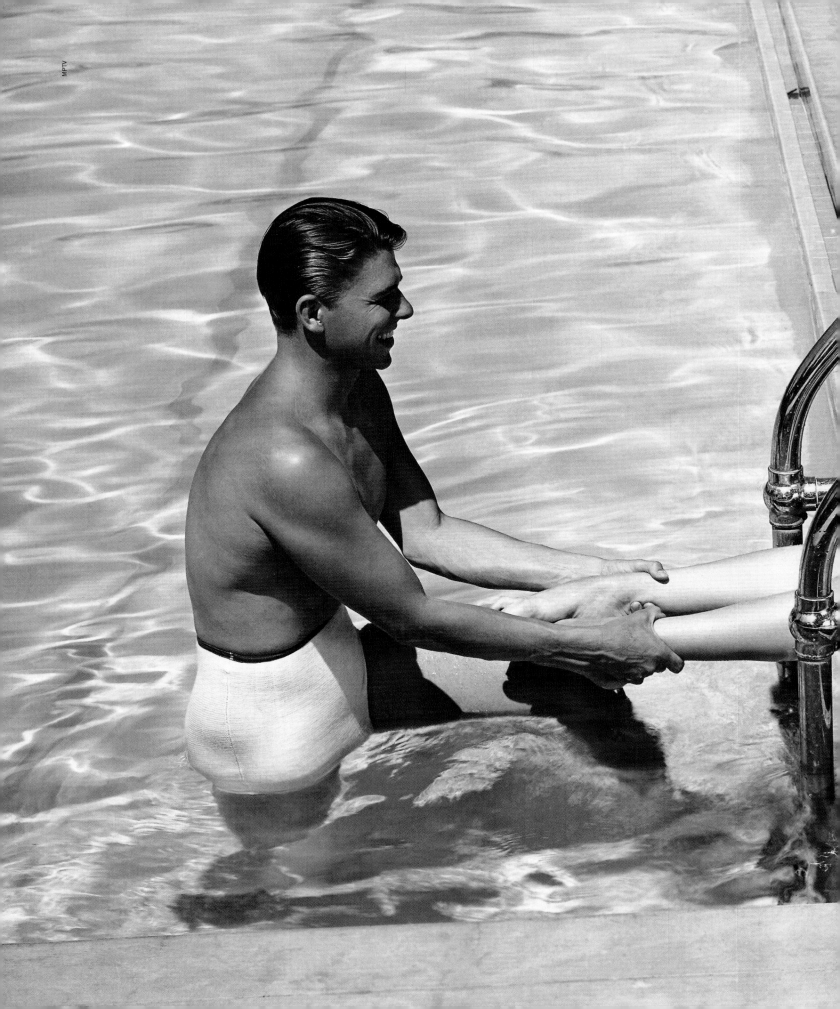

"We do the same foolish things that other couples do, have the same scraps, about as much fun," said Reagan in a 1941 press release. "The Reagans' home life is probably just like yours, or yours, or yours." Except for the pool, of course.

PHOTOFEST

MOVIE STILL ARCHIVES

bring them to life for his listeners with all the appropriate bells and whistles: the crack of the bat, the roar of the crowd. He broadcast 600 games over four years and became not only a source of news but of reliability for millions. Hugh Sidey, who many years later would cover Reagan as a *Time* magazine editor, was a boy in Dust Bowl Iowa in the 1930s, and once mused that Reagan, calling a baseball game, always gave him the feeling that life was going to get better.

Dutch Reagan, now a well-known broadcaster enjoying his celebrity, was, in 1937, ready to attempt a big leap. The Chicago Cubs' spring training camp was

A star is born: Two of Reagan's early films, *Knute Rockne* (above) and *Kings Row* (right), made him a household name. Although he would never be known as an actor whose skills approached those of costars Pat O'Brien or Ann Sheridan, he turned in fine performances in the films—two of his favorites.

Warners' publicity stills portrayed a wholesome, happy, smiling Reagan (opposite). It helped that the image matched the man, but in any event, to adoring fans, the image *was* the man (above). Part of Reagan's appeal was that he was safe at a time when America needed to feel safe. He was not marketed as a playboy but as a good guy and loyal husband—and that took no role-playing.

on Catalina Island off the California coast, and Reagan coaxed WHO into sending him to Hollywood to file reports. He then had a friend of a friend set up a screen test at Warner Bros., and after filling in blanks that transformed Eureka College's drama club into some kind of semipro theatrical troupe, he showed up for an interview with agent Bill Meiklejohn. "I have another Robert Taylor sitting in my office," Meiklejohn told Warners' casting director Max Arnow, who agreed for the most part with the assessment. Reagan was told to ditch the "Dutch" nickname, lose the eyeglasses—and report for work in June, at $200 a week. Adieu, Des Moines.

Like other Hollywood male actors, Reagan was handsome, preternaturally photogenic and well-spoken. Unlike some of them, he was not a naturally gifted actor and frequently came across as one-dimensional. But, rare among them, he was sober-minded and willing to work as hard as he had to for success. On his first day on the set he had trouble reading the script because of his bad eyes (he had worn horn-rims since he was 13). He struggled through the day, then resolved to memorize all his lines before showing up each morning—something he would do throughout his career.

The film *Brother Rat* (1938) is significant for two reasons: It marked Reagan's

33

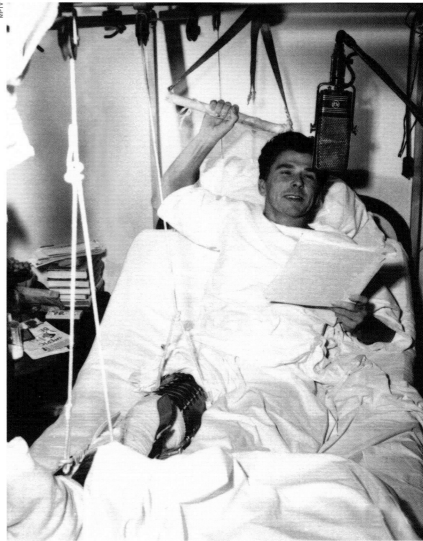

In 1940, University of Southern California art students chose the 6′1″, 180-lb. Reagan—32″ waist, 41″ chest—as their "20th Century Adonis," he of the perfect physique. Reagan said thanks by posing for a sculpture class. In real life, no one's perfect: Reagan was hospitalized with pneumonia in 1947, and in 1949 (above) was laid up after breaking his leg in six places playing baseball.

first big popular success, and on that production he met the actress Jane Wyman, whom he would marry in January 1940. That year—1940—turned out to be a very good one for Reagan, as his portrayal of the doomed Notre Dame running back George Gipp in the film *Knute Rockne—All American* represented a critical breakthrough. Reagan was well-suited to capture Gipp's athleticism and his brave stoicism in confronting a fatal illness. The actor knew it, lobbying hard for the role. Other performers, he said later, "could have played the part better, but no one could have wanted to play it more than I did." And no one could have foreseen how useful an association with

Gipp—not to mention the rallying cry "Win one for the Gipper!"—might be in a later career.

Slogans from Reagan's early movies became part of who he was and who he would become. In *Kings Row* (1942) he gave perhaps his finest performance, as a playboy whose legs are needlessly amputated. When he awakens after surgery, the character looks down and cries out, "Where's the rest of me?"—a question Reagan would challenge himself with in the years to come, and also the title of candidate Reagan's 1965 memoir.

"THE HOPEFUL REAGANS," declared the press release. "They Are Looking Forward to More of Everything Good—Including Children." Maureen, above, was born in 1941, and Michael was adopted in 1945. But everything else was not, in fact, good—and one afternoon Wyman simply told Reagan to "get out." As she put it in her succinct courtroom statement suing for divorce: "There was nothing in common between us, nothing to sustain our marriage."

Left and above: At his ranch in Northridge, Dutch always loved horses and was an excellent rider. In more than one movie, he refused to yield the saddle to a stunt double, and he often executed his own jumps. His three California retreats, with their combination of sun and trails, would over the years be sources of revivification for Reagan.

In wartime Hollywood, Reagan was something of an odd duck. Having enlisted in the 14th Cavalry Regiment of the U.S. Army Reserve in 1937, he was called up after Pearl Harbor. While he certainly appeared 1A, his poor eyesight kept him from combat, and eventually he was assigned to an Army Air Corps motion picture unit in Culver City, Calif. He made 400 training films, appeared opposite Joan Leslie in *This Is the Army* (1943) and, before being discharged in late 1945, was promoted, which yielded a valuable portfolio of photographs depicting Captain Reagan in uniform.

He stood out among his colleagues in

other ways, too. Moralistic, sober and monogamous in Sodom, he was seen by some as a bore. Brazen Bette Davis thought him "a silly boy." Hollywood's liberal intellectuals considered him and his Midwestern attitudes shallow, while the town's revelers couldn't understand his abiding passion for politics. This was chiefly manifested, at the time, in the active role he played with the Screen Actors Guild. He had served on the board as early as 1941, and in 1947 he succeeded Robert Montgomery as president. In the turbulent Red Scare period, when Congress was weeding out Hollywood's

communists, Reagan was a strong, stalwart leader. In '47 he told the House Un-American Activities Committee that, while communism was no doubt an evil, any blacklisting or censorship of his fellow actors was unwarranted. What one commentator called "a fine statement of civil-libertarian principles" got him branded a dangerous liberal by others. As a union activist, Reagan at one point received death threats and began packing a pistol for protection. Even as his acting career was stalled (one pedestrian film after another, a stream of mild second-banana parts, a highlight of sorts being his

Reagan was a seven-term president of the Screen Actors Guild in the 1940s and '50s. In October 1946 (above), Jane Wyman, Henry Fonda, Reagan, Boris Karloff and Gene Kelly discussed crossing a picket line at an emergency meeting of the union. The following October, Reagan testified before the House Un-American Activities Committee (opposite). In 1947 he was finally fitted for contact lenses, and rarely again appeared in public wearing glasses.

He made some good pictures—really! *Bedtime for Bonzo* (1951, left) was an amiable screwball comedy. In 1950's poignant *The Hasty Heart* (above), Reagan played opposite Patricia Neal. In *The Winning Team* (1952, right), he was winning as Grover Cleveland Alexander.

famous performance opposite Bonzo), Reagan became obsessed with his real-world role as a political figure.

Jane Wyman sued for divorce in 1948, complaining among other things that her husband "talked about politics at every meal." Reagan put on a brave face, joking publicly about the film for which Wyman won her '48 Oscar: "I think I'll name *Johnny Belinda* as the co-respondent." In fact, he was devastated. He was seen at parties with tears in his eyes. He descended into "a lonely inner world," he admitted much later. "My loneliness was not from being unloved, but rather from not loving . . . Real loneliness is not missing anyone at all."

Actors William Holden and Brenda Marshall (his wife) attended Ron and Nancy at their wedding on March 4, 1952. The newlyweds honeymooned in Phoenix (above). In the fall of '52, Patti Reagan was born, and Dad campaigned as a Democrat for Eisenhower.

In the early '50s a pretty, big-eyed actress named Nancy Davis heard that her name had been attached to left-wing groups then under investigation. Nancy, from a well-to-do, conservative background in Chicago, went to SAG for help in clearing her name. Her hero at the union, Ronald Reagan, allowed her to help him in turn. "Although he loves people, he often seems remote, and he doesn't let anybody get too close," Nancy wrote years later. "There's a wall around him. He lets me come closer than anyone else, but there are times when even I feel that barrier."

Presidents in the Movies

Ronald Reagan was our only actor-President, but there were lots of other actors who portrayed the President. Here are examples from the intersection of Sunset Boulevard and Pennsylvania Avenue.

Anthony Hopkins as Richard Nixon
In 1995 director Oliver Stone, who had made revisionist history with *JFK,* struck again with *Nixon.* He cast an Englishman in the title role.

Charlton Heston as Andrew Jackson
In 1953's *The President's Lady,* Heston was cast as Tennessee's favorite son. He would again play his Old Hickory five years later in *The Buccaneer.*

Ralph Bellamy as Franklin D. Roosevelt
In 1960, Bellamy reprised his Broadway triumph in the film version of Dore Schary's play *Sunrise at Campobello.*

Nick Nolte as Thomas Jefferson
The U.S. ambassador fell for artist Maria Cosway (played by Greta Scacchi), according to 1995's *Jefferson in Paris.*

**Henry Fonda
as Abraham Lincoln**

The critic Pauline Kael considered 1939's *Young Mr. Lincoln,* about an Illinois country lawyer, "one of [director] John Ford's most memorable films."

**Cliff Robertson as
John F. Kennedy**

In 1963, months before JFK was assassinated, a movie depicting his World War II heroism was released. Kennedy himself had picked Robertson for the lead in *PT 109.*

John Travolta as "Jack Stanton"

Emma Thompson and Travolta were not Hillary and Bill Clinton—sure—in 1998's *Primary Colors,* based on the book by Anonymous, not Joe Klein.

**Alexander Knox
as Woodrow Wilson**

The character actor Knox was superb in the 1944 biopic *Wilson;* he garnered one of the film's 11 Oscar nominations. *Wilson* took home six statuettes.

A Time of Transition

Ronald Reagan, the movie star, was on his first tour as General Electric's front man/pitchman/booster/glad-hander/communicator. The plan was for Reagan, the new host of the television show *General Electric Theater,* to visit 139 plants across the country, bucking up 250,000 employees. He would listen to their concerns and share his thoughts. This mightn't have been everyone's idea of a good time, but it sure was Reagan's.

Kicking off the tour at the giant turbine plant in Schenectady, N.Y., he had a ball. He signed hundreds of autographs, had his back slapped by a hundred guys, sent a hundred gals swooning.

As the night wound down, a request came via Reagan's speechwriter Earl Dunckel. There was a convention of high school teachers in town, and their speaker had taken ill. Could Mr. Reagan take his place? "Dunk, let's give it a try," he replied.

The next day, Ronald Reagan took flight on education, offering everything he remembered—facts, fancies, theories. Four thousand teachers sat rapt, then leapt to their feet and cheered. The thunderous applause lasted 10 minutes. Earl Dunckel, off to the side, shook his head in wonder.

Reagan was 43 and a fading star when he signed to host General Electric's weekly anthology in 1954. His association with the company not only allowed him to perfect meet-and-greet skills that would serve him immensely well, it also kept him before the public at large: *General Electric Theater* was one of TV's top-rated shows during the late '50s.

Greetings from Las Vegas

R onald Reagan, joyous in his new marriage, was miserable as an actor. Warner Bros. had dumped him and offers were few. What films he did land were B-minus. "*Tropic Zone* and *Law and Order* both gave me that I-don't-want-to-go-out-in-the-lobby feeling," he recalled. On occasion, he turned down work because he felt victimized by the 91 percent tax bracket; he became a crusader against an "evil" tax system that soaked the rich—including glamorous Hollywood movie stars. Reagan eventually went into debt, in part because the Internal Revenue Service made him a poster boy for his new issue by smacking him with a back-taxes assessment.

Needing money, Reagan accepted a two-week gig in 1954 as emcee at a two-bit Vegas nightclub in a hotel chillingly

Well, the Coconut Grove doesn't come cheap. Reagan played Vegas in 1954 (above) for the money, and shilled for Rheingold beer in 1955 (below). He and Nancy enjoyed a splendid evening at L.A.'s chichi Grove in '57 (opposite).

Double duty: Hosting G.E.'s show (left) and meeting the rank and file. The plant tours sharpened Reagan's political skills as well as his ideas. At one factory he shook 2,000 hands, at another he signed 10,000 photos. At Appliance Park in Louisville, Ky., Reagan walked 46 miles of assembly line (or so he claimed). He returned after dark and walked the night shift.

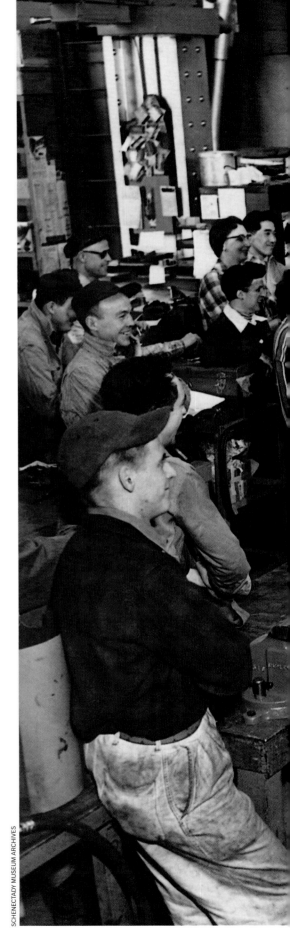

named the Last Frontier. Taking the stage, he said, "When it was announced I was going to do a floor show, someone said, 'What's he going to do?' That's a very good question—I wish I had a very good answer—so does the fellow who asked me—he runs this place." (Ra-ta-*boom!*)

"It was a great experience," Reagan said later, finding that silver lining. "But two weeks were enough."

What next? Well, for a Hollywood actor in 1953 there was one venue just as dicey as a Vegas dive, and that was TV. Jungle law said if you opted for the small box, you were through on the big screen. But Reagan could refuse no longer. The offer he accepted—to host a series of dramas sponsored by G.E. at an annual salary of $125,000—was a good, respectable one. (The biggest benefits of this deal wouldn't be realized for another decade.)

Reagan was not hired merely to be host of, and occasional actor in, the tele-plays. As roving ambassador in the G.E. universe, he sought to explain management to labor. This marked a third stage in his relationship with workers. The son of a working stiff, he had nevertheless derided the Screen Actors Guild when he got to Hollywood. Then, coaxed by a fellow actor, he had become a union stalwart. Now he was a missionary for a notoriously antiunion company. "Boulwarism," after G.E.'s fierce vice president Lemuel Boulware, was a dread term to labor lawyers, but Reagan was management's gung ho foot soldier among G.E.'s employees. That he was able to develop not only a constituency but also a cult among the working class is yet more evidence of the man's innate charisma and nonpareil salesmanship.

As Reagan was evolving into a different kind of public figure, his politics were shifting too. It wasn't just taxes and Boulwarism, it was everything. His problems

with the IRS led to other conservative impulses: antiwelfare, anti-big-government. With each passing day, the hard times of Dixon receded further, and the influence of years among the privileged gained purchase. And then there was the Nancy factor. Whereas Jane Wyman had grown so weary of Reagan's political obsessions that she showed him the door, Nancy, imbued with conservative values, listened intently to her husband's speeches. As he drifted right, she assured him it was the right way to drift.

Reagan often said that changing parties was as hard as changing religions—explanation for staying a Democrat so

Hellcats of the Navy (1957, opposite) was Reagan and Davis's only feature together and would have been Reagan's last film except that the prospective television drama *The Killers* (above, featuring Angie Dickinson) was deemed too violent for TV and was released in theaters in 1964. In 1954, Reagan was targeted by James Dean on *G.E. Theater* (right).

long. But finally there was no room in a party dominated by Kennedyism and heading toward LBJ's Great Society.

He was giving a speech near his home in Pacific Palisades in 1962. The themes were reflective of his conservative views, and in the middle of his talk one woman in the audience couldn't take it anymore.

"Mr. Reagan!" she shouted, gaining her feet. "I have a question. Have you registered as a Republican yet?"

"Well, no, but I intend to."

The woman stormed the stage. "I'm a registrar," she said, and she thrust a form at him. He signed, and that was that: Ronald Reagan, Republican.

The Reagans, along with actor Don DeFore (to Nancy's right)—as well as Andy Devine, John Wayne, Jane Russell, Linda Darnell and other stars—got a charge out of the rabid, placard-carrying audience at an anticommunism rally at the Hollywood Bowl in 1961.

The Great Communicators

By the time Ronald Reagan made the nickname his own, there had already been several Presidents who had a similarly uncanny ability to connect with the American people.

Abraham Lincoln
Lincoln didn't simply dash off the Gettysburg Address on an envelope; he prepared it with care. A great debater as well as orator, he handwrote five versions of the speech, which he delivered on November 19, 1863.

Theodore Roosevelt
T.R.'s dynamism was heroic—one time, literally so. Challenging for the White House in 1912, he was shot by a would-be assassin. He gave his speech, then sought a doctor.

Executive Mansion,

Washington, _____, 186

Four score and seven years ago our fathers brought forth, upon this continent, a new nation, conceived in liberty, and dedicated to the proposition that "all men are created equal."

Now we are engaged in a great civil war, testing whether that nation, or any nation so conceived, and so dedicated, can long endure. We are met on a great battle field of that war. We have come to dedicate a portion of it, as a final resting place for those who died here, that the nation might live. This we may, in all propriety do. But, in a larger sense, we can not dedicate— we can not consecrate— we can not hallow, this ground— The brave men, living and dead, who struggled here, have hallowed it, far above our poor power to add or detract. The...

CLOCKWISE FROM TOP LEFT: BROWN BROTHERS; FPG; UPI/CORBIS-BETTMANN; PAUL SCHUTZER; CORBIS-BETTMANN; LIBRARY OF CONGRESS

Franklin D. Roosevelt

From 1933 through 1944, FDR gave 30 Fireside Chats. For his New Deal he asked a "spirit of mutual confidence and mutual encouragement," which is just what the radio chats fostered.

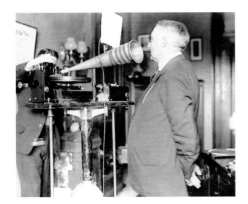

Warren G. Harding

By the time Harding took office in 1921, Marconi and Edison had changed the ways a President could communicate. He could take to the airwaves, or wax his eloquence.

John F. Kennedy and Richard Nixon

When JFK bested Nixon in four debates during the '60 campaign, another new criterion was established. A great communicator now had to be not only forceful and eloquent but telegenic. Great hair helped, as Kennedy and Reagan learned.

Governor Reagan

He stood in a light blue suit that picked up his light blue eyes; his left hand was stuck deep into his pants pocket. He gestured with his right hand, moving it around, touching the podium with his fingertips. About to deliver a punch line, he touched his right eyebrow. The joke went over well. The audience, tipped it was coming, had grown anxious, then had responded with a big laugh.

He was asked a question. He cocked his head to the right, not unlike a fighter sidestepping a jab. "Well." He said it with emphasis—"Weellll"—while wearing an easy smile. Then he answered.

One day in the '60s, when young people were at the barricades on college campuses across the country, the question to the governor was this: "Aren't these kids just rebelling against the principles and standards we were raised on and which we've been trying to pass on to them?"

"Perhaps," Reagan said, "young people aren't rebelling against our standards. Perhaps they're rebelling because they don't think we are living by the standards we've tried to teach them."

The hall was silent for a moment, then trembled, then erupted. He did know how to work a crowd.

Soon after his inauguration as governor of California in January 1967, Reagan took control of the state's Republican delegation as a favorite son for the 1968 presidential primary—a token effort that did nothing to slow the rise of Richard Nixon but that indicated Reagan might want to take control of future national conventions, too.

REPUBLICAN
NATIONAL
CONVENTION
1968

At the '64 Republican convention (opposite), Ronald Reagan, aging movie star, worked the room, expressing support for Barry Goldwater. That support reached a national TV audience on October 27 when Reagan delivered his famous speech *A Time for Choosing* (left). "We can preserve for our children this last, best hope of man on earth," said the new political star.

Ronald Reagan became very good at disclaiming. In the early 1960s, friends were urging the former union chief to consider political office. He'd smile and say thank you and then, "Well, ahh, no, I don't think so." In 1961 the California state Republican chairman said at a news conference that the party's best chances to wrest the governorship in 1962 lay with Richard Nixon and that strong-spoken actor fellow, Ronald Reagan (who wasn't yet a Republican). Replied Reagan: "It would represent too much of a change in my way of living and what I'm trying to do." As if to emphasize, when his contract with G.E. expired, Reagan let it be known to Hollywood friends that he would like to resuscitate his movie career. He narrated *The Young Doctors* in 1961, and when

The Killers metamorphosed from a television production to a feature film, he was back on the big screen. But that would be the end of the movie career: A man with Reagan's political inclinations and personal ambition could disclaim only so long.

In 1965, Reagan, now visible primarily as the host of another TV anthology, the oater *Death Valley Days,* was asked by Republican politicos to be cochairman of the California Citizens for Goldwater committee, an effort to elect conservative Arizona Sen. Barry Goldwater President. Reagan, a true believer in Goldwater conservatism, said sure, this I can do. He traveled the state giving "The Speech," which was basically a harangue against big government and the welfare system. In late summer, party bosses again came to Reagan with a proposition: If they paid for

some national TV time, would Reagan give a speech boosting Barry? Reagan said sure, this I can do.

A Time for Choosing was "The Speech" writ much, much larger. It, and the speaker, were magnificent, and when Reagan summed up with "You and I have a rendezvous with destiny," Joe Sixpack turned from the tube and said to the missus, "Hey, why ain't Ronnie running?"

But Ronnie wasn't, and Barry got whomped—one of the worst thrashings in presidential election history.

Reagan emerged from the debacle of 1964 not only unscathed but a political star. His magnetic delivery of A Time for Choosing had drawn a thousand letters of congratulation and invitation, as well as a million dollars to Republican coffers. Reagan's suitors would press their suit harder this time. They came to his

In 1965, Bill Ray visited Pacific Palisades and took these rarely seen pictures for LIFE. By then, Reagan's family was complete. Maureen and Michael were grown; Nancy and Ronald's daughter Patti, born in 1952, wasn't home, but Ron, born in 1958, was. Reagan is acting here: By his kids' accounts, he was an aloof dad.

house and told him he was the man to beat Pat Brown for governor. "I kept saying no," Reagan remembered later. "I had a good job and a good life, and at 54, the last thing I wanted to do was start a new career."

The political operatives asked Reagan to at least test the waters with a swing around the state. The response to his tour was such that Reagan was compelled to run. The race against Brown, a liberal who was seeking a third term, was vicious. While Reagan was only six years the younger man, he would do impressions on the stump of a doddering Brown (never worrying, certainly, that the issue of a candidate's age might plague him, too, one day). Brown, for his part, kept asking voters if they wanted an actor for governor. The way he sneered "actor," it equated with idiot.

He was ready for the role, expert at pressing the flesh or riding a horse (here in San Jose's Mexican Independence Day parade during the '66 campaign). Herbert Gold called him "a heavenly Pop politician in the paradise of Pop art."

In the early '60s the idea of people like Ronald Reagan being active in politics was, to many, ludicrous. Electing an entertainer to high office was a bridge not to be crossed, just as the election of a Catholic President was an impossibility before John F. Kennedy. The idea that actors do nothing but pretend was hammered home even by some of Reagan's showbiz brethren, including an old liberal-leaning compadre from SAG. "I've

played many roles before the camera," Gene Kelly said in a political commercial. "I know I could *play* the role of a governor but that I could never really sit in his chair and make decisions affecting the education of millions of children."

As it happened, Californians like their actors, or at least they liked this actor, plenty. Reagan beat Brown by nearly a million votes; it was a landslide of LBJ proportions. Overnight he was the leader of the country's most populous state and, also, the national leader of the conservative movement.

The very moment Reagan achieved the State House he started disclaiming again—"Well, ahh, no, I don't think so"— about designs on the White House.

COURTESY RONALD REAGAN LIBRARY

Reagan won big in '66 (left), then got down to business with aides (above, from left) Lyn Nofziger, Tom Reed and Art Van Court. As governor, Reagan had to overcome his fear of flying. LIFE photographer John Loengard said of the photo opposite: "He was this happy because he was back on the ground."

Some well-scrubbed young people carried his posters, others picked a fight. In February 1967 in Sacramento (left), he confronted University of California students demonstrating at the capitol against budget cuts and the introduction of tuition.

Meanwhile, he set about building a reputation as a strong, innovative governor. Some things might have been anticipated—his opposition to handgun control, his support of capital punishment and, in his first term, his tough response to the People's Park takeover at the University of California at Berkeley, which saw the National Guard patrolling city streets for a full 17 days. But other initiatives remain surprising all these years later. He signed a liberalized abortion law; his much-lauded welfare reforms included a 41 percent increase for the neediest; he put on the books the toughest water-quality standards in the country; he signed several measures banning discrimination against women and one that protected rape victims from public questioning about their sex lives. Reagan's government commissions were multicultural—

he appointed more minorities than had any previous California governor—and he saw to it that many bilingual services were added for Spanish-speaking citizens (even as he fought Cesar Chavez's efforts to unionize migrant farmworkers). In 1972 he told Equal Rights Amendment lobbyists that they had his "full support." As President, Ronald Reagan would flip on several of these issues, but during eight years as California's governor he was building a record that would make it easy—enticing, even—for those who would come to be known as Reagan Democrats to join him in his tent.

Among the many people dismayed by

Richard Nixon's resignation was Ronald Reagan, and he had personal reasons. The rise of Gerald Ford to the presidency put a crimp in Reagan's designs on the 1976 Republican nomination. He made a charge anyway, and it was a strong one. Ford remembered later: "Some of my closest advisers . . . had been warning me for months to prepare for a difficult challenge from Ronald Reagan. I hadn't taken those warnings seriously because I didn't take Reagan seriously." Pat Brown had made the same mistake.

Ford survived Reagan but lost to Jimmy Carter. Reagan survived 1976 with a million dollars left over, and he used this

The derision aimed at Reagan "the actor" engendered a campaign backlash and drew cronies such as Bob Hope, John Wayne, Dean Martin and Frank Sinatra to the fore. Sinatra became a particular friend of the Reagans (opposite) and would be a frequent White House guest.

to launch, in January 1977, his Citizens for the Republic political action committee. Carter hadn't been inaugurated yet, but the 1980 presidential race had already begun. There was no more disclaiming; Ronald Reagan needed no more convincing. He was ready for his rendezvous with destiny.

Prominent First Ladies

Some Presidents' wives were all but invisible. Some others, like Nancy Reagan, held the public eye. And a few even held real power.

Edith Wilson

Some were powers behind the throne. Was Woodrow Wilson's wife the power *on* the throne? Some say she was in 1919 and '20 after first a breakdown, then a stroke, left the President severely diminished. The smart, strong Mrs. Wilson was an able deputy.

Dolley Madison

During a British attack in 1814, Dolley grabbed the Declaration of Independence, the Constitution and a portrait of George Washington.

Abigail Adams

Her husband, John, the second President, called her Partner. She groomed their son John Quincy to follow Dad's path.

Harriet Lane

Her uncle, the bachelor James Buchanan, leaned on her for hostessing in 1857, and the 26-year-old became D.C.'s darling.

Caroline Harrison

Benjamin's wife was the "best housekeeper the White House has ever known"—sumptuous praise in the Gilded Age.

Florence Harding
Warren was pudding next to the formidable Flossie. "Well," she said after the 1920 election, "I have got you the presidency; what are you going to do with it?"

Jacqueline Kennedy
JFK's wife presided as queen of Camelot, imbuing the White House with glamour and style while hosting new kinds of guests, like French man of letters André Malraux (above).

Eleanor Roosevelt
Feminist, diplomat, crusader: FDR's wife proved that the First Lady could be an overt—and effective—political being.

Hillary Clinton
An official aide to, and defender of, her husband, she began her own bid for public office while still First Lady.

President Reagan

One day in 1982, as Ronald Reagan was in the White House reading *The Washington Post,* he came across a disturbing item. A black family, the Butlers of College Park, Md., had been harassed. A cross had been burned on their lawn.

This was 1982, not 1962, and Ronald Reagan was now President of the United States, not a B-list actor hanging out by the pool in Pacific Palisades. He could do something about this.

As leader of the Free World he was a busy man, but he ordered his schedule cleared and summoned the motorcade—the whole sirens-blaring motorcade. In College Park, the presidential limo pulled up curbside; Ron and Nancy Reagan got out and crossed the Butlers' small lawn. "They were a nice couple with a four-year-old daughter and a grandma, a most gracious lady, living with them," Reagan said. "Their home was comfortably and tastefully furnished. We enjoyed our visit, and when it was time to leave they saw us to our car." Reagan made a bit of a show in bidding farewell, waving to neighbors who had gathered.

"Needless to say," he recalled with satisfaction, "this fine family had no further harassment."

"There is, in America, a greatness and a tremendous heritage of idealism, which is a reservoir of strength and goodness. It is ours if we will but tap it. And because of this—because that greatness is there—there is need in America today for a reaffirmation of that goodness and a re-formation of our greatness."—Ronald Reagan, 1981. The opinion was an honest one, for there was in him a tremendous heritage of idealism, a reservoir of strength and goodness.

He once said that "nothing thrilled me more than looking up at a windblown flag while listening to a choir sing 'The Battle Hymn of the Republic,' my favorite song." From 1981 through '88, he would have many an opportunity to experience that thrill from a special vantage point. But first he had to win the role.

In 1980, Ronald Reagan, former actor and ex-governor, knew something about winning a role. He knew about forceful gestures and seizing the moment. For example, George Bush had beaten him in the Iowa caucuses and was giving him trouble in the polls on the eve of the New Hampshire primary, making hay with assaults on Reagan's "voodoo economics." But at a debate in Nashua, Reagan refused to be cut off, declaring, "I paid for this microphone!" Indeed, Reagan's campaign may have paid for the hall, and certainly there were aspects of Reagan's "trickle-down" economic plan that may have looked like voodoo, at least hoodoo—

Even before he said he was running, he was running; even when he was resting, he was running. He had a huge war chest left over from 1976 (opposite, campaigning in Tampico, Ill., in front of the building in which he was born). With the money, he formed his political committee, then retired to plot his strategy (above, at his California ranch).

At the Kentucky Derby in 1980, the candidate tried out the winner's circle. He said he was a "citizen politician" who was running on behalf of his fellow citizens. He asked the electorate that summer: "If not us, then who? If not now, when?"

suddenly, none of it mattered. Bush was a wimp, Reagan was a warrior, and in flinty New Hampshire, where the state motto is Live Free or Die, warriors crush wimps every time. Reagan thrashed Bush in the primary, 51 percent to 22, and cruised to his party's nomination. Sixty-nine years old, with his last, best chance to be President, he was playing to win.

If George Bush, a bona fide World War II hero, could be made to look weak by Ronald Reagan, then mild-mannered Jimmy Carter could be made to look anemic. Carter's economic program had failed miserably, and he had, only shortly before the national campaign began, seemed to castigate his countrymen for a sullen state of affairs in America, citing "a crisis of confidence . . . that strikes at the very heart and soul and spirit of our national will." Reagan said there was no spiritual crisis that would not be cured by a switch in tenancy at 1600 Pennsylvania Avenue: "I find no national malaise, I find nothing wrong with the American people." Joe Sixpack turned to the missus and said, "Is Jimmy trying to blame us for this hostage thing? I'm voting for Ronnie."

In January 1979, Iranian zealots had forced the shah to leave; in November they had taken 52 American hostages—diplomatic emissaries of the "Great Satan." As the days of the hostage crisis

MICHAEL EVANS/CORBIS-SYGMA

were tallied by news anchors, respect for Jimmy Carter evaporated drop by drop. Reagan finished him off in the "There you go again" debate of October 28 when he summed up for the American people thusly: "Are you better off than you were four years ago? . . . Is America as respected throughout the world as it was?"

Had the mullahs' prisoners been released in 1980, then in all probability Carter would have prevailed. As it was,

Reagan won the election by 10 percentage points, Republicans took control of the Senate, Democrats lost 31 seats in the House, and on January 20, 1981, Americans watched split-screen coverage of Ronald Wilson Reagan being sworn in as the 40th President while a 444-day nightmare ended with the release of the hostages, who flew from Tehran 28 minutes after Reagan took his oath.

Reagan strove to appear fresh and dif-

"This country doesn't have to be in the shape that it is in." So spoke the challenger in his October 1980 debate with Carter. As the candidates kissed their wives (above), Carter's campaign was crashing and Reagan's, opposite, soaring.

On January 20, 1981, the Reagans took over the White House. The President recalled his father's old shoe business when he said, "I'm back living above the store again." Shortly after his swearing-in by Chief Justice Warren Burger, he joked, "It's been a very wonderful day. I guess I can go back to California, can't I?"

ferent. The first President inaugurated on the West Front of the Capitol, with its sweeping view of the great monuments, he pledged in his address "an era of national renewal." His dashing performance over the next several days was beyond boffo. The inauguration, a three-day, $8 million bash—which kicked off with an $800,000 fireworks display, featured nine balls and starred A-list talent from Johnny Carson to Frank Sinatra—was a smash; Gary Wills called it "Hollywood on the Potomac." The release of the hostages had spurred a national euphoria, and it seemed as if every citizen from Portland to Portland was dancing at the party. The glamour was all the more pronounced for its stark contrast with the cornpone image of the Carter White House. It was as if Ron and Nancy were sweeping out any straw left behind by the hillbillies from Georgia, proclaiming a second coming of Camelot. (In fact, it was almost precisely like that: The Reagans reinstated the White House trumpeters, banished by the Carters; a color guard to precede the presidential

The Reagans and
friends, including
Frank Sinatra, danced
the night away.
The photo above
displeased Michael
Deaver, who felt
Sinatra's alleged
mob links made
him too hot for the
White House.

family's entrance was restored as well.)

Nancy, a self-proclaimed "frustrated interior decorator," raised nearly a million dollars among rich friends to help her spiff up the mansion. She accepted from a private donor a 220-place setting of china, the first new china in the White House in nearly two decades. She presided at elaborate gourmet dinners. *The Wall Street Journal* reported, "In the early days, the Carters didn't give their guests anything to drink. Then they added table wine . . . But now, with the Reagans, booze is back."

After the first flush of excitement wore off, critics began disapproving of such splendor, saying it was offensive at a time of widespread economic misery. A hot-selling postcard in 1981 showed "Queen Nancy" in a crown, and a reporter wrote that she "was using her position to improve the quality of life for those in the White House." Mrs. Reagan was hurt by the broadsides but did nothing to change her ways. Her disapproval rating in the first term climbed to the highest of any modern First Lady.

Ronald Reagan said once, "I remember John Kennedy saying that when he came into office, the thing that surprised him the most was to find that things were just as bad as he'd been saying they were. In my case, the biggest surprise was find-

The puritans had been routed, prohibition was over, the booze was back. On his first workday, Reagan was all business in the Oval Office (above). But not long after, at a White House party in honor of Walter Cronkite's retirement from CBS, a hearty toast was enjoyed by the President, the honoree and Vice President Bush (second from right), among others.

ing out that they were even worse." He meant the economy. "I arrived in the White House as the country was experiencing what many called its greatest economic emergency since the Depression . . . My advisers and I had begun working on a recovery plan the first day after the election. The morning after Inauguration Day, we began implementing the plan. Its basis was tax reform."

Whether Reagan's supply-side economic recovery program, which argued that tax cuts all the way up the economic ladder (big business included) would stimulate prosperity all the way down, was a disaster for the poor during the 1980s, or whether it was the bedrock on which the fantastic growth of the 1990s was built, would prove a debate never to be settled.

Reagan cast his attention unwaveringly upon the economic plan during his first weeks in office, and it was a topic he would concentrate on in his speech at the Washington Hilton to the Construction Trades Council on March 30. He put on a new blue suit that morning and a favorite old wristwatch that Nancy had given him. He felt good, but the speech

March 30, 1981: As Secret Service agent Parr (behind Reagan) pushed the President into the limo, Parr's colleague Timothy J. McCarthy was wounded (above, foreground; in background, other agents cover fallen press secretary Brady, who is facedown). Hinckley is seized (right). At the hospital, Reagan asked, "Does anybody know what that guy's beef was?" Later, while Hinckley's mental illness didn't satisfy those who wanted his scalp, it was enough for Reagan: "He wasn't thinking on all cylinders."

91

Remedies for the healing President came in all shapes and sizes. A distraught Nancy arrived at the hospital bearing Ron's beloved jelly beans. The White House staff posed for a huge get-well card and sent copies to the four men wounded by Hinckley.

was only politely received. "I think most of the audience were Democrats," he said.

He left the hotel through a side entrance and passed the ever-present photographers. He was about to climb into the limo when he heard something—"just a small fluttering sound, *pop, pop, pop*"—to his left. He turned and said, "What the hell's that?" Secret Serviceman Jerry Parr knew what it was and threw Reagan into the car. "I landed on my face atop the armrest across the backseat and Jerry jumped on top of me," Reagan remembered. "When he landed, I felt a pain in my upper back that was unbelievable." He yelled for Parr to get off him, thinking the agent had broken one of his ribs. "The White House!" Parr shouted, and the car sped off. Reagan tried to sit up. He coughed. That was when he saw "the palm of my hand was

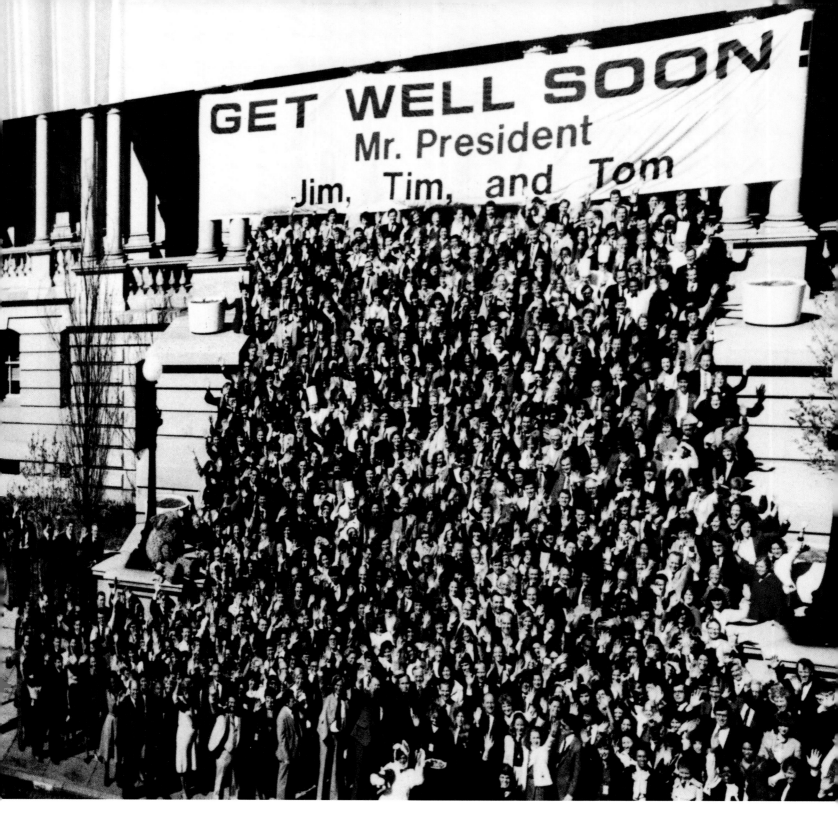

GET WELL SOON!
Mr. President
Jim, Tim, and Tom

brimming with extremely red, frothy blood." Parr saw the hand too, and told the driver to head for George Washington University Hospital instead.

Assaults on U.S. Presidents have been made by men and women, the politically motivated and the frustrated, sane men and madmen. And what was John W. Hinckley Jr.? He was a 25-year-old son of a Denver oil executive. He was a man who, on March 30, was packing a .22-caliber pistol, despite the fact that he had been arrested on a concealed weapons charge in Nashville a few months earlier. He was mentally ill. He had been in treatment before and at one point had developed an obsession with Jodie Foster after seeing her in *Taxi Driver.* In that film, a character played by Robert De Niro tries to assassinate a senator in hopes of attracting a woman's attention.

On August 13, 1981, he signed his tax bill on a foggy day at Rancho del Cielo. "I've been told that some members of Congress disagree with my tax-cut proposal," he had said in a speech. "Well, you know it's been said that taxation is the art of plucking the feathers without killing the bird. It's time they realized the bird doesn't have any feathers left."

Hinckley squeezed off six shots outside the Hilton. Press secretary James S. Brady was hit in the head and would be paralyzed for life. A police officer and a Secret Service agent also were wounded. The bullet that caught Reagan ricocheted off the limo, then bounced off a rib and lodged in his lung, an inch from his heart.

The nation did not know, at the time, just how critical the President's condition was—and this had everything to do with the brave, graceful manner with which Reagan confronted the situation. He tried to walk into the hospital under his own power until his knees buckled. Lying on the gurney, he told one surgeon, "I hope you're a Republican," to which the loyal Democrat replied, "Today, Mr. President, we're all Republicans." When Nancy arrived at her husband's bedside, he used a line from the boxer Jack Dempsey: "Honey, I forgot to duck."

Reagan's recovery from his brush with death was remarkably quick, and though not fully healed, he left the hospital 12 days after entering. During that time his popularity had soared to new heights, and now aides James Baker and Michael Deaver persuaded him to use this to advantage in selling his economic plan. Less than a month after the attack by Hinckley, who was meantime heading to a psychiatric facility, Reagan lectured

Michael Deaver once suggested that Reagan spend less time at Rancho del Cielo. The boss looked his aide in the eye and said he could question anything except the visits to the ranch.

Congress on the wisdom of supply-side thinking. The address helped shore up the bipartisan coalition Reagan needed for this and other legislation. Also, with the assassination attempt he took on the armor that would lead to what Deaver termed his Teflon presidency. For seven more years, critics could assail Reaganomics or Iran-Contra all they chose, but if they attacked the man himself, a figure beloved by his countrymen, they did so at their considerable peril.

While there was this arguably positive fallout from Hinckley's assault—an upsurge in devotion, a Teflon coating—

there were curious aftereffects as well. Reagan wrote in his diary, "Whatever happens now I owe my life to God and will try to serve Him in every way I can," but Nancy turned ever more fervently to astrology to help her guide the family. It was rumored that the precise timing of Reagan's inauguration ceremony as governor had been dictated by the planets, and now Nancy insisted that the President's schedule be subject to the influence of her stargazers. Reagan's wife grew more protective of him, and so did his staff, the Secret Service, everyone. This led not only to frustrating episodes on airport tarmacs—Reagan cupping a hand to his ear, indicating to reporters who were a football field away that he couldn't hear them—but also to a gradual disengagement on the part of the Chief Executive.

Reagan, while an impenetrable man with few intimate relationships, had always been a gregarious, handshaking public figure, eager to greet a starstruck fan of *Kings Row,* an assembly-line worker at a G.E. plant or a Democrat primed for conversion. Now no such interaction was possible. He was walled off, and it sapped his spirit. In retrospect, it seems clear that Reagan more purely enjoyed the first nine weeks of his presidency than he did the next seven years, 10 months.

But he served out all that time, the first President since Eisenhower to finish two terms. And an eventful two terms they were. By the end of 1981 he had signed the biggest tax cut in history (25 percent over three years) as well as a budget that was $44.3 billion less than Carter's fiscal '82 budget projection, even

President Reagan, Anglophile, had a close working relationship with Conservative Prime Minister Margaret Thatcher and enjoyed a good laugh or ride with Queen Elizabeth II. "I must admit," Reagan said, "the queen is quite an accomplished horsewoman."

Evenings formal and informal: In 1984 (left) the President caught the news before a state dinner. In 1983 (above) he worked the phones in casual attire. "Most nights after six p.m. [he] would be wearing his nightclothes," said aide Michael Deaver. "The Reagans are probably the biggest pajama fans this side of Hugh Hefner."

though Reagan's contained a $28 billion increase in defense spending. Instead of promoting prosperity, however, Reaganomics ushered the country into a recession. Bankruptcy hit a half-century high, unemployment approached 10 percent (its highest level since the Depression), and an already huge deficit was being padded by the hour. Reagan, shifting gears, asked for the largest tax increase in U.S. history and got it. In 1983 the economy began to revive and unemployment began to drop (it would reach a 15-year low of 5.5 percent by the end of his presidency). Some things got better while some got worse: Domestic prosperity picked up even as the trade deficit quadrupled, making the U.S. the world's largest debtor. The stock market soared to an all-time high just before it crashed. The 508-point fall on October 19, 1987, represented the worst percentage drop in Dow-Jones history. Reaganomics was a roller coaster. The country shut its eyes tight and hoped for the best.

Volatility wasn't restricted to the mar-

On November 4, 1983, at Camp Lejeune, N.C., the Reagans prayed during a memorial service for 241 servicemen killed in the bombing in Beirut and 18 others felled in Grenada. "This is not the happiest of my days as President," said Reagan, "but it's one of my proudest."

kets. Reagan fired 13,000 striking air-traffic controllers in 1981 and called in military personnel to keep the airports open. He elevated conservative Justice William Rehnquist to Chief Justice of the Supreme Court, meanwhile appointing the even more rigid Antonin Scalia to the bench. He tried to install Robert Bork and Douglas H. Ginsburg, but the former was turned down after bitter partisan Senate debate, and the latter withdrew his name after admitting to past marijuana use. (Reagan also named Sandra Day O'Connor to the court early in his tenure, fulfilling a campaign pledge to nominate a woman; later in his second term he promoted the moderate Anthony M. Kennedy after Bork and Ginsburg crashed.) Running for reelection in 1984, Reagan and his vice president and eventual successor, George Bush, beat Walter Mondale and Geraldine Ferraro by the second greatest plurality in a presidential election. Whether Reagan was doing a great, good, adequate or uneven job, Americans loved him all the same.

In January 1986 the space shuttle *Challenger* took off from Cape Canaveral and, to the horror of millions of television viewers, exploded in midair. Aboard was a teacher from New Hampshire, Christa McAuliffe, who had won a contest allowing her to be an astronaut. What would—

At the 1984 Republican national convention in Dallas, the First Lady waved to her husband, the party's nominee-in-waiting, who was watching from a hotel suite with his vice president. The song that played as Nancy waved was "You Are the Sunshine of My Life." In the First Lady's speech, she urged, "Let's make it one more for the Gipper!"

what could?—the Great Communicator do with such a tragedy in his State of the Union address, only hours away?

When faced with specific cases (as opposed to abstractions like "the welfare class"), Ronald Reagan was an innately compassionate man, and there can be little doubt that such affairs as the *Challenger* disaster—or the permanent injury of his friend James Brady, or the killing of 241 Marines when their compound in Beirut was bombed by terrorists in 1983—affected him deeply. An example: Once, a lone-wolf kidnapper threatened to kill his victim unless he got a call from the President. Chief of Staff James Baker was horrified when his boss told him to place the call. Baker talked Reagan out of it and grew increasingly watchful of Reagan's propensity to act on passion, on *feel*.

The *Challenger*, its explosion replayed endlessly on TV monitors and then in the national subconscious, was paradoxically a technological tragedy and an intensely personal one. Reagan would write that McAuliffe's visit to the White House made the disaster "seem even closer and sadder to me." He did the right thing. He canceled the State of the Union address

For a 1985 session with the First Couple, photographer Harry Benson brought a backdrop to the White House (left), then got some memorable up-close-and-personal shots.

and consoled his countrymen. In a moving broadcast, he paraphrased from a sonnet written by an American flier killed in World War II. "We will never forget them," said the President, "nor the last time we saw them this morning as they prepared for their journey and waved goodbye and 'slipped the surly bonds of earth to touch the face of God.'"

Earlier in the day, he and House speaker Tip O'Neill had had acrimonious discussions about Reagan's efforts to cut spending. But O'Neill knew a real thing when he saw one, and said of the President's elegiac speech, "It was a trying day for all Americans, and Ronald Reagan spoke to our highest ideals."

The AIDS epidemic, which erupted

A target once, Reagan, when he wasn't in conference (above, with aides Dennis Thomas, Pat Buchanan, Adm. John Poindexter and David Chew) or isolated in the Oval Office (opposite), moved inside a scrum of Secret Service agents (left).

during his presidency, provides another example of his dealing with an issue only when it was personalized. In the first half of the '80s he thought AIDS was like "measles and . . . would go away." He had nothing against homosexuals, beyond what he called his "old-fashionedness," but many conservatives were telling him to stay away from this issue. Then his friend Rock Hudson, who had been a guest at a recent state dinner, died of complications of AIDS in October 1985.

On July 4, 1986, the Reagans were aboard the USS *Iowa* in New York Harbor to take part in Hollywood producer David Wolper's whiz-bang salute to the century-old Statue of Liberty. The President reviewed 33 vessels from 14 nations, but not the 200 Elvis look-alikes in Wolper's finale.

Shortly afterward, Reagan told the Health and Human Services Department that "one of our highest public-health priorities" was the fight against AIDS.

As for Iran-Contra, the great scandal of the Reagan years: Was it at all personal or wholly political? What did the President know and when did he know it? Was he even paying attention?

As background for an assessment of Iran-Contra, it is useful to look at the Reagan White House's foreign policy in toto. It was defined from Day One as strongly anticommunist and antiterrorist. On March 8, 1983, in a speech in Orlando, Fla., he famously called the Soviet Union an "evil empire" and he backed the Strategic Defense Initiative, an antimissile defense system that would cost billions and was derided by his critics as "Star Wars." Reagan bought Stealth bombers and MX missiles like so many jelly beans, and over a period of six years he shoved a $150 billion defense-budget increase into the evil empire's face.

Then when Moscow blinked and tensions began to thaw, he dealt one-on-one with Mikhail Gorbachev, a man whom, during the Geneva summit of 1985, he had come to know and trust. "I couldn't help but think that something fundamental had changed in the relationship between our countries," Reagan said of

At Geneva (above) and in Washington (left), Gorbachev and Reagan worked to change the world order. Reagan felt a "chemistry" with Gorbachev, "something very close to a friendship."

the Geneva meeting. Reagan and Gorbachev negotiated a reduction in the nuclear stockpile and, eventually, an end to the cold war. Like little kids with a new best pal, each hosted a summit sleepover, and in 1988, Reagan stood at the Berlin Wall and stated: "General Secretary Gorbachev, if you seek peace, if you seek prosperity for the Soviet Union and Eastern Europe, if you seek liberalization, come here to this gate. Mr. Gorbachev, open this gate. Mr. Gorbachev, tear down this wall." He had got to a point in the relationship where his friend—not too strong a word—would listen. The Wall would fall 10 months after Reagan left office.

Back to Iran-Contra: Though Reagan had condemned Iran's holding of hostages in 1980, his administration secretly sold weapons to that country during 1985-86 in exchange for the release of five Americans being held in Lebanon. Millions of dollars from the arms sale were then buried and transferred to the Contras, who were rebel forces in Nicaragua fighting against the leftist Sandinistas—transferred in violation of U.S. policy. Would Ronald Reagan really deal with Tehran? Would he support an effort that flouted Congress? It was clear from the outset that Lt. Col. Oliver North might: Before being convicted of obstructing Congress and other charges (convictions later overturned), he shredded so many documents that the machine jammed twice. But Ronald Reagan?

The President testified that he did not remember authorizing the deal. In a statement to the nation he elaborated somewhat: "The fact of the matter is that

Ron and Nancy (above, on their last day in the White House) bid sentimental farewell. Reagan said that, as President, "you spend a lot of time going by too fast in a car someone else is driving and seeing the people through tinted glass—the parents holding up a child and the wave you saw too late and couldn't return. And so many times I wanted to stop and reach out from behind the glass and connect."

there's nothing I can say that will make the situation right. I was stubborn in my pursuit of a policy that went astray."

No matter what his supporters believed, they were left with dismay. Either he was finally being dishonest after a career of pointing up dishonesty in others; or he was out of touch and freelancers like North were running amok in the White House; or he was fading, losing his memory as sometimes happens with people of 76. Whichever, it was distressing.

Reagan had never been a workaholic Chief Executive, and he found vacations

The torch having been passed, the Bushes were elated, the Reagans resigned. Their relationship had traveled a long road. In 1980, Reagan wondered at his running mate's lack of "spunk" but over eight years grew to like the man immensely and campaigned for him energetically in 1988.

at his 688-acre retreat in the Santa Ynez Mountains near Santa Barbara an important escape. JFK had his Hyannisport, Nixon his San Clemente, and Bush would have Kennebunkport, but perhaps no President ever drew more from his "weekend White House" than Reagan did from Rancho del Cielo. "This is the place where I restore myself," he said.

Everyone in the country knew this, and so when, on January 20, 1989, he handed over the presidency to George Bush and headed west, people felt good for Ronald Reagan. He left the White House with the highest approval rating of any President since Eisenhower.

On that last day, Rex, the Reagans' King Charles spaniel, scooted across the lawn and the President said softly, "There he goes, that's his last walk." Nancy spent the morning wiping away tears. The President's aides, too, were teary-eyed as they surrounded him in the Oval Office. Reagan took out his laminated card that could be used to order a nuclear-missile launch and asked, "Who do I give this to?"

The Notre Dame football team, national champs that year, dropped by and gave Reagan the letter sweater once worn by the real Gipper. His staff gave him a bridle for the hours he would spend riding through the California hills, watching the sun set into the Pacific.

Assassinations...

Four United States Presidents were slain while in office, and four others, including Ronald Reagan, were attacked by would-be assassins.

Abraham Lincoln, 1865
Lincoln, attacked once as a President-elect, was killed by Southern sympathizer John Wilkes Booth, an actor, at Ford's Theatre. Booth was shot in the manhunt.

James A. Garfield, 1881
Charles Julius Guiteau, frustrated in his bid for a diplomatic job, shot Garfield on July 2; he lingered for 80 more days. Guiteau was hanged.

John F. Kennedy, 1963
JFK was murdered as his motorcade rolled through Dallas. His assassin, Lee Harvey Oswald, was killed two days later by Jack Ruby.

The Body passing the Treasury.   State Funeral of President McKinley
Copyrighted 1901, by William H. Rau.

William McKinley, 1901
At the Pan American Exposition in Buffalo, McKinley was shot by an anarchist named Leon Czolgosz. Even as Washington mourned McKinley (above), New York State moved against Czolgosz. He was electrocuted only 53 days after the attack.

...and Near Assassinations

Gerald Ford, 1975
On September 5, Squeaky Fromme took aim at Ford in Sacramento, and Sara Jane Moore shot at him 17 days later in San Francisco (above). He was unscathed; the women got life.

Andrew Jackson, 1835
Richard Lawrence's assault on Jackson in the Capitol Rotunda was the first attempt on a U.S. President's life. Lawrence, a housepainter, fired at Jackson from six feet but didn't nick him. Found insane, Lawrence was committed for life.

Harry S Truman, 1950
Two Puerto Rican nationalists, Oscar Collazo and Griselio Torresola, attacked Blair House but didn't reach the President. Torresola was killed at the scene. Collazo was wounded (right); he served a life term in prison.

The Legacy

In 1954, Ronald Reagan made a film called *Prisoner of War.* It was about American servicemen who were taken captive during the Korean conflict. While it was far from his best movie, the subject matter resonated for Reagan. It was a patriotic film, of course, and contained tales of quiet bravery, personal heroism. The character he played, Web Sloane, was an intelligence officer who allowed himself to be imprisoned in order to confirm that torture and brainwashing were taking place in Korean camps.

Many times, citing *Prisoner of War,* Reagan would tell his family and others about the horrible treatment that American POWs had received at the hands of the North Koreans. One night late in 1993 the Reagans were having dinner. On this occasion, Ronald's daughter Maureen was telling the war stories, much the same ones her father had told years before. "But now he seemed to be hearing me tell the stories for the first time," Maureen noticed. "Finally he looked at me and said, 'Mermie, I have no recollection of making that movie.'" When his daughter heard this, she suffered what she would call a "click of awareness."

President Reagan, in a 1982 speech to the British Parliament, referred to the Berlin Wall as "that dreadful gray gash across the city . . . a grim symbol of power untamed." In that address he boldly predicted communism would be consigned to "the ash heap of history." By September 12, 1990, when Citizen Reagan took a hammer and chisel to the Wall, the hammer and sickle in Moscow was coming down too.

R onald Reagan's beloved mother, Nelle, was, in her latter years, what was then called "senile." Her son realized this, of course, and as early as the 1980 campaign, Reagan promised to have his doctors watch him closely for signs of senility, a catchall term for the depredations of old age. By that time most researchers believed that pathological changes in the brain owing to a disease called Alzheimer's were responsible for many of the cases in which old people drift toward dementia. Candidate Reagan said in 1979 that if his doctors found signs that he was fading, he would resign.

He did not, and after serving two terms, Reagan retired to the ranch. He rejoined a private citizenry that was much changed. Reaganomics had started a shift that would continue through the 1990s,

a realignment under which America's rich and powerful grew richer and more powerful, as the disenfranchised sank further. In 1987, 20 percent of U.S. children lived in poverty, representing a 24 percent increase during the Reagan years. In 1989 the wealthiest 40 percent of U.S. families controlled 68 percent of the wealth, while the poorest 40 percent controlled 15 percent: the biggest gap in four decades for which such statistics were kept. Global politics, too, had changed. Most significantly, the cold war was over, the superpowers' nuclear stockpiles were being downsized, and there seemed a sense that Eastern Europe was ready for something truly revolutionary.

Reagan would watch the previously unthinkable happen from Rancho del Cielo. He would marvel as democracy spread west across Europe and in 1990 would himself take a hammer to the wall

Out to pasture at Rancho del Cielo: Reagan and Gorbachev laugh about their gunslinging days (above). Always proper, the former President still dressed for work in his retirement (right).

that had symbolized the Communist–Free World divide. His legacy to the world was not a monument that could be seen but, rather, symbols, barriers and governments that were vanishing.

He left his nation with an optimism that was far removed from the malaise perceived by his predecessor, Jimmy Carter. Since audiences enjoy gung ho speeches, early in his retirement Reagan was able to perform as the embodiment of positive thinking. He made a bundle giving speeches; a 1989 trip to Tokyo brought $2 million for two 20-minute talks and some handshaking. It was the ultimate extension of his old G.E. gig.

In the early '90s his appearances became fewer, his public manner more

disengaged. Other people experienced
that click of awareness.

In 1994 doctors at the Mayo Clinic in
Minnesota diagnosed the former President's illness, and Reagan, in an emotional
handwritten letter, told his countrymen

**In Simi Valley in 1991, President George
Bush and predecessors Reagan, Jimmy
Carter, Gerald Ford and Richard Nixon
(left to right, in reverse historical order)
gathered for the dedication of the
Ronald Reagan Presidential Library.**

that he had joined the four million of them who suffered from Alzheimer's. The old radio man was, in a sense, signing off: "At the moment I feel just fine. I intend to live the remainder of the years God gives me on this earth doing the things I have always done. I will continue to share life's journey with my beloved Nancy and my family. I plan to enjoy the great outdoors . . . I now begin the journey that will lead me into the sunset of my life. I know that for America there will always be a bright dawn ahead.

"Thank you, my friends. May God always bless you."

And that was the Great Communicator's valedictory. His wife and children became his spokespeople and delivered updates. Nancy, always by his side at the ranch or strolling on the beach, saw her own popularity rise as her evident devotion brought respect from past critics. By humanizing Alzheimer's disease, the children helped raise public awareness of a condition that afflicts more than a fifth of Americans after age 85. Michael said candidly in 1995, "He's a vibrant guy who's not so vibrant anymore," and Maureen testified movingly about her father's condition before Congress in 1999.

Eventually, Reagan could no longer enjoy the glories of Rancho del Cielo, and the property was sold in 1998 to Young America's Foundation, an organization dedicated to teaching "future generations of young people about Ronald Reagan's legacy." Ron and Nancy moved permanently to Bel Air.

That's where famous old movie stars live out their lives. It's rarely a retirement spot for sons of the Midwest dust bowl, or even for former U.S. Presidents. But then, nothing was ordinary or predictable about Ronald Reagan's journey from Tampico. It was wholly unpredictable. It was, in every way, extraordinary.

The Reagans enjoyed their early retirement years at the ranch (right) and celebrated Ron's 89th birthday in Bel Air (above). "When our children turn the pages of our lives," President Reagan said in his farewell address, "I hope they'll see that we had a vision to pass forward a nation as nearly perfect as we could."